INTEGRATION
of
MAN and SOCIETY
in
LATIN AMERICA

PREPARED FOR PUBLICATION UNDER THE
SPONSORSHIP OF CATHOLIC
INTER-AMERICAN COOPERATION PROGRAM
(CICOP) LATIN AMERICAN BUREAU, U.S.C.C.

CONTRIBUTORS

Ricardo Arias Calderon   George Cabot Lodge

Marina Bandeira   John Mackay

Ernest Bartell, C.S.C.   Jorge Mejia

Robert Bilheimer   Joseph Michenfelder, M.M.

Adolfo Bonilla   José Miguez-Bonino

Ildefonso Cabrera   Edward O'Brien

Antonio Casas-Gonzalez   Gustavo Perez-Ramirez

John D. Early, S.J.   José Ignacio Rasco

Michael Francis   John Santos

Gustavo Lagos   J. Mayone Stycos

Henry A. Landsberger   Leon Josef Cardinal Suenens

Jorge Lara-Braud   Carlos Talavera

Pablo Latapi, S.J.   Eduardo Vallarino, Jr.

Key Yuasa

INTEGRATION
of
MAN and SOCIETY
in
LATIN AMERICA

SAMUEL SHAPIRO
Editor

UNIVERSITY OF NOTRE DAME PRESS
NOTRE DAME – LONDON

Library of Congress Catalog Card Number: 67-28682
Manufactured in the United States of America

Contributors

Ricardo Arias Calderon is professor of ancient and medieval philosophy at the University of Panama and director of *Presente*, a quarterly devoted to cultural and social problems.

Marina Bandeira de Corvalho is secretary general of the MEB (Brazilian Adult Education Movement).

Ernest Bartell, C.S.C., is an assistant professor of economics at the University of Notre Dame.

Robert S. Bilheimer is the director of International Affairs Programs for the National Council of Churches of Christ in the U.S.A.

Adolfo Bonilla has served as secretary for Central America of CLASC (Latin American Confederation of Christian Trade Unionists).

Father Ildefonso Cabrera, now living in the United States, was formerly coordinator of IERAC (Ecuadorian Institute for Agrarian Reform).

Antonio Casas-Gonzalez is an economist in the Economic and Social Development Division of the Inter-American Development Bank.

John D. Early, S.J., is a professor of behavioral science and pastoral theology at Woodstock College.

Michael Francis is an assistant professor of government at the University of Notre Dame.

Henry A. Landsberger is a professor of economics in the New York State School of Industrial Labor Relations, Cornell University, Ithaca, New York.

Gustavo Lagos is the director of INTAL, a research institute in Buenos Aires.

Jorge Lara-Braud is the director of the Hispanic American Institute at Austin, Texas.

Pablo Latapi, S.J., is the technical director of the Center for Studies in Education in Mexico City.

George Cabot Lodge is a professor in the Graduate School of Business Administration at Harvard University.

John A. Mackay is president emeritus of the Princeton Theological Seminary.

Father Jorge Mejia is the editor of *Criterio,* a quarterly devoted to religious and cultural topics, in Buenos Aires.

Joseph Michenfelder, M.M., is the director of the Catholic Information Service in Lima, Peru.

José Miguez-Bonino is the president of the Evangelical Theological Institute in Buenos Aires.

Edward O'Brien is the assistant food program officer for the Catholic Relief Services of the United States Catholic Charities.

Father Gustavo Perez-Ramirez is the director general of ICODES (Colombian Institute for Social Development) in Bogotá, Colombia.

José Ignacio Rasco is an adviser to the Inter-American Development Bank.

John F. Santos is the chairman of the Department of Psychology at the University of Notre Dame.

J. Mayone Stycos is the director of the International Population Program at Cornell University.

Leon Josef Cardinal Suenens is the Archbishop of Mechelen-Brussel in Belgium.

Monsignor Carlos Talavera Ramirez is the director of Archdiocesan Social Secretariat in Mexico City.

Eduardo Vallarino, Jr., is an officer of the Instituto Centroamericano de Administración de Empresas in Managua, Nicaragua.

Key Yuasa is the director of the Department of Assistance of the Japanese Evangelical Federation of Brazil.

Preface

The Integration of Man and Society in Latin America, the theme of the fourth annual meeting of the Catholic Inter-American Cooperation Program, opened up to the contributors to this volume the widest perspectives. "Integration" is one of those protean words, like "imperialism" and "revolution," which can mean very different things to different people. The dictionary gives as its essential meaning "to bring together into a whole; to make up or complete." In the United States it is primarily used to refer to desegregation of schools and housing, and the entrance of American Negroes into full citizenship. But in the Latin American context, as the papers printed below demonstrate, integration has been taken to mean such diverse things as

a changed world view of the individual,

improved marital adjustment and better relations between the sexes,

the turning of marginal peasants and slum-dwellers into participating, job-holding, literate, voting members of society,

better communications between religious leaders and officials, and between various ecclesiastical communities, an effective role for the Church in social and economic development,

cooperation between Catholics, Protestants, and non-Christians in the work of development,

the joining together of Latin American nations in a Common Market and, perhaps, eventually, into a United States of Latin America,

the improved functioning of the universities as agents of rapid change,

the development of effective labor unions,

the creation of a social conscience among United States and Latin American businessmen and politicians,

United States cooperation in Latin American development,

common programs for the development of frontier regions and an ending to border disputes.

Given such a broad interpretation of the theme, it is natural that the papers in this volume, along with others which had to be omitted for want of space, should deal with almost every major aspect of Latin American society from the psychology of the individual to the role of that area in world history and contemporary affairs. CICOP has brought together businessmen, union leaders, and scholars, cardinals, bishops, priests, and laymen, politicians and professors, Catholics, Protestants, and non-Christians, Latin Americans, North Americans, and Europeans, theoreticians and men of action, united only by their common concern for the future of Latin America's 240 million people. To participate, even peripherally, in CICOP's work is an exhilarating experience, for in the coming together of so many men and minds from such different backgrounds there is real integration and true ecumenism.

The genuinely cordial relationships between CICOP's organizers and the many Protestant participants was perhaps the most striking feature of the 1967 assembly. Most of the old sterile animosities, Protestant provocation and Catholic intransigence alike, seem, happily, to have been buried. The papers by Protestant leaders reflect their reaction to the changed atmosphere brought about by the Vatican Council. And Catholic spokesmen, realizing the enormity of the task of development that confronts Latin America, are at last prepared to welcome all the help they can get. CICOP's plans call for further collaboration with the National Council of Churches, and one may hope that much of the energy that formerly went into polemics can now be devoted to cooperation and development.

The job to be done is indeed a staggering one. Mexico, for example, which began a social revolution more than fifty years ago and enjoys special benefits because of its proximity to the United States, is one of the largest, most advanced, and relatively most prosperous nations in Latin America. And yet, as a study by Manuel Loya Mocias (quoted in an unpublished CICOP paper) shows, three out of five Mexican families have a monthly income of less than 750 pesos (60 dollars), and one in five less than 300 pesos (24 dollars). People at such low levels of income and life are cut off from the modern society around them; they produce little, consume little more than bare necessities, are illiterate, have nothing to do with banks, churches, newspapers, the post office, or any governmental agency except the police. To bring them and their children into the modern world is the great task that confronts the societies south of the Rio Grande. And it is to this central theme that, in one form or another, the papers in this volume address themselves.

As CICOP's activities broaden in scope and grow in size, it is useful to review the organization's history and purpose. Founded in 1963 by the United States Bishops' Committee for Inter-American Cooperation, CICOP was designed to increase understanding, friendship, and mutual concern among thoughtful and competent people in both halves of the hemisphere. Its founders and participants hope to encourage concerted action for the betterment of all the Americas by the presentation of information in an unadulterated way, by the dispelling of ignorance, myths, and stereotypes concerning Latin America, and by supplying historical, social, economic, and religious facts. Its bias is progressive, but it provides a platform for the expression of varied views, even on such controversial issues as birth control, United States military aid programs, and the struggle between the AFL-

CIO and the Christian Democratic trade union movement. As Father Louis M. Colonnese, administrative director of the United States Bishops' Latin America Bureau puts it,

CICOP is an organization for dialogue between Latin American and United States leaders and people of good will in general. Its private and public meetings are an occasion for the candid expression and appraisal of ideas, for discussion of plans, and, increasingly, of joint planning efforts with other groups. It is a service which the Bishops of the United States, through their official agency, the Latin America Bureau, place at the disposal of the American public. It is intended to serve as an honest speaker, an exact interpreter, and, hopefully, a prophetic voice. It should, above all, assist in the formation of a national conscience as regards our relationship with the Latin American nations and their people.

As CICOP continues to grow, it becomes impractical to list the names of the hundreds of people who make its meetings possible. Even the briefest paragraph of acknowledgment, however, must begin with Richard Cardinal Cushing, whose warm support has from the beginning been CICOP's greatest single material and spiritual asset and who this year had the satisfaction of bringing the meeting to his own beloved Boston. Official sponsorship by the hierarchy has been ably directed by the Most Reverend Coleman F. Carroll, Bishop of Miami and vice-chairman of the United States Bishops' Committee for Latin America. The actual work of organizing the conference, selecting speakers, coordinating workshops, and handling the complicated logistics of such a meeting fell to the CICOP Program Committee, composed of North and Latin American, lay and ecclesiastical, leaders. Outstanding among the many non-Catholic contributors was the Rev. Dana Green, director of the Latin America Department of the National Council of Churches of Christ in the U.S.A., whose assistance helped to bring a large number of Protestant leaders into the Conference. The editor, finally, wishes to acknowledge the absolute freedom with which he was permitted to select and revise the papers which follow.

University of Notre Dame   Samuel Shapiro
August, 1967

Contents

Contents   xiii

PART ONE

THE INDIVIDUAL
AND THE FAMILY

Personal Values

JOHN SANTOS

There are some considerations which are basic for an understanding of Latin American behavior, personality, and thought characteristics. The first factor which might be considered is one which influences many facets of life in Latin America, namely, the commitment to self and family. There is very much of the I-you, we-they attitude. In many respects the self tends to be rather confined. It extends primarily to the immediate family and perhaps a core of close friends but drops off sharply beyond this restricted range. This drop-off, of course, is not unique to Latin Americans, but the sharpness is in some contrast to North Americans. This is not to say that there is an unawareness of community or national affairs, or a lack of knowledge about international affairs in the large cities, but rather that Latin Americans tend to invest relatively little energy, emotion, or concern in those aspects of reality falling outside of the self-family range. This is certainly strikingly different from North American society, where closer ties often seem to develop between neighbors and friends than amongst members of the family. Some specific examples of these strong family ties in Latin America come readily to mind

3

along with indications of protected privacy and attempts to maintain the separateness of family units. In the former case may be cited the tendency of children to remain close to parents and relatives even after marriage, whereas here there is a strong tendency to move away as quickly as possible. In the latter case may be mentioned the high walls that are built around homes and the fact that outsiders do not enter property, yards, or homes of others without proper courtesies and approval.

This degree of commitment to self and family is an important factor to keep in mind because it seems to influence behavior and decisions more deeply and extensively than it does in North American society. At the same time it greatly restricts the degree of commitment that is possible to the community or to the nation. This statement is based on the assumption that we have a limited amount of energy available to cope with all internal and external problems and realities. Thus, we attend to and react to some problems, people, and things at a cost of neglecting others. And if a large proportion of energy is directed toward or expended for self and family interests and goals, this will leave relatively little available for problems beyond this restricted range or realm of concern.

Moving beyond this first consideration, we might speculate about the type of personality characteristics that are encouraged and reinforced by the Latin American family and social system. To increase its vitality, long life, and survival the family probably encourages self-orientation, family-orientation, and the development of individual power and influence by means of which the individual will be able to protect the self and the family. This last emphasis understandably leads to a great concern with personal power and the demonstration of its possession in a variety of ways. One aspect of the demonstration of personal power and bravery has been discussed extensively under the heading of *machismo*. It should be kept in mind, however, that *machismo* has more relevance to interpersonal interactions and dominance than to encounters with the physical environment.

This appropriately leads to the next consideration which has been beautifully handled by Dr. Rogelio Diaz Guerrero, a Mexican psychiatrist and experimental psychologist, who suggests that in understanding Latin Americans and comparing them with Anglo-Americans it is essential that attitudes and reactions toward the physical and interpersonal realities be taken into account.[1] Briefly, he suggests that Anglo-Americans tend to view the physical reality as something to be subjected to their will. The success of American technology he considers to be a result of this orientation. Latin Americans, on the other hand, are seen as fatalistic in their attitudes toward nature. They feel subjugated by it and therefore have done relatively little to bring the physical reality under their control. This suggests an interesting comparison that might be made between fictitious and folk heroes in Anglo and Latin America. In corroboration of Díaz Guerrero's point of view it might be pointed out that the North American heroes such as Paul Bunyan, John Henry, Pecos Bill, and Davey Crockett were outstanding primarily because of their tremendous capabilities for dealing with realities and overcoming great physical tasks, dangers, and hardships. According to Díaz Guerrero's analysis, this type of hero might be expected to be much rarer in the folklore of Latin American cultures. Latin heroes would be expected to be outstanding for their patience in dealing with personal hardships and tragedies, in being especially adept in interpersonal relations, in dealing with authority and the social system rather than the physical reality.

Díaz Guerrero also points out that if attitudes toward interpersonal relations in Anglo-Americans are closely inspected, they are found to regard these relationships as much more static, difficult, and threatening than do Latin Americans.[2] The Latin tends to view the interpersonal situation as very attractive, dynamic, and fluid because there are two people involved: they can influence one another and they can both do something about the interaction. Therefore a great deal of pleasure and satisfaction is anticipated from interpersonal interactions. Díaz Guerrero suggests that because of their orientation Latin Americans would rather lose an argument than lose a friend, whereas North Americans prefer to win the arguments. If we are willing to speculate and extrapolate the above considerations regarding interpersonal relations, it is not too difficult to see how they may be related in one way or another to a variety of behavior, reactions, and attitudes of Latin and Anglo-Americans toward the community, the nation, social movements, civil rights, and such. Latin Americans are not likely to be attracted by situations lacking in opportunities for interpersonal interactions and involvements, whereas Anglo-Americans are likely to be attracted by movements and causes which allow them to become involved at a "safe" distance. For Latins, ritualistic involvement at a distance in civil rights movements, in organizations for the protection of this or that, leaves a lot to be desired because it simply is not direct, meaningful, or attractive enough.

It is worthwhile at this point to consider the degree to which the immediate and overt act is emphasized in Latin cultures. It appears that what is said or done at any given point in an interpersonal contact or interaction is very meaningful and important, but the follow-up, the ultimate consequences, the final goals, are often de-emphasized, neglected, and forgotten. This obviously means that under most circumstances planning is difficult, if not impossible, on a short- or long-term basis. This brings up the whole question of promises and their function in the interpersonal situation. The utility and psychological implications of promising has been given some attention in the psychiatric and psychoanalytic literature, but there obviously is not time here to cover these analyses. For the present purposes, however, it should be pointed out that in Latin America much more than in Anglo-America the promise is a quick, natural, easy gesture. It is, of course, made in the fervor and involvement of a moment of interpersonal encounter, and is prompted by an eagerness to say the polite thing at the right time.

However, these promises so easily and graciously made, like most plans which involve commitments far beyond the moment of encounter, are just as easily forgotten. To say simply that the gesture is insincere or meaningless would do an injustice to the personal involvement that Latin Americans experience in interpersonal contact and would miss the whole point. It is, nevertheless, undeniable that the making of the gesture is of the utmost importance because it helps to generate warmth and friendliness in the interpersonal encounter for the parties who are playing the friendship game. Projecting the promise into the future or inquiring about specific details could be embarrassing if pursued with too great vigor and would certainly detract from the appreciation of the moment or suggest a lack of courtesy or confidence. Therefore it is avoided or relegated to a position of minor importance. Of course, there is also a component of utility in such promising. It protects the self from the embarrassment of not being able to aid someone who has a problem, and it avoids having to admit helplessness and lack of personal power and influence in a face-to-face encounter. The promise therefore serves to protect the self, it may be temporarily reassuring and therapeutic for the other person, and it undoubtedly helps to preserve the cordiality of the interpersonal situation.

Gradually now we see personality characteristics emerging in which there is a stronger commitment to ideas than to action, to plans than to end results, to the immediate rather than to the ultimate. All of this suggests a greater tendency to be controlled by the pleasure rather than the reality principle. There also seems to be a stronger tendency to employ denial and compartmentalization as mechanisms for handling problems rather than compulsive confrontation, guilt, anxiety, and ulcers.

Another key to consider in understanding Latin American behavior is the reaction to authority. There seems to be some tendency to maintain certain ritualistic vestiges of respect for authority at a superficial level. At the same time there also seems to be a strong need to depreciate and question the intentions of authority. Great emphasis is placed upon bypassing, outmaneuvering authority and the "system." The Brazilian writer Vianna Moog has discussed the subtleties and skills that are developed in outmaneuvering and bypassing the system in terms of the *jeito*.[3] He defines the *jeito* as the famous Brazilian "way" of doing things, the "gimmick," the indirect and delicately complex means to an end, the difficult and circuitous route which suggests that in Brazil the shortest distance between two points is not necessarily a straight line.

The Latin's superficial deference and grudging admiration and

respect for authority, along with the need to demonstrate that
authority can be outmaneuvered, neutralized, and made impotent,
makes sense in the context of strong father-figures, *machismo,*
and the need for a symbol to fight, to overcome and defeat, in
proving one's personal power and influence. It may also explain
the subtle combination of respect and hate for the military strong
man in Latin America, reactions to the United States and her great
economic and military power, reactions to the Church, the peculiar combination of disregard and respect for scholars as "nice" but
ineffectual people, and the position of women in Latin society.

The reaction of Latin Americans to authority and the strong
commitment to the self and the family, to ideas rather than
action, to circumvention rather than direct attack, to interpersonal
rather than physical realities, should have some predictable consequences and effects in relation to government and the economy.
Silvert, for instance, has suggested that "the fruits of the industrial society will not flower best on the Iberian tree." At least
some part of the explanation of the economic problems in Latin
America may well be the lack of personal confidence in the future
of the country, in the stability of business organizations, currency,
and the government which often develops from many sad and
discouraging experiences. To some extent it may also be related
to the previously mentioned tendency to protect the self and the
family at all costs, which would understandably lead to "playing
it safe," sending money out of the country, or holding on to it in
the form of hard cash, land, or tangible material possessions. The
notions of investment in the future of the country and planning
for a rainy day have not been feasible with the people in general
because of the limited resources and finances available. But even
where resources, money, and potentialities for profit and advancement have been good, saving has not been too popular.

In addition to what has already been mentioned, there also
seems to be a tendency to underevaluate national products and
national potential and to overevaluate things foreign and European. This seems to be true even in those instances where national
products and potential are good and comparable to foreign products and potential. In Latin America there are quite a few exam-

ples of ample potential for vital and productive economies which have been demonstrated by the success with which foreign capital has managed to exploit situations. Foreigners have been able to operate as outsiders or naturalized citizens in reaping huge profits. It must be kept in mind that a lack of confidence in one's own potential and capabilities can often work as effectively to hinder effort and performance as a real lack of potential.

So far as governments in Latin America have been concerned, there has too often been a toleration of corrupt and ineffective political regimes and of erratic and selfish leadership which goes far beyond reasonable limits. Expectations with respect to governments and politicians and their intentions are extremely poor. There has also been a tendency toward passive acceptance of impossible conditions and unacceptable performance rather than a willingness to deal with problems and do something about them even if this would be painful and require self-sacrifice. Thus action is often delayed until only drastic measures can bring about a realignment of forces, if not a real solution to the problem. This may cause the great patience and frustration tolerance of the Latin to be pushed beyond the breaking point. Then hostility and aggression erupt and produce bloody revolution and chaos. A strong leader often emerges who eventually substitutes one form of authoritarianism for another. The cycle then begins again because the basic problem has not been eliminated. In general, Brazil has been an exception to this process in that she has not seen many bloody days in the past. But it is certainly not difficult to predict that if real progress and change are not forthcoming soon, then more and more drastic solutions will be sought as more and more drastic ones fail.[4]

Extensive and meaningful social integration is difficult even in a highly developed economy with extensive educational systems and relatively weak class lines such as those which exist in the United States. We are presently becoming painfully aware of this. However, social integration in a poorly developed economy with a weak educational system, with strong class lines and strong commitments to the self and the family, is obviously much more difficult. The problems are certainly increased when personal contacts with other class groups are extremely limited in the lower educational system and become even rarer in the secondary system and at the university level. Under these circumstances the possibilities for understanding the plight of the "others," the openness to contacts, the mobility that is provided through education, intermarriage, and the like, are minimized. Further, whatever class prejudices and misconceptions exist tend to remain intact, uninfluenced and unmodified by personal experiences and "outside" sources of information. The system therefore tends to maintain itself through the deprivation of information, and about "other" groups it nurtures rationalizations which may employ ideas such as genetic inferiority and lack of motivation. In addition, the strong family ties and the pressure for frequent family contacts which compete with "outside" interests and contacts should again be mentioned here as a contributing factor. While it may not be too desirable from a Christian point of view, family ties may first have to weaken somewhat in Latin societies before extensive and meaningful social integration can take place, and commitment to the welfare of the larger community and the nation can produce progress and modernization for the masses to any significant degree.

The influence of the Church in the development of values, motivation, and behavior in Latin America is both obvious and disappointing in many ways. For the most part it has seemed that only a thin veneer of Christianity has been developed rather than any real appreciation or respect for man, his rights and dignity. This, of course, is true not only of Latin America. In the case of Latin America, however, the problems can undoubtedly be related to the lack of sufficient personnel, the magnitude of the job, as well as some obvious lack of concern for the well-being of the masses. In many ways it seems that the Church has missed an opportunity to contribute to the well-being and progress of man in Latin America which perhaps is unparalleled in history. Since it is healthier to be concerned with what can be done in the future rather than to fret about the mistakes of the past, it would seem that the Church should quickly address itself to this question. There is little doubt that the Church can still serve one of the most important roles of any institution in Latin America in encouraging modernization and progress if it is willing to become less traditionalistic and more involved in giving encouragement and backing to the people and the programs which are likely to succeed in bettering the lot of the masses. This would mean, for instance, that instead of encouraging participation in long and arduous pilgrimages, recitations of the rosary, and the like, a greater emphasis would have to be placed upon participation in building, sanitation, agricultural, and other action programs. Some segment of the Church in Latin America is already oriented in this direction, but unfortunately it is still too small. Latin America presents an excellent opportunity for the Church to put its energy where its words are and to demonstrate that it recognizes and is concerned with the total well-being of the individual, that it recognizes that man's physical well-being has important implications for morally relevant behavior and spiritual beliefs.

NOTES

1. Rogelio Diaz-Guerrero, "Neurosis and the Mexican Family Structure," *American Journal of Psychiatry,* Vol. 112, No. 6 (1955), 411–417.
2. Rogelio Diaz-Guerrero, *Mexican Assumption about Interpersonal Relations.* A Review of General Semantics. Vol. XVI, No. 2, 185–8.
3. Vianna Moog, *Bandeirantes and Pioneers* (New York: George Bragiller, 1964).
4. John Santos, "A Psychologist Reflects on Brazil and Brazilians" in *New Perspectives of Brazil,* ed. E. Beklanoff (Nashville: Vanderbilt University Press, 1966).

Birth Control

J. MAYONE STYCOS

At the turn of the century the combined population of the United States and Canada approximated the current population of Brazil. By the end of this century it may have multiplied four times and reached two-thirds the population of today's crowded India. In reviewing the growth patterns of the United States the National Academy of Sciences noted recently that "rapid population growth will create difficulties in reaching America's noble goals of optimum education for all, universal abundance, enriched leisure, equal opportunity, quality, beauty and creativity."[1] An American Assembly Conference warned the United States about "increasing dangers in the continuation of (its) present rate of growth that would double the population every forty years with the prospect of constricted social opportunities and progressive crowding."[2]

At the turn of this century all of Latin America was populated by about 63 million persons, a figure well under the present population of Brazil. At current rates of increase, by the end of this century Latin America will have multiplied its population ten times, perhaps to match the current population of China. Indeed, "the increase in the population of Latin America during the last

12

half of this century may equal the total increase in population of man during all the millennia from his origin until 1650."[3] A Pan-American Assembly on Population held in Colombia in 1965 concluded that "Most Latin American nations . . . have rates of population growth which are high, both in terms of their growth of national product, and in comparison with the demographic growth of nations in other areas or eras . . . the population of the region will double in about 25 years, but the number and severity of the problems will increase by an even higher factor."[4]

Thus, rapid population growth is a fact and a social problem for both continents of this hemisphere. The Catholic Church has been deeply involved in this particular social problem, which is intimately involved with the very purposes of family life and sexuality. On the North American continent the hierarchy has been especially outspoken and activist in the sphere of family planning, since the issue was forced upon them by militant non-Catholic, and often anti-Catholic, groups. Since there has not been, at least until recently, any significant challenge to the Church on this issue in Latin America, it is to the United States which we must turn for the most official Church pronouncements on the question of population problems and the means to solve them.

Two especially important statements on these matters have been promulgated by the United States Catholic bishops within the past decade. It will be useful to compare these statements and utilize them as a point of departure. On November 26, 1959, the Catholic bishops of the United States issued a statement referring to the population explosion as a "terror technique phrase . . . a smoke screen behind which a moral evil may be foisted on the public." They referred to "hysterical terrorism and bland misrepresentation of data" and charged that to speak of a population explosion in the United States "is the sheerest kind of nonsense."[5] On November 14, 1966, the United States bishops approved another statement on birth control.[6] Whereas the earlier statement was remarkable for what it said, the more recent document is remarkable for what it does not. Gone is the vituperative tone, gone is the dismissal of population as a problem, and gone, by and large, is any significant attack on the concept of family planning. Instead the guns are trained on government coercion in the field of family planning. The bishops refer to the "threats to the free choice of spouses," to the "right to found a large family," and to the evils of "coercing the underprivileged to practice birth control." In my opinion this is not only change but change in a direction which can prove to be highly constructive. For in defending the rights of couples to have large families, the bishops implicitly defend their right to have small ones.

In a recent speech to the American Association for the Advancement of Science I discussed the political dangers of excessive demographic activism on the part of the United States, a matter fully appreciated in the bishops' statement.[7] Today, rather than concentrate on the negative aspect of their message, let me elaborate the positive: "the freedom and responsibility of spouses to make conscientious decisions in terms of nuptial love, determination of family size, and the rearing of children."

Freedom. What does freedom to determine one's family size mean? Certainly it means the absence of coercive measures such as the application of specific legal or economic sanctions on the large family. But just as the illiterate's liberty to vote is a hollow freedom, so is the ignorant man's freedom to control his family size a meaningless, if not dangerous, freedom.

Studies conducted in the United States and Latin America disclose great ignorance about population, about sexual functions, and about the means for controlling reproduction. For example, when a national sample of North Americans was asked to specify the population of the United States, not more than one in three persons could come within 25 million of the correct figure. Even fewer had any realistic notion of how rapidly the population is growing.[8] In Latin America recent surveys show that not only ignorance but serious error is characteristic of the average adult's view of sexual matters. Seventy-one percent of a national sample in Costa Rica thought that a man's fertility varied with the weather, and 77 percent that the fertile period occurs just before and after menstruation.[9] Precisely those who most need information, moreover, are the least likely to have it. A recent study conducted in the city of Medillin, Colombia, found that prior to marriage only 29 percent of those with less than three years of schooling, but 76 percent of those with seven or more years, knew anything about how a baby is born. Two-thirds of the poorly educated group, but only a third of the better-educated women, said they knew nothing about menstruation prior to its onset.[10]

The frequent opposition of Church groups to sexual education and to the spread of information on medically acceptable means of contraception has done nothing to foster the Church's support of freedom in the family sphere. As many sad parents have discovered, ignorance as a method of sexual control is self-defeating. "Responsible paternity requires," says the National Academy of Sciences report, "that couples of all social strata have the ability and means to limit births when they wish to do so, in accordance with their personal convictions . . . the freedom to limit family size to the number of children wanted when they are wanted is, in our view, a basic human right."[11]

Thus far we have been referring to the means by which family size goals may be realized. But what of the goals themselves? "Freedom is endangered," say the bishops, "when persons or agencies outside the family unit . . . presume to make the decisions as to the number of children or the frequency of births in a family." The Bishops were of course referring to the state, but why should the statement not apply equally to any institution, including the Church? It is often said that Church teaching refers only to the *means* for achieving the number and spacing of children, rather than to the ends themselves. Yet Catholics and non-Catholics alike associate the Church with the large-family ideal. Are they entirely in error?

Pope Pius XII continually extolled the large family, and even Pope John in 1960 cautioned the faithful not to "be afraid of the number of your sons and daughters. On the contrary, ask Divine Providence for them, so that you can educate them for this benefit, for your own honor in later years, for the great welfare of your fatherland, and for the external homeland for which we are tending."

In the United States, according to a *New York Times* article, "parish approbation customarily was reserved—in many parishes it still is reserved—for the big Catholic family. Mothers with plans to limit the number of their children have often faced parish censure. 'When the Catholic Mother of the Year turns out to be a woman with three children instead of eight or nine, I'll believe the church word has reached down to my level,' a mother in Chicago said smiling."[12] The smiling mother's statistics were suprisingly accurate. The number of children of the National Catholic Welfare Conference's Catholic Mother of the Year has averaged 8.2 over the past decade,[13] in a period when the average Catholic couple's maximum expected number of children was less than four.[14]

In a survey in the summer of 1966 in the metropolitan area of San Juan, Puerto Rico, we asked 650 married women, "What does the Catholic Church say about the number of children which a family should have: that it ought to have many children, the number of children which can be properly brought up or does the Church say nothing about this?" Only a fifth of the women said that they did not know or that the Church does not speak on the subject. Fully two-thirds believe that the Church says a family should have many children. It is of interest that when asked whether or not they agreed with the position they attributed to the Church, 60 percent disagreed with the Church if they thought it favored large families, but only 7 percent disagreed if they thought it favored the number which could properly be brought up.

Judgment. In the view of the bishops, spouses have not only the freedom but the "responsibility to make conscientious decisions" in this area. Citing a passage from the Second Vatican Council's Constitution on the Church in the Modern World, they maintain that "the decision concerning the number of children they will have depends on the correct judgment of the parents and it can in no way be left to the judgment of public authority."

If decisions on family size are to be left to the correct judgments of parents, it would seem reasonable that parents should be aided in achieving their family size goals if (1) their judgments could be determined and (2) their judgments be "correct" or "responsible." The first is essentially a question for the demographer; the second a question for the theologian or moralist. But even the theologian, in order to determine the morality of a judgment or desire, requires accurate information both on the nature of the judgments and the individual justifications for them.

I need not tell Catholic priests about the problems of securing reliable information from human beings on sensitive or embarrassing topics, nor about the problems of securing an unbiased sampling of the population, so that we may make correct inferences about "the average person." Suffice it to say that over the past decade there have been major scientific advances in the collection, processing, and analysis of social-psychological data dealing with human motivations concerning reproduction.

Indeed, we have learned immeasurably more about people's judgments on family size in the past ten years than in the previous hundred. For the United States, for example, we now know that from 80 to 85 percent of Catholic men and women regard four or fewer children as their ideal, and that their desires in this regard are not very different from those of non-Catholics.[15]

In Latin America a series of systematic surveys has recently been conducted in major Latin American cities by the United Nations Latin American Demographic Center in collaboration with Cornell University. Carefully trained local staffs interviewed representative samples of approximately two thousand women of childbearing age in each of the following cities: Bogotá, Caracas, Lima, Mexico City, Panama City, Rio de Janeiro, San José, and San Salvador. In all instances women were asked the following question: "If you were to start a family now, how many children would you want?" The number desired ranged from an average of 2.4 in Rio de Janeiro to 4.1 in Mexico City, or from a quarter to half the number of the average North American Catholic Woman of the Year. We then classified the women in each city according to the frequency with which they receive Communion. In no city did the difference in ideal number of children vary by as much as one child between those who receive Communion less than once per year and those who receive twice or more per year.[16] Another kind of datum is provided by a recent public opinion survey conducted in seven Brazilian cities. While the

average family in these cities had only between three and four
living children, only about a quarter of the couples planned to
have more children.[17]

But this is what people *want*. Are such desires based on selfishness, hedonism, or irresponsibility? Are the lower-income populations of Latin America capable of reaching "correct judgments"
in the light of their low levels of education? I believe that we
often underestimate both the intelligence and responsibility of
the uneducated. To illustrate what I mean, let me give you some
examples of what poorly educated Latin Americans say when they
are questioned in this area. My first illustrations are from Mexican women interviewed by Father Alfonso Orozco Contreras in a
family planning clinic in Mexico City.[18] For example, a twenty-
nine-year-old woman with five children reported:

> I came to the clinic because since I am not able to support them, I no
> longer want to have more children. I now have five, why more when with
> these I already have too many? Two or three would be enough. I know that
> the Church says we should not try to avoid having children, but I believe
> that it is a greater sin to have them and not educate them. The point is not
> only to bring them into the world but to educate them also. I am not in
> accord with those families who have ten or twelve children but can only
> half dress and feed them, turning them into beggars and delinquents. Many
> say that pills are used so as to keep a slim figure, but these people do not
> know that what we want is something much more important: our home,
> children, and husband.

Another thirty-five-year-old patient of the clinic said:

> Religion says that we should accept the children that God sends, but my
> personal opinion is that it is a much greater sin to have children one can't
> educate. Of course, I would not discuss this with any priest because it is my
> own personal feeling. I believe in confession and all, but I have not confessed
> this. Also, I do not feel I am living in sin because I believe it to be good.
> I have seen many children who are almost in misery and never go to church.
> On the other hand, if you ask the families why they have so many children
> they answer "because it is a sin to prevent them." They are not faithful
> church attenders but resort to the Church to justify a large family. I really
> believe that if they were better church members they wouldn't have so many
> children. They consider it a sin to avoid having children, but on the other
> hand they find it very normal not to fulfill their obligations as parents.
> Doesn't this seem like a contradiction?

Another said:

> I know that according to my religion I am doing wrong because I have not gone to confession and I have not wanted to confess, but I would like to see them with nine children and begging bread and milk with not enough to go around, or walking without shoes or with torn clothes because they do not have means to buy them. Also, if I have not gone to confess and do not go, they will not be charged with my sin.

It might be thought that the desperation of poverty drives such women to desire to limit the size of their families and that if their economic level were improved, they would desire more children. While there may be some truth to this argument, as the standard of living rises we can also anticipate comparable increases in the standards for responsible parenthood. In short, the number of children viewed as adequately supportable may decline. A Puerto Rican mother with some high school education explained the process with admirable clarity when she was interviewed by one of our students this summer:

> If I have to send my children to school, I have to dress them properly. One, two, or five is not the same as ten. . . . One lives here as one's neighbors. A poor woman sees her neighbors send their children to the *Colegio* nicely dressed and neat; she feels sad because she can't have her children the same. She decides, well I have already have five and I'll have no more.[19]

And what of the males' sense of responsibility? Much has been written, largely by journalists and pseudosociologists, about the Latin American complex of *machismo*. In my earliest investigations in Puerto Rico I used this presumed drive to manifest virility as a major hypothesis in accounting for high birth rates. Research proved me wrong, and proved that lower income Puerto Rican males had attitudes far more responsible than had ever been supposed. When we asked them how a man could prove he was an *hombre completo* or a *macho,* they cited the need to prove one was not sterile, but they added that beyond this point manhood was demonstrated by being able properly to support one's children. As phrased by a sugar cane cutter with three years education: "to be an *hombre completo* a man should have a wife and children, and that these should be well fed and have clothes to wear and the necessary things to live well."[20]

The bishops noted that "free decision is curtailed when spouses feel constrained to choose birth limitation because of poverty, inadequate and inhuman housing, or lack of proper medical services." This may well be, and it behooves governments to move with all due haste to remove poverty from the face of the earth. But what can the individual family be expected to do in the meantime? Reprehensible as our social system or our leaders may be, in the face of today's poverty can a poor family's desire for a moderate number of children be considered anything other than responsible parenthood? I would say that such motives, in the face of religious and legal obstacles and almost a conspiracy of silence on the part of our mass media, is magnificent tribute to the "correct judgment" and "conscientious decision-making" of the common man. The fact that he often fails to *achieve* these goals is no reflection on his judgment or responsibility, but a reflection on the forces which deny him adequate knowledge and facilities to realize the dictates of his conscience.

In the case of Latin America there is a great thirst for knowledge and a great need for enlightenment. When asked whether information on birth control should be disseminated, an overwhelming majority of the women in the Latin American cities covered in our survey answered affirmatively. In Medellin, a conservative Colombian city, where over three-quarters of the sampled women attend church every Sunday, close to nine out of ten felt that contraceptive instruction should be available in public facilities, and only a quarter of these felt that only instruction in periodic abstinence should be offered. In the United States eight out of every ten Catholics interviewed in a recent national sample felt that "information on birth control ought to be easily available to any married person who wants it"; and six out of every ten felt the government should "give aid to states and cities for birth control programs if they request it."[21]

To many intellectuals the key to freedom is knowledge, and institutions which are viewed as suppressing knowledge are regarded with particular suspicion. In a series of lengthy interviews conducted with Colombian intellectuals this summer, in

speaking of the role of the Church and population problems, one
of them put it this way:

> To my view all the purposeful hiding of knowledge is immoral, be it
> political knowledge in a totalitarian state or birth control [knowledge] in a
> religious state. The worst example is what happens economically when a
> selected group keeps a new technology to itself and does not allow other
> groups in the society to benefit from it. Our higher classes are using birth
> control quite widely, although they would never admit it because they
> maintain a facade of religiousness to appear as favorites of the Church. But
> it is these same people who oppose birth control in the general population.
> It is this kind of double standard that I see as the highest immorality in
> the world.[22]

Nevertheless, despite imperfect knowledge, despite the absence
of public facilities and the benediction of their Church, Catholic
women of both continents are increasingly turning to contraception, and, in the United States at least, to highly effective means.
According to the results of national samples, by 1955 57 percent
of married Catholic women had practiced contraception. By 1965,
however, the proportion had risen to 78 percent. Moreover, while
the proportion of users of the rhythm method remained at the
same level (about 25 percent), the proportion of users of other
contraceptive methods rose from 30 percent to over 50 percent.[23]

In Latin American cities, too, surprising proportions of women
have practiced contraception, from 40 to 65 percent of currently
married females. Women who attend church regularly are somewhat more likely to practice rhythm, but the differences are not
great, and most contraception is by other means. Indeed, one of
the pressing social problems of urban Latin America is the high
incidence of induced abortion, a good indication that women
will resort to illegal, dangerous, painful, expensive, and irreli-
gious measures to control their fertility if other means are not
provided.[24]

It may not be true, as a Colombian intellectual put it to one of
our interviewers recently, that "this problem will ultimately either
finish the Church or transform it," but we can all share with
Father Gustavo Perez of Colombia the "unrest and the hopes of
all those who wish a resolution of the conflict between religious

norms and social realities."[25] I have attempted to indicate some
of the social realities as revealed by modern demographic research
and to show how these realities relate to the norms promulgated
in the 1966 statement of the North American bishops. In this
connection I should like to repeat the final recommendation of
the Pan-American Assembly on Population:

Religious leaders should be continually provided with the best available
scientific information on biological, social and economic aspects of population
problems. This information should be made available to all levels of the
church hierarchy. In turn, religious leaders of all faith should intensify communication with scientists in order that the public may fully comprehend the
continual development of church thought.[26]

What is the importance of this dialogue? It has been well
phrased by Paul VI, who on June 23, 1964, stated, "The Church
has to proclaim such laws of God in the light of scientific, social
and psychological truths which, in recent times, have received
new and most ample studies and documentation."

(In response to questions, Doctor Stycos made the following
comments.)

First let me comment in regard to statistics on the number of
children born into consensual unions. As far as Latin America is
concerned, the quality of the data vary very much from country
to country. But between the census data and the surveys that
have been done recently, we have a pretty good indication of the
extent to which children are born out of legal wedlock. One question of particular interest to us is whether these nonlegal unions
or nonreligious unions are more or less fertile than legal unions.
We did very exhaustive studies on this in the British Caribbean,
and there we discovered that the problem is the reverse of what
we had expected: the less legal the union, the less fertile it was,
and if you legalized most unions, you would raise fertility, not
lower it. Evidence from some other Latin American countries,
however, indicates that the pattern we find in the British Caribbean may not hold in Latin American cultures. We find in some
countries that there is a higher fertility on the part of common-
law unions than in others, although it is very difficult to separate
this from the educational status and other factors.

With regard to other remarks, I am very pleased that neither commentator wished to accept my proposition that the Church was pro-natalist. I am absolutely delighted to be proven wrong on this issue. My point here is that while it may not be that Church teaching has been pro-natalist in any official sense, in some way Catholics have come to feel that the Church is encouraging large families. Our studies have indicated that Catholics believe this is the case. Now if the Church does not believe this, it should take pains to disabuse the population about this issue. I do not wish to take a stand on that. I would just refer you to the scholarly work* of Professor Noonan which examines carefully the whole history of the Church with respect to this issue and has a great deal of information in it on the pro-natalist history within the Church.

I also appreciated Bishop Arias' comments about responsible paternity. I feel that his point about the importance of scientific knowledge in this area was very well taken. For the past decade I have been one of the people who has been urging greater scientific research not only on the biological but also on the sociological and moral aspects of this problem. As of ten years ago there was practically no research conducted in either of these areas. We did not know what people thought about the subject, nor did we really know in any scientific way what the biological consequences of the use of contraceptions were. I would not say that we know them with 100 percent accuracy today. But there is a new spirit among the scientific community, a new interest in turning their attention to this problem. Both social scientists and biological scientists have become seriously interested, for the first time in man's history, in social and biological aspects of human reproduction. We have managed for the first time, in the past decade, to attract people of high caliber in these areas into the study of human reproduction. There is no doubt that we need to increase our knowledge, and I am personally optimistic. I believe that within the next decade we will really have some major breakthroughs in our scientific information.

Where I would differ somewhat from Bishop Arias is in the

* John Thomas Noonan, Jr., *Contraception: A History of Its Treatment by the Catholic Theologians and Canonists* (Cambridge: Harvard University Press, 1965).

strategy adopted. Must we really wait until the last scientific results are in before the Church or other groups seriously come to grips with this question? I would say if we do that, given the current rates of population growth, we will be in trouble because as we know science moves rather slowly. I would like to see the Church deal with this question just as soon as it can. Of course it is doing this to a very large extent. My point here is that if the Church can keep itself informed about what is developing on the scientific side, and in the same way the scientists keep themselves informed of what is happening in Church thinking on the moral side, we can reach an agreement on this question and move ahead to implement our decisions.

Finally, on the question of the economic and social problems of the world coming first, problems as pressing as food or the distribution of the wealth of this world, again I could not agree with the Bishop more. These problems are number one on our world priority list. If I were here speaking as an economist, I would certainly speak about these kinds of problems, and if you ask me as a human being, I would place these problems first. I believe that birth control in and of itself is neither good nor bad. Unless we have a good objective there is no point in it at all. The difference here again, as I see it, is that whatever economic progress is made, whatever plans for education or medical improvement there are, can be accelerated by slowing the rate of population growth. Slowing of the population growth alone will not solve the problem, of course. But nations must face this dilemma, that much of what they do in improving the distribution of wealth or improving the gross national product will be eaten up by the population growth. I think a nation which emphasizes economic development and its usual ingredients, but at the same time gives ample attention to slowing rates of population growth, will develop much faster than one that pays no attention to the population question.

NOTES

1. National Academy of Sciences, *The Growth of U.S. Population* (Washington, D.C., 1965).

2. P. M. Houser, ed., *The Population Dilemma* (Englewood Cliffs, N.J.: Prentice-Hall, 1963), p. 181.

3. Harold F. Dorn, "World Population Growth" in J. Mayone Stycos and Jorge Arias, eds., *The Population Dilemma in Latin America* (Washington, D.C.: Potomac Books, 1966), p. 21.

4. First Pan-American Assembly on Population, Final Report, August 11–14, 1965.

5. National Catholic Welfare Conference, "Explosion or Backfire," November 26, 1959.

6. National Catholic Welfare Conference, "Statement on the Government and Birth Control," November 14, 1966.

7. J. Mayone Stycos, "Defusing the Population Bomb in Latin America" (1966), mimeographed.

8. "American Attitudes on Population Policy," *Studies in Family Planning*, No. 9, January, 1966. For a good study of ignorance on sexual matters see L. Rainwater's report of a lower income group in a North American City, *And the Poor Get Children* (Quadrangle Books). For an analysis of the ways in which lower class Latin American culture discourages communication on sexual topics see J. Mayone Stycos, *Family and Fertility in Puerto Rico* (New York: Columbia University Press, 1955).

9. F. B. Waisanen and J. T. Durlak, "A Survey of Attitudes Related to Costa Rican Population Dynamics" (San José: American International Association for Economic and Social Development, 1966), mimeographed.

10. Preliminary tabulations from a study conducted by Mario Jaramillo and Robert Hartford. The data are based on a subsample of 290 cases from the larger sample of about 2,000.

11. National Academy of Science, *op. cit.*, p. 22.

12. George Barrett, "Catholics and Birth Control," *New York Times*, August 5–8, 1963.

13. Judith Blake, "The Americanization of Catholic Reproductive Ideals," *Population Studies*, Vol. 20, No. 1 (July, 1966).

14. R. Freedman, P. K. Whelpton, and A. A. Campbell, *Family Planning, Sterility and Population Growth* (New York: McGraw-Hill, 1959), p. 285. Data are for 1955, and for couples in which both husband and wife are Catholic. "Most likely" expected number of births is 3.4, and "maximum" expected 3.8.

15. J. Blake, *op. cit.*

16. J. Mayone Stycos, *Contraception and Catholicism in Latin America*, forthcoming.

17. "Pesquisa de Opiniao Publica Sobre a Convenencia do Uso de Anticoncepcionais" (Brazil: I.B.O.P.E., July, 1966) (mimeographed).

18. Padre Alfonso Orozco Contreras, mimeographed paper based on interviews with sixty patients of the Asociacion Pro-Salud Maternal, Mexico City, no date (c. 1966).

19. Interview No. 5, by Betsy Cohen, August, 1966.

20. J. M. Stycos, *Family and Fertility in Puerto Rico.*

21. "American Attitudes on Population Policy."

22. Interview No. 53, by Sergio Sismondo.

23. Charles Westoff and Norman B. Ryder, "Methods of Fertility Control Used in the United States: 1955–65." November, 1966 (mimeographed).

24. For a brief review of the studies on incidence of abortion see J. Mayone Stycos and Jorge Arias, ed., *Population Dilemma in Latin America* (Washington, D.C.: Potomac Books, 1966), pp. 237–240.

25. Gustavo Perez, "Family Planning—Current Perspectives" in *Population Dilemma in Latin America,* p. 212.

26. First Pan-American Assembly on Population, *op. cit.*

Indian Populations

JOHN D. EARLY, S.J.

A discussion of efforts of United States members of the Christian community working in the Indian areas of Latin America is a highly complex subject, and the following can be only a very brief, general sketch of what I consider to be the anatomy of the problems facing the American Christian community in this work.

For the sake of simplification we can divide the Indian populations of Latin America into four types.

The first are the isolated Indian groups who have little or no contact with the outside world and the national culture of the territory in which they reside. These are usually tribes that have retreated to the interior in the face of the expansion of Europeans. The territory in which they live may be noted on a map as belonging to a certain country, but actually the central government has no effective control over these regions. The numbers included in such Indian populations are impossible to estimate with accuracy, but it is a small proportion of the total Indian population of Latin America. We will not deal with this Indian type here because few Christian groups and no American Catholics to my knowledge are working with this type of Indian population. However, a number of the remarks we shall later make apply a fortiori to this group.

The second type is what Steward calls the corporate peasant. These Indians have been able to retain some of their communal land, live apart from the local Latin culture, and marry within the group. "The in-group feeling associated with corporate-peasant isolation gives rise to local distinctiveness in dress and other overt features. The corporate-peasant culture, however, has a continuity with village culture of aboriginal times as far as family life, farm practices, food habits, religious and social practices are concerned. But it has also incorporated many Spanish features with aboriginal features and patterned them in what is a new subculture or subsociety of the larger nation." This type of Indian population has a distinct culture that is quite different in many respects from either Latin or United States culture, even though it has borrowed some traits from the Spanish. In this paper I shall discuss this type of Indian population.

The third type of Indian population is the hacienda or *finca* peasant. These are farm workers who live on the large plantations run by the Latin owner or his representative. The Indian's whole life is encompassed by the confines of the plantation. Steward notes, "Under this arrangement, the worker's family patterns and indeed a considerable amount of his previous culture may be preserved, provided only that it does not conflict with the larger hacienda pattern. The hacienda, however, insists on conformity within the paternalistic arrangements. The workers remain illiterate, they become Catholics, and they follow the political dictates of their *hacendado*." This type of Indian is a partially acculturated Latin, and no longer can be considered simply as Indian. A number of the remarks we shall make about the corporate-peasant Indian will also refer to this group.

Finally there is the fully acculturated Indian Latin peasant. These are people who racially may still be full-blooded Indian or mestizo, but due to the historical processes of the last four and a half centuries they have lost their Indian culture and today are Latin peasants. Latin peasantry, whether it be Indian, mestizo, or white, is a fascinating area of study, but this is not our topic.

At this point it would be logical to give a detailed description of the life and customs of a corporate-peasant Indian group. But a description of a distinct culture in a short space is not very practical. I shall instead give an impressionistic, oversimplified picture of what I have observed throughout many parts of Latin America to be a common American approach in work with the corporate-peasant Indian groups. A parish will be founded by taking over a ruined church, restoring it, and establishing a parish program. This will include the performance of the traditional liturgy in the church and the training of a group of Indian catechists who in turn will preach the word of God. This will lead to a certain amount of mechanical ritual practice by the Indians. However, as with a number of Catholic groups, it will often be difficult to distinguish this ritual practice from superstition. The middle-class American will usually be overwhelmed by the poverty of the people. He will establish a medical clinic and operate it himself, in spite of his lack of training, if no one else is available. He may attempt to found some kind of agricultural cooperative.

After a short time he will begin to see some manifestations of the Indian culture. The Indian religion may make its appearance. However this is different from the American priest's, which represents to him that of the one, true religion. Hence these strange customs are considered automatically pagan and superstitious, and are to be eradicated with all possible speed. The ideal here seems to be to found a parish among these Indians just like the good, old Irish or Italian or mixed parish that the priest came from back in New York, Boston, Chicago, or San Francisco. After all, that is Catholicism, and that is what he is here among these Indians to do—start a Catholic parish.

Now my thesis is that this good, simple, straightforward American is at best giving a good example to the Indians, ministering in a very limited way to their material needs, but probably is not communicating the Christian message to the hearts of his Indian parishioners. At worst he may be destroying the Indians' pride, self-respect, and dignity by attempting to destroy their culture and by not being able to give them anything else to put in its place. The drunken, degenerate Indian who is no longer an Indian but has not been able to become a Westerner is the sad sight in

many areas where representatives of Western culture have introduced a process of aborted change. And missionaries of the Christian community have more than once made their contribution to
this state of affairs. This type of service of the Christian community in the integration of the Indian is at best highly inefficient
for all the resources of manpower and money invested in it. And
at its worst it is a human catastrophe that can be called Christian
service only by an Alice-in-Wonderland use of words.

What is the difficulty here? I believe its roots are quite deep,
and it is worthwhile to take a few minutes to examine them. I
believe one difficulty is theological. It involves the question, What
is the meaning of Christianity and what is its relevance for human
development? Perhaps it is assumed that all members of the
Christian community, especially those engaged in formal church
work, know the answer to this problem. However I am not quite
sure. Certainly the present convulsion of change in the Church
shows that there is much disagreement on this fundamental question. And it would be naive to believe that this confusion does
not reveal itself among the personnel of the Christian community
working with the Indian populations in Latin America. Here, a
number of burning theological issues must be faced by any personnel of the Christian community with a Western background
when they attempt to communicate the Christian message to
someone from a non-Western culture. The simple assumption that
seems to underlie much of the present work with the Indian populations—that we all know what Christianity is and therefore our
only job is to communicate it—must be challenged and examined.

Another difficulty, not unrelated to the theological problem, is
psychological. This is the problem of self-knowledge. Do I really
understand myself and my own background? Do I really understand what it means to be a member of the middle class in the
United States with all the values, prejudices, and ways of defining reality that are typical of middle-class existence? Do I understand what it means to be a member of a particular ethnic group
in the United States? And, finally, do I understand what it means
to be an American, with all of the values, prejudices, and ways
of looking at things that are typically American. If a person has

no sensitivity to all these ingredients that make up his own background, how is he going to be effective among a group that has none of this background? Is he really going to communicate Christianity, or will it be some middle-class, Americanized version of it?

Again, the simple assumption that seems to underlie much of the present work with Indian populations in Latin America is that these problems to not exist. To my mind this is a most dangerous assumption. These theological and social-psychological problems have far-reaching ramifications. The process of self-examination that they demand must be carried out as part of the general personal formation received in the various religious and lay groups of the Christian community. Whatever position one may take on these questions, the simple assumptions that prevent them ever being discussed must be blasted away in this age of reform.

In addition to these more general problems, I believe there are several areas of very specific difficulties for the Christian community in their service of the Indian populations. The first concerns liturgy and catechesis, the two principal means of communicating the Christian message. The current liturgical and catechetical reform has many valuable aspects for work with the Indian populations. Much of this reform, however, is still taking place within a Western context and needs a different development to deal with the problems of Indian populations. Here we need much professional work in the fields of linguistics and languages, ethnology and anthropology, as well as some creative theological thinking. The necessity of learning the Indian languages seems almost obvious. Yet the very few members of the Christian community working in these areas who know them leads one to conclude that it really is not important. It is true that a fair number of the corporate-peasant type of Indian can understand some Spanish, but for many, communication with the heart is not had by means of a language which is not well understood. The need to learn, in great detail and with deep understanding, the customs of the Indian groups again would seem to be an obvious fact. Yet our missionaries never do this. Once professionally trained people have captured the linguistic structure of the language, its cognitive patterns, the social customs of the group, its system of law and morality, then some theological analysis needs to be done. And this does not mean that a theological judgment will be passed on various Indian forms by simply using the norms of Western Christianity. Here is an area for much creative theological thinking, an area scarcely touched by the professional theologians since the days of Ricci in China and de Nobili in India.

Rather than speak about possible theological, catechetical, and liturgical developments, however, I should like to focus on the institutional prerequisites for any significant work of this kind. Before projects are initiated among the Indian populations, it is necessary to train personnel in the Indian culture. To neglect the Indian culture, to act as if it does not exist, is an insult to these people. To send personnel among them on the assumption that these human beings have nothing of human value in their culture, that it does not need to be understood, that they are all wrong and the American groups all right, is intellectually a stupidity of the highest order and morally a paternalistic disdain of the Indian which is completely alien to the Christian spirit. Therefore I would seriously propose that the bishops and religious superiors in conjunction with the American and Latin academic communities establish institutes of human development for the study of linguistics, anthropology, theology, agronomy, and so on in the various Indian areas where members of the Christian community are working.

These institutes would require professionally trained people to staff them. They would do the linguistic, anthropological, and theological research needed as a basis for any realistic program and would also train new personnel coming into the area. The institutes must be cooperative efforts between the various American groups and the representatives of the local Latin communities. Protestants already have several such institutes, such as the Summer Institute of Linguistics. And these institutes must receive realistic support in both money and manpower. The ecumenical aspect of such institutes cannot be emphasized too strongly. If Catholics and Protestants are going to fight with each other, and the various Catholic groups are going to fight among themselves and the various Protestant groups do the same, then we come back to the problem previously raised: What is the meaning of Christianity and its relevance for human development? I do believe that until such institutes are started and the basic research performed, much of the service of the Christian community to the Indian populations at best will continue to be haphazard, inefficient, and often irrelevant, and at worst will destroy the Indian's pride and dignity in exchange for a paternalistic handout.

Another problem of the Christian community working with Indian populations centers around what is often called community development work. The words "community development" have been used in many senses. Often the term refers to economic development alone. More recently it has been expanded to include the development of all the material services of the community. I would prefer to use it in an even larger sense—the development of the fullest potential of the human community. In this sense a realistic liturgical and catechetical program is a part of community development. But here let us give a few thoughts to some of the other basic elements. There are usually three core programs: agriculture, education, and health, which may in turn be broken down into a number of smaller programs.

The agricultural program leads one into such projects as teaching agricultural techniques in order to increase quantity and variety of yield, road building to open up markets, supporting land reform, and perhaps even attempting to introduce light industry in areas where population is increasing and there is no more available land. Any attempt at agricultural and economic development should take into consideration regional or national development plans that may be projected by the government.

Education may mean the teaching of Spanish, literacy programs, and perhaps the opening of an elementary school if the government is unable to do it. In the words of the distinguished Peruvian lawyer, Roberto MacLean y Estenos,

We must do more than instruct the Indian; we must think about educating him. It is not enough to teach him to read and write in order to free him from want, to make him a citizen and to incorporate him in the national life. Often it happens that . . . the Indian who has learned to read and write gradually becomes maladjusted to his social environment, thinks that he is superior to his own family and social group, withdraws from his community and becomes an exploiter of his own Indian brothers. We need more than mere instructors, that is those who lack mature education, who have made a superstition out of method and are incapable of projecting themselves beyond the school walls. The Indians need educators who enter into the lives of their students, understand them, stimulate them and show them life in all its potential richness.

A health program means above all public health measures. There are two principal enemies of Indian populations. The first is malnutrition. Frequently this is not so much due to lack of food as due to the lack of variety and balance in the diet. Protein deficiency is common because of the absence of fish and meat. The other problem is bad water. Intestinal difficulties are constantly occurring for this reason. When the human organism is under attack from malnutrition and bad water, it becomes easy prey for many other types of pathology like pneumonia, tuberculosis, and malaria. Clinics and hospitals are helpful, but public health programs should receive priority.

It should be emphasized that community development is an organic reality that demands a variety of different programs. The attempt to establish a Christian community by introducing only one or two specialized programs is narrow-minded. As MacLean y Estenos has pointed out:

to implement only one of these programs, betters only one aspect of community life to the neglect of others. This is like trying to write on a piece of paper in a wind storm, like trying to plough the sea or like trying to preach a sermon in an empty desert.

This is a fruitless effort, a waste of time. The lack of education and the presence of precarious health nullifies any upraising of the level of life. Nor does it help the Indian only to teach him some Spanish or only to try to indoctrinate him in a religion whose essence he does not understand. And not only are you not helping him, but you are receiving him and exploiting him as you lead him to believe that now he is a citizen of the national community when he can hardly spell and write his name. You put before his eyes the dazzling promise of political rights, without giving him at the same time economic liberty, healthful living conditions, and a standard of life and cultural level he needs.

It has been asked by a number of people, including some of

the Christian community currently engaged in work with Indian populations, Why should the Church become involved in literacy, education, health, and economic programs? Some say that this is not the function of the Church, that the service of the Christian community should be restricted to the administration of the sacraments and preaching the word of God. It is true that in more developed nations these functions are taken care of by the government. But many governments are simply not in close contact, or present in only a bureaucratic form, with their Indian populations. It takes courage and sacrifice to live among these populations, and these the bureaucratic spirit generally lacks. In short, if private segments of the Christian community do not undertake this work, it is highly doubtful that anything will be done in many areas. But it also means that the missionaries will be hoping to work themselves out of jobs once the development matures. The objection to the Church running community development programs may be based upon an identification of the Church with the priest. It may be questioned whether all the aspects of community development belong to the role of the priest. Certainly from the viewpoint of professional training the laity are better prepared. Perhaps the day of exclusively clerical Christian service to the Indian communities is finished. Future service should be a team effort involving both priest and laity.

In promoting a community development among Indian populations the Christian community is helping to integrate the Indian community in the national culture. Rapid integration as such, however, should not be the goal. Too rapid a rate of development in the Indian areas can have the effect of destroying the local culture without really substituting anything in its place.

It is sometimes argued that what was previously said about language, liturgy, and catechesis encourages the Indian to retain his own culture and discourages him from integrating into the national community. This objection oversimplifies the situation. To encourage a liturgy and catechesis adapted to the Indian culture and in his own language does not mean that one is discouraging change. The liturgy and catechesis themselves will be a change for him, even though they are different from the Western forms. With the other programs of community development, they can help the Indian to interpret the change he is undergoing, so that some of the shock and discontinuities of change can be mitigated. To charge that the use of Indian languages and a catechesis and liturgy adapted to his culture means that one is discouraging all change indicates that one fails to appreciate the complexities and different possibilities that are available.

Finally, I believe that the service of the Christian community to the Indian populations should be professional service in all the areas where there exists a body of technical and professional knowledge. Christian justice demands that one know what one is doing. To offer Christian service and to refuse to prepare oneself professionally for it is a contradiction in terms. Thus there is need of professional preparation in linguistics, anthropology, theology, medicine, nursing, agronomy, education, literacy, and language programs. It is true that professional preparation is no panacea for solving all problems or developing Christian community. The professional is not the messiah. But good will without professional competence is always an inefficient, often dangerous, incompetence which is difficult to distinguish from injustice.

In discussing the problems and needs of the Indian populations we have so far not mentioned physical plant. This may appear to be a minor item which does not really need discussion. But the physical level of life in these areas is rather meager, unbelievable in fact to middle-class Americans. He was not brought up in such circumstances and probably could not survive if he tried to live at the physical level of the Indians. Thus in all prudence he needs to make allowances for himself if he is to survive in the area and do his work. Yet the obsession to build and install machinery that seems to grip many Americans in the Indian areas appears pathological. The attempt to re-create a little bit of the good, old United States, with a parish house, school, and compound just like those back home, goes far beyond the dictates of necessary protection. The social and psychological gulf which unnecessary buildings and machinery put between the priest and his congregation is at times scandalous. The Americans have achieved a great reputation for their *cordon sanitario*, the sanitation belt, the isolation they put between themselves and the people they are there to serve. Perhaps the contradiction that this situation poses is best expressed this way. How can one in honesty and justice presume to share the Eucharistic meal in church with those with whom he would never share a meal in his or their home because of the *cordon sanitario*? It seems to me this contradiction must be faced up to.

I realize that during the course of these remarks I have been critical of American Christian service to the Indian populations of Latin America. I have not given the other side of the coin, the efforts and achievements that can be praised (and there do exist a number of such situations.) If my remarks have any impact, investigation will be made, and I am sure the good work will quickly be discovered and emulated. I should explain also that some of the criticism in my remarks has been learned the hard way, by my own mistakes and foolishness. I do not claim the role of the just man. And, finally, the basis for this composite picture is all of Latin America. Various areas have differing circumstances and needs which would require many qualifications on my remarks.

Christian service to the Indian populations is a particular embodiment of the Christian life. The Christian life is not simple. Neither is this particular type of service.

The Campesinos

GEORGE CABOT LODGE

It is no more possible to generalize about rural Latin America than it is about other parts of the region. Close to 70 percent[1] of the population live in rural communities or in isolation, with different kinds of problems and opportunities, subject to a wide variety of economic, social, and political forces. There are, for example, the traditional, hierarchical, and more or less organized Indian communities of southern Mexico, Guatemala, and the Andes; the transplanted, socially decomposed, and politically disorganized communities of Indians found, for example, in the Bolivian tin-mining areas; the diffused and scattered mestizo communities mingled with the old hacienda structures; the relatively modern towns and villages inhabited by wage earners from surrounding cattle or sheep ranches or plantations of banana, sugar, cotton, or coffee; the ramshackle clusters of migrant, seasonal workers; and the more prosperous communities which are emerging around large, modern commercial farms and food-processing industries.

There are without doubt many other categories of rural communities in Latin America. In this paper, however, we shall discuss only one, the casual, mestizo community, typically composed of squatters, tenant farmers, small—very small—landowners, and a few large landowning families whose land is used marginally and inefficiently for grazing, perhaps to grow some sugar cane and maybe some rice or corn.

Veraguas Province, Panama, is a useful example of this type of community. Bishop Marcos McGrath initiated a movement there in 1963 which has developed admirably, and several of us from the Harvard Business School have had the good fortune to be associated with him in these efforts. Much of the following is drawn from that experience, although it is presumed to have a far wider application.

The Character of Veraguas

Veraguas Province, with a total population of 130,000, is divided into eleven districts, stretching from Santa Fe on the Caribbean to Montijo on the Pacific. Most of the commercial, professional, and educated inhabitants reside in the cities of Santiago and Sona. The remainder of the population consists mainly of *campesinos* living in a variety of settlement patterns. There are several larger rural towns such as San Francisco and La Colorada, with populations of about 1,000 persons, which, while populated by *campesinos*, are in constant communication with Santiago and are thus being influenced by a more urban type of life.

Outside the larger towns, and generally throughout Veraguas, are smaller population groups living in pueblos. These small villages, inhabited by thirty to one hundred families, may be the seat of a school district and have a chapel, one or two *tiendas* (stores), a few water pumps, and perhaps a dance floor; but usually there is no focal point to the community. While a few huts may be concentrated around a cleared area of land, many are scattered within a radius of one or two miles.

Finally, outside the *campesino* pueblos live numerous isolated family groups consisting of as many as ten members. Usually these families are poorer than other campesinos, none of them have attended school, and they are highly superstitious.

While some pueblos are near the Inter-American Highway and others on secondary roads, many can be reached only via rutted dirt roads, passable sometimes by Land Rover and much of the time only by horse or on foot. In the rainy season, sudden cloud bursts turn such roads into muddy quagmires and swell streams into impassable and dangerous rivers. As a result, there is irregular communication between Santiago and many of the pueblos.

Campesinos are for the most part marginal, subsistence farmers. They are marginal in that a decline in the price of rice and/or corn in the national market will have grave consequence upon them. We estimate that the average income in Veraguas is roughly forty-five dollars a year. They are subsistent in that little excess production is ever available for sale. A year of bad weather, for example, can have catastrophic effects upon families. In 1965 a late rainy season caused the rice harvest in Veraguas to be small and late. As a result, many families were reduced to eating corn tortillas three times a day, day after day, and were close to starvation. Most of the children are undernourished, and a flu epidemic spreads quickly in some of the villages since most members are too weak to resist it. Under these conditions it is not surprising that the *campesinos* are sometimes termed "static," and are hesitant to introduce any changes which might jeopardize their tenuous present state.

Over the years the destructive practice of slashing and burning the scrub, planting for one or two seasons, and then moving on, has caused a great deal of erosion, particularly since land was not fertile in the first place. At the same time the large cattle owners and cane growers in Veraguas have been slowly moving their fences outward, leaving the *campesino* less land on which to grow corn and rice and forcing him into the mountains in the northern part of the province.

On top of the basic production problems are others of a social and political nature. Most rural towns are isolated from each other, with little or no communication between them. Within a community there are few "strong men" or dynamic leaders. The *tienda* keeper is often a leader in a sense, partly because of his better economic position, greater education, and business ability, and partly because of his origin. The *tienda* keeper may not have been a *campesino* originally. Often he is a migrant from Panama City, the Canal Zone, or some other urban area. Leaders have seldom developed from within the *campesino* community, and the *campesinos* who have attended school often leave their communities for Panama City.

Partly as a consequence of his agricultural wanderings, the *campesino* is seminomadic. He moves from plot to plot, sometimes changes houses, and occasionally moves to a new village. Many of the *campesino* communities around Santiago are not more than forty or fifty years old. The founder of such a community may still be living and able to recount how he cut down the trees and scrub to form what is now the village's central green.

The only groups which work together within the community are the communal work forces, or juntas, formed for special tasks. Little exact information is available about these groups. Some consist of four to five members, while others have as many as twenty. There are different kinds of juntas. Some work on communal projects such as a chapel or a school. Others contribute their labor to a neighbor to help him build a house. The caller of the junta need only supply food and drink to his helpers. Still other juntas consist of a labor force that works in rotation on each member's land, a more efficient process than if each worked alone. In addition to his work in the group, or junta, each of the members takes a square plot, called the *tarea,* which he works alone. There is no substantial feeling of cooperation or community; junta activity is a rare and scattered experience.

The problem of political leadership arises from the splintered social organization of the *campesino* communities. Even if well-trained leaders were members of the communities, well-organized villages would not develop quickly. The problems that many of the Peace Corps volunteers in Veraguas have experienced in forming clubs attest to this point. For one reason or another, villagers just do not show up at the club meetings.

There appears to be little economic motivation in the communities. A *campesino* owning twenty cattle and ten hectares of land may live in poorer conditions with less material accoutrements (except for a radio) than his nonlivestock-owning and landless fellow villager. The motivation and values of *campesinos* are complex and mostly unknown.

The outside society (with a few significant exceptions) does little to help the *campesino*. Most members of the Panamanian business community view the *campesinos* as neither potential producers nor potential consumers. Only a few businessmen have ever visited the rural areas of Panama; indeed, hardly anybody in Panama City has ever been to Veraguas. The national government has little sense of identity with Veraguas. Its reach, control, and influence are limited. It is regarded generally with either indifference or suspicion.

The Circle of Problems

It is in such a setting that we can see the problems of Latin America, rural and urban. A brief list follows:

Low living standards, inadequate and poorly distributed purchasing income and land.

Wide and growing gaps in income between rural and urban areas, as well as between different regions within a single country.

Rapid population growth, about 2.8 percent a year, set against an economic growth rate of less than 1 percent per capita.

Population flow of surplus rural labor to urban areas, to create slums, unemployment, dislocation, and unrest.

Inadequate education and skill training which causes a frustrating lack of opportunity.

Rigid hierarchical social structures which choke off opportunity for those who manage to obtain some education.

Inadequate and inflexible credit and market systems which lead to abuse, exploitation, high prices for the consumer, and low return to the farmer.

Insufficient and inefficient agricultural production.

Low consumer buying power.

Centralized industry, concentrated in urban areas, which detracts from rural development and employment opportunities.

Lack of trust and communication among men and social groups, to screen and isolate vast sectors of society and the economy from one another.

Political instability and corruption which arise from the lack of a broadly based popular organization, as well as limited and polarized centers of powers.

The remnants of feudalism, reflected partly in paternalism, which linger on to stifle change, initiative, confidence, and dignity.

THREE HYPOTHESES

This partial list of problems is sufficient to suggest several hypotheses. First, the above problems are parts of a circle, for they are interrelated, self-supporting, and self-infecting. They cannot be treated effectively when they are separated one from another. Much of the disappointment with our government aid program stems from our attempt to do just this. As a nation of specialists, which intensively trains and consequently admires experts, we tend to isolate problems, frequently artificially, for the application of expertise. Thus we send in an agricultural technician who thinks he can solve all the problems of farm production by introducing new varieties of seed or fertilizer.

The second hypothesis which can be drawn is that these problems result from two general inadequacies: lack of motivation and insufficient organization. Untouched by a sense of nationality or community, apprehensive about the simplest of changes—including, for example, the introduction of fertilizer—and vulnerable to any organized group that wants to exploit him, the Latin American *campesino* lives a lonely and isolated life.

Concern with sheer survival retards and depresses any motivation for additional achievement. Without motivation, organization is difficult; and without organization, real and lasting development is impossible.

The injection of material or technical assistance into areas such as these accomplishes no purpose. Indeed, it can be harmful in several ways:

1. The introduction of an administrative bureaucracy without local roots is apt to bring corruption and smother the delicate

tentacles of what some day might be real local government and local organization.

2. The people are inclined to look increasingly for outside help and so are to that extent discouraged from organizing to help themselves.

3. Material is of no value unless its recipients are clear regarding its purpose.

This leads to the third hypothesis, which is that economic and social development, to be real and effective, must be preceded by a measure of political development, or, in other words, by motivation and organization. Economic development must be designed to serve and promote political development, with economic need acting as a useful lever for motivation and organization.

The steps appear to be: First, there must be a measure of agitation, that is, people must be clearly aware of a need which is more compelling than their fears or their concerns with sheer survival. Once they are agitated, they can move to fulfill this need and organize themselves to do so. Organized, they are committed and thus are part of an institutional structure which can set about meeting the manifold problems which beset them. It is in this way that the revolution can be made constructive, and its noblest purposes served.

This process of development is filled with risks and dangers, for in any society there are always forces present whose interests are offended by change. A movement for change, therefore, needs the protection and guidance of an authoritative force. It also needs the capacity to communicate up the hierarchical ladder in order to explain itself. Communication is generally difficult in a developing society. In Latin America relatively few people can talk to the *campesino* and be understood, believed, and trusted. He likewise can talk to few in authority. He needs help in building the communication "bridges" as well as the political, social, and economic links which will make him part of the national system. The process needs material, technical, and managerial assistance, all carefully applied so as to serve an organizational or institutional end.

A variety of forces are striving to fill the motivation-organization vacuum of the developing world today: the old elites, including landowners and merchants; the new elites, such as industrialists and manufacturers; the military; various sorts of demagogic movements; the Church; cooperative organizations; and labor unions. Apart from these, but no less important, is the large, modern, foreign-based industrial enterprise. Of special importance is the modern, integrated food company which within a single managerial network can drastically reshape a wide variety of economic, social, and political structures in the rural areas where food crops are grown, in the urban areas where they are sold, and at every stage in between. The direction and result of the revolution currently under way in Latin America will be largely determined by what combination and balance of forces prevail, and what engines of motivation and organization they are able to devise and set in motion.

CRITERIA FOR SUCCESS

For such an engine to be successful in rural Latin America it must make an integrative, as opposed to a specialized, approach.

It must deal more or less simultaneously with a broad spectrum of rural needs including, for example, improved food production, preservation, and processing; removal of obstacles and distortions in the market, credit, and transport systems; and increased motivation and organization required to produce a stable and representative political formation.

It must have sufficient authority to be heard and believed by the *campesino* as well as by the power elite in the capital city. It must have access to both, and at least the partial confidence of both. It must have the sustained capacity and will to protect the newly developing rural structures which it encourages against the forces of the status quo and other predatory elements outside.

NOTES

1. Cole, *Latin America, An Economic & Social Geography* (London: Butterworth), p. 17. Cole finds that 28.5 percent of the population in Latin America in 1960–1961 lived in towns of more than 50,000 inhabitants.

Integration of the Rural Population

ILDEFONSO CABRERA

This treatment of the rural population will begin with a sketch of the present state of the Latin American peasant. It is not my intention to investigate why and how the peasant finds himself in such circumstances, but rather to deal only with the existing situation. Afterwards, I shall enumerate the principal causes which are bringing about a change and ask at the same time whether this change conforms to Christian ideals. Finally, I shall close by indicating certain facts which deserve attention if we are really interested in bringing about the integration of the peasant into a life of well-being and social dignity that accords with Christian principles.

I believe it useful to make some preliminary statements in order to avoid false interpretations. First of all, the term "peasant" in this context does not refer to a racial or ethnic group. It refers to those people who have been born in the rural areas and have made these areas the perimeter of their activities. I am, consequently, including under this term the Indian or native who is already incorporated into the civilized way of life. Furthermore, in view of the broadness of this field and the lack of detailed information, my appreciation will necessarily be general and global.

Using socioeconomic criteria, we may divide the Latin American peasants into three main groups. First, there is the peasant who, notwithstanding the changes which have come about in the past, continues to be dominated by a patron who continues to exploit him without respect for the fact that the peasant is a human being. Next, there is the peasant who has taken the first step toward his liberation, with or without the patron's approval, thanks to the changes that have occurred in recent years. Finally, there are a very few peasants who are presently enjoying a more dignified life, due more to good fortune than anything else.

It would be interesting to present figures and percentages which would give a more precise idea of these three groups. I have, however, found this to be practically impossible. I believe that I am not mistaken, in any case, when I say that the first group will decrease with the passing of time, if only because all peasants are conscious of the fact that their state must change, that they deserve something better, that if their ancestors were slaves, they should not have to be.

The first class of peasants is usually made up of farm workers who have no shelter or land of their own. They live in one- or two-room huts where poverty, dirt, and disorder reign. These huts shelter not only three to eight members of the family but also domestic animals such as chickens, dogs, cats, pigs, and even sheep.

The diet of these peasants consists of whatever crops are produced by their gardens. Meat, milk, and eggs are luxuries. They could have these, but they generally do not because they prefer to sell them in order to have the money needed to buy salt, sweets, clothing, and perhaps some medicines.

Peasants of this class work most of the week on the farms and receive a salary which varies between ten and twenty-five cents per day, payable to them not weekly or monthly, but whenever the patron feels like it. Besides their salary, which can be reduced or eliminated whenever the patron desires, they are permitted to cultivate a patch of land for themselves. Usually this land is of very poor quality. We can add to this group those peasants who are not bound to any particular farm but who work wherever there is work offered to them. These generally receive a higher salary, but their economic situation is as bad or even worse.

The cultural level of these peasants is very low. The few who are literate are considered to be very important. We must keep in mind that as soon as a peasant learns to read and write, he usually tries to leave in search of better opportunities in the cities. If he stays in his community, he becomes a leader. The masters, with few exceptions, keep their workers from learning to read and write because if they permit this, it would mean a loss to them. There is no entertainment geared to the mentality of these people. Their only past-time is usually drinking, as I can testify from personal observation in my own country, Ecuador.

The following facts are the outstanding ones in the life of the peasant:

A tremendous respect, amounting even to fear, for the patron, who is owner and lord of the peasant's possessions, family, and will.

A great love for the land.

A great desire to become educated, especially among the young.

The principal factor which distinguishes the second group is the fact that by having some property they have become independent of their masters. They have acquired a certain amount of self-confidence, although they must continue their battle for a decent life. They live from what they can produce, from raising and selling domestic animals or perhaps from some small industries. Their homes are usually in small groups along the roads and have a more solid aspect. Uncleanliness and disorder, however, continue to prevail. These conditions are no longer the result of poverty, but of the lack of education and good habits. As far as cultural matters are concerned, we may say that even though the adults are illiterate they are very anxious to have their children learn to read and write.

Since this group enjoys a certain income, they frequently become intoxicated and show off their generosity at family and religious celebrations. Their diet is better, as they can afford to purchase more and different foods. When sick, they visit the doctor. They are more communicative in their behavior. In this class of people as in no other group there is a desire to become united. They are always interested in becoming members of unions, syndicates, or cooperatives. Their greatest danger? The city, where they acquire vices. Their greatest problem? The battle to enhance their income and field of action.

The third and smallest group is made up of economically independent peasants. Because of their assets and relatively good income they have taken a further step toward social integration. They are citizens who produce and consume. Although their participation in political and social matters is limited, they are conscious of them and take part in accordance with their capabilities. Their standard of living is still rather low, but their state of independence has placed them in another category. Their economic freedom is evident by the house they live in and their manner of dress, as well as the social life they enjoy. These peasants have completed their primary education and in some instances their secondary education. They educate their children in colleges and universities. Many of them, encouraged by their economic well-being and attracted by the environment of the cities, leave their farms.

The peasants can thus be divided from a socioeconomic point of view into three large groups. From a religious aspect, however, there can be no classification. The problem is almost the same for all.

Many things can be said for and against the Spanish and Portuguese conquistadores. But we cannot deny that their missionaries planted the seed of Christianity in this hemisphere. Unfortunately, the Church for many years has felt satisfied with merely maintaining the Faith among the people. Very little has been done to have the people live their Faith. The Church may have its excuses, but the fact is that Christian principles have remained inactive. This statement applies both to peasants and to those who are already integrated in the social life of their countries.

To be a Catholic to the majority of Latin Americans signifies merely (1) to believe in God and (2) to be baptized. Frequent reception of the sacraments, responsibility for common sanctification, the doctrine of the Mystical Body of Christ—these are truths which just recently have started to be explained to them. As we might expect, it will be a long time before these truths are understood and practiced.

With regard to the peasant I may summarize his religious state by saying that he has the Faith. He manifests it by the acknowledgment of God and respect for the authorities of the Church. He receives the sacraments of baptism and matrimony, and has veneration for the saints and the dead. His religious beliefs, however, need to be purified of many superstitions. He needs a religious instruction which must be presented in such a way that it will make religion, not a collection of inoperative principles, but a guide of personal and social life.

I have given you some idea of what the peasant is. Now I would like to say something in regard to what has influenced and continues to influence the change that is taking place in his beliefs and his life.

There is, in the first place, the old, yet new, ideas of social justice which have received so much impetus during recent years. I say old because they have been proclaimed by the Church since the beginning of Christianity, interpreted and oriented in hundreds of pastoral letters and encyclicals. I say new because in reality they had never been so stressed as they have been recently in what refers to Latin America. For a long time the principles of social justice proclaimed by the Church of Christ have been dormant. They did not exist except in religious textbooks until the enemies of the Church led the social revolution in Mexico in 1910. We must sadly recognize that the social revolution in Latin America has not been under the leadership of the Church. Only recently has the Church tried to lead the revolution because she has now realized that she is called to do so by the requirements of justice and charity, and because if something is not done, the Christian traditions which have made South America a land of God will be lost.

I certainly do not wish to deny that there have been bishops of great vision who saw the danger long ago and who have valiantly fought in their respective dioceses. Such are Bishop Larrain of Tolca, Chile, and Bishop Proano of Riobamba, Ecuador. Men like these, unfortunately, have been very few.

A second great force for change is the drive for agrarian reform. This is not the moment to analyze if the agrarian reforms have been carried out under Christian principles or if they were legal or illegal. Let us accept the fact that they have come about.

In many cases, unfortunately, agrarian reforms have not achieved the desired goals. There have been many failures and disappointments. But we must not forget that an agrarian reform is not a simple process of dividing lands. It is a complicated and lengthy affair which demands time, money, vision, and professional methods. Agrarian reforms have in any event been the first step toward the liberation of thousands of peasants. They have given, not property titles, but rather titles of freedom, to innumerable peasants who had been slaves to their patrons. They may still be poor, but they are free. It is true that in many cases agrarian reforms have reduced production and have created problems for the peasants. But these temporary setbacks cannot be compared with the fact that they have achieved freedom.

It is the obligation of the Church today to act as guardian and see to it that present-day agrarian reforms are developed under Christian principles. If the Church cannot claim to have given birth to these reforms, it should adopt them as illegitimate children rather than abandoning them to their often irresponsible progenitors.

Another cause which is encouraging this change in rural Latin America is the cooperative movement which is being developed with sacrifice and success in various countries. Let us thank God that the Church has her representatives in this movement. There are various priests dedicated to it; one might make special mention of Father Pablo Esteel and his cooperative institute in Panama City.

What is the general attitude of the peasants toward this movement? At the beginning they are doubtful. They are not familiar with the principles of mutual cooperation. But once they understand what this movement is and once they experience it in some way, they accept it and are convinced that this is the way to progress. They learn to rely on their own efforts and not wait for a gift from the strong ones. The cooperative movement is being accepted as a fair solution to economic problems and a repudiation of the communistic and capitalistic systems.

It should be mentioned, finally, that the programs and leadership of the Alliance for Progress are another cause which is aiding the peasant. The programs of the Alliance present many problems, but they are effectively helping to bring about change in Latin America.

Let us, then, ask ourselves if the peasant in Latin America is on his way to integration? If by integration we understand the efforts of men to shape their personal unity in relation to a social unity, we must categorically answer *yes*.

What I am now going to say will scandalize many people. I personally believe that although the Cuban Revolution has been a cross for the Cuban people, it has also been a blessing for Latin America. Why? Because with its cry of rebellion, whether just or unjust, Christian or non-Christian, it has been the voice that awoke the inhabitants of Latin America and North America from the contented apathy or indifference in which they were living.

Before the Cuban Revolution the Latin American peasant would say, "I was born poor and will die poor. I am a peasant and will die a peasant. God bless the master who feeds me." But it is not like that today. Now he knows that he deserves and has a right to a better life, and he is aware that he must fight to obtain what is due him. Under no circumstances am I in favor of what happened in Cuba. Not at all. I simply say that Cuban Revolution brought many people to face reality.

We can sum up by saying that today's peasant is ready to follow any leader who promises a change. He does not care how it comes about. The peasant will not stop to analyze the principles motivating the change or the leader. He and his family are suffering from hunger, cold, and lack of clothing, and this is sufficient to cause him to join the battle for change.

Now is the time when we must provide the peasant leaders who will insure a democratic and Christian future. This is the moment for action, and the sooner the better, because the social, agrarian, and industrial revolution will not wait; it will go on. It is too late to stop it or even slow it down. The Latin American peasant has begun his march toward integration, and this integration will take place with or without the Church.

Let us now ask ourselves in a more definite way if the Church's social doctrine has inspired the revolution? It is my opinion that the voice of rebellion of the peasants in various Latin American countries has not been the fruit of a Christian conscience. It is simply the desperate cry of men who cannot continue living in these conditions. It has been the lament of those who are tired of a life of misery.

The peasant has voiced his cry of rebellion, not as a Christian, but simply as a man who wants to subsist. He has not acted in a Christian way because he knows so little about Christianity. Religion to him is a series of abstract truths which must be believed. Religion to him has no value or principles which he must live up to. To believe and to practice are to him two completely different things.

If the peasant is working to better himself, it is not because he is conscious of his Christian dignity; it is simply because he is hungry and naked. Can we blame him for this? Certainly not. It is not his fault that religion has no application to his daily life. What then is happening to the peasant? It is simply that, tired of a life of slavery, he has followed the voices of the first leader who came around. We can be sure that he is learning well and rapidly. We have evidence that this is so.

The rural population is beginning to organize and shows capabilities for effective political action. This is true even among the Indians. The nearly spontaneous movement of the Bolivian Indian peasants following the 1952 revolution which dictated the sweeping character of the Bolivian land reform is the most striking example. More recently the Cuban peasants have been effectively mobilized in support of a revolutionary programme. Venezuela has had an important, organized peasants' organization since 1959. In Brazil and Chile peasants' organizations held their first National

Congress in 1961. The Congress in Brazil was attended by 1,500 delegates and 3,000 observers.

In conclusion, if the Church today does not inspire leaders for the peasant masses, there is the eminent danger of leftist leaders taking command. I have pointed out that the Church's doctrine did not inspire the social revolution in Latin America. The people have acted as Christians or anti-Christians.

And what can we say about the patrons and other masters upon whom the peasants have depended or continue to depend? There have been a few who have acted in the name of Christianity. But the great majority will recognize the rights of the peasants, not in the name of Catholicism or charity, but just because there is no other way. Rather than perish in a rebellion, they prefer to recognize the peasants, although their hearts break when they do so. The shameful part is that among these masters there are Catholic dioceses which continue to scandalize humanity as owners of enormous amounts of land.

It is interesting to note that just as the peasants are conscious of the need for a change which must take place peacefully or by violence, the masters are also conscious of the fact that they must surrender some of their privileges, that it is impossible to continue the old system.

I sincerely believe that very few of the Latin American rich are still enjoying their possessions and privileges. They are in a very uncertain situation. They may have wealth and legal titles to properties, but they no longer possess the absolute security of old. Their attitude is defensive. There are thousands who have fearfully sold everything and deposited their money in foreign banks. They now live off the interest paid to them by these banks. They are aware that the peasants have endured much, and patience has now run out.

Let us conclude by saying that even though the peasants have been born Christian, the social revolution was born without religion. This is the moment to Christianize it. And if the Church does not hasten to give it a Christian name, its name will be communist. It is necessary to take up much time in saying what has been accomplished up to now in order to orient the socioeconomic revolution in Latin America.

Almost every diocese at the present time has some kind of program in favor of the peasant. There are pastors and priests who, no matter how limited their means, are doing something to start or continue some project. In some places there is such a desire to help the peasant that I fear too much attention is being given to the socioeconomic aspect with the danger of minimizing the religious aspect of reforms.

It is a consolation for past neglect to know that today the Church is more than ever conscious of its obligation to act. Recently, in a speech to the graduating class of the University of Notre Dame, Cardinal Landazuri said, "The mission of the Church in Latin America is to be a servant to a society in revolution. . . . We are aware of the social revolution now in progress. We identify with it."

It is also, unfortunately, true that there remain dioceses whose hearts break at the thought of giving to the poor even part of their enormous estates. But not all the fingers on the hand are the same. There are exceptions in every situation.

Let us turn to the Pan-American aspects of aid to peasants. We know that the Latin American bishops are working with great enthusiasm, but what can we say about the North American bishops? Not satisfied with sharing surplus wealth with us, North America sent its priests, religious, and laymen to share in our desire to live the apostolate in Latin America. In the name of justice and charity the Latin Americans thank you and bless you for what you have done and are doing.

Both hierarchies, united in love of Christ and his Church, are eager to save Latin America. The task is an arduous and difficult one.

In his book *Latin America,* Peter Nehemkis comments on the adjectives "critical" and important used by Presidents Kennedy and Johnson when referring to the Latin American situation.

Latin America is critical and important, but not because of the probability of another Cuba, although that contingency cannot be ignored. The real trouble lies much deeper. It is the despair and hopelessness of the ordinary people, the cynicism and social irresponsibility of most of the rich, and pervasive corruption in high places, the sense of inferiority and insecurity of the people, the emotional identification of the middle class with the institu-

tional status quo . . . the contempt for and indifference toward the Indian
population and paralysis of the will which prevents action for social reform.
These are the manifestations of clinical disorder. For the true matter is that
Latin America is a sick society. It is sick politically, it is sick economically,
it is sick spiritually.

We should not fear this sad, but realistic, vision. Let us balance
it with the optimistic vision of the Church. Cardinal Ritter's words
are comforting:

> Against this complex background, a tapestry woven of social, economic,
> and religious threads, there are some who can see Latin America rejecting
> entirely her Christian past to embrace new structures, perhaps communistic
> in form, or perhaps godless and amoral in some way. It is my judgment that
> this will not be the final eventuality, for there are already signs that the tide
> is really turning in favor of Latin America's people. Further, we can abso-
> lutely be sure that what happens in Latin America in the future will depend
> significantly on the Church there and in the United States.

At this point I should like to enumerate three of the principal
problems facing Latin American peasants. Then we can discuss
what might be done in favor of the peasant in order to integrate
him into a national life under the flag of Christ and his Church.

First, as it is well known, there is a tremendous imbalance in
the possession of land, with the degrading fact that in some
countries the Church is numbered among the landowners. I shall
not go into details; let us just remember that some 60 percent of
the population lives off the land and that there are nevertheless
thousands of peasants who do not have the satisfaction of owning
a patch of land. The second problem, as important as the first, is
the lack of an education which would prepare the peasant to be
a good citizen and a Christian useful to God and his country.
There is an urgent need for educational institutions which can
take care of the social and economic needs as well as the spiritual
and corporal needs of man. The education should be focused on
the children. Little can be accomplished with the adults, but the
children are the hope of tomorrow. A third problem is the lack of
capital. It is not enough for the peasant to have land and be able
to read and write. He needs money and credit to help him achieve
a better economic status. But the banking firms of Latin America

are out of reach for the peasant. He cannot comply with the bank's requisites.

Each of these problems is serious and needs to be solved. But it must be understood that the Church is not expected to find a solution to all of them. Other agencies both native and foreign are at work. I believe that the Church should concentrate its energies on education, and upon the children above all. Integration is a process that demands time and ideals, but Christian ideals cannot be implanted if not in school.

Right now there are numerous projects and programs of a socioeconomic character on which the Church is spending thousands of dollars and assigning hundreds of people. How much have the results obtained changed the Christian way of life of the peasant? Probably very little. If all this effort were directed to education, I am sure that a Christian future for the Latin American peasant could be assured.

I would like to close with some final observations which I direct to those in charge of programs in Latin America. There is no doubt that much is being done to aid this area. But there is much disorder in the effort. There is need for planned action in a coordinated manner. We need plans which would orient and direct the action in precise fashion, not just in one country but throughout Latin America.

If we do not work in such a manner, we will only be handing out remedies that will alleviate the situation but will not cure the illness. We must keep in mind that we are facing a revolution, and we must, therefore, prepare a strategic plan that will insure our victory. A lack of coordinated action is causing us to lose money and time.

If the bishops have preference for specific projects in their own dioceses, it is their responsibility to take care of them. But projects supported from outside need broad criteria of judgment and should be studied by a committee in charge of the entire program. Bishops in some dioceses are acting with narrow interests in view. If they could act with a catholic point of view, the results would be of greater benefit to their dioceses as well as to the whole Church.

Taking advantage of the experienced people here, we might well study the problem and develop a coordinated plan. And then we could create a committee of priests, sisters, and lay people to direct and supervise the programs under the auspices of the hemispheric hierarchies. This committee should emphasize the programs dealing with education.

These two conclusions may seem very inadequate when they are measured against the problems facing Latin America. But we should not be building castles when what we really need are simple houses. We should not draw up long lists of projects and programs, but start at the beginning. If we could develop a sound plan of action, with means and authority to decide and act, it would be the best guarantee for a better future for the rural population of Latin America.

PART TWO

INTERMEDIATE
STRUCTURES

Private and Public Schools

PABLO LATAPI, S.J.

The objective of CICOP was once defined by Bishop Marcos McGrath as "an opportunity for Latin American Catholics to explain their Church to North American Catholics." With this aim in mind I shall attempt to set forth the principal functions of education in the integration of Latin America and try to explain the problems which confront the Christian community in private and public education while contributing to that integration.

Education can, in the first place, be considered as a process of transmission of values. Of the totality of cultural values, education selects certain formative ones that must be transmitted to the next generation for the conservation and progress of that society. The transmission of values contributes to the integration of society by establishing common value-orientations and making all members of society share in these values.

If we compare the value-system contained in Latin American education with the anthropological, psychological, social, cultural, and historical conditions of the Latin American nations, we find an inadequacy of the former with respect to the latter. The culturally more mature countries of the Latin American continent have become conscious of this inadequacy, rebelling against cultural eclecticism and manifesting their eagerness to discover their proper identity. Latin America is not an extension of Spain, nor the sum total of European and North American influences, nor a backward realization of Western culture. It is rather a melting pot of cultures, a product certainly of multiple influences, but also an amalgamation with aboriginal elements in different stages of cultural fusion. The cultural identity of each Latin American society is only in the process of discovery, and as yet the value-orientations that can be considered fundamental and specific to each Latin American culture are controvertible.

The value-system implicit in the educational curriculum of Latin America is substantially an eclectic result of imported Western traditions. The philosophers of Latin American education have lacked as yet a solid anthropological basis in order to define the cultural identity of each society of this continent. This definition of our cultural identity is indispensable to establish clear value-orientations that would give us the profile of our educational ideal.

Beyond establishing common value-orientations, education promotes integration in a social system by increasing the degree in which members of society participate in these value-orientations. It is evident that since a conscious definition of fundamental values is as yet lacking in the societies of Latin America, the social participation in these values is, at best, partial and often disoriented.

It may be helpful to compare the process of cultural fusion in Latin America with the same process in the United States. The "American Way of Life" that has made a nation from the melting pot of immigrants in this country was sufficient to define the value-orientations which would be assimilated and which would be workable in the new American society. On the contrary, Latin America had to accomplish the mixing of Spanish or Portuguese cultures with pre-Columbian cultures. Only after three centuries of disregard for our ancient aboriginal values during Colonial times has a gradual discovery of these values taken place and a tentative effort for cultural integration begun. The foregoing is most valid, of course, for those Latin American countries where ethnic and cultural mixing has been more intense. Only to a limited degree does it apply to countries such as Argentina, Chile, or Uruguay, where cultural amalgamation has been so different.

Beyond transmitting common values, increasingly shared by members of society, education contributes to integration by creating functional patterns of behavior. In Latin America the deficiences described above explain why education has not been able to create these consistent patterns of behavior. This is obvious, for example, in such areas as civic life, religious behavior, political consensus, and readiness to accept social reforms. Education in Latin American countries has a tremendous task to accomplish in order to attain this integration of conduct among the different social groups to prepare the process of development.

At this point I would like to analyze other integrating functions of education which are proper to it as an organized institution. First of all education should identify and train talented persons. It is the educational system, when adequately coordinated and expanded, that permits the use of talent for the benefit of the social system. But the lack of educational opportunities in our countries is one of the principal obstacles for exploiting the fundamental resource of Latin America. This lack of educational opportunities is at the same time one of the principal obstacles to the integration of Latin American societies, since it causes an enormous dissimilarity among members of society in their appreciation of values, in their behavior, in their participation in social benefits, in their contribution to community progress, and even in some regions in their ability to communicate through a common language.

Education also promotes the just distribution of social opportunities. Social justice is, in fact, fundamentally the result of a just distribution of educational opportunities. Since social justice is one of the indispensable conditions for integration, it is evident that the deficiences in educational justice are impediments to integration. During the last thirty years Latin America has made an extraordinary effort to establish a public educational system, open to all without distinction of social class. Nevertheless, in a greater measure than in the more highly developed countries the social conditions of the family continue to prevent an equal access to education. To this circumstance must be added that education in Latin America is still considered more as a "symbol" (symbol of status and prestige) than as a "function" (a means to attain a functional role). The development of social mobility in Latin American societies, which requires that educational opportunities be distributed, not according to the economic position of the family, but according to individual talent, is as yet in an embryo stage in half a dozen Latin American countries, and in almost all of them is very far from maturing.

Finally, there is education's contribution to economic growth. Although economic progress is only a part of integral development, it is a fundamental factor. The function of education in regard to economic progress envisages not only a necessary change in mentality to adjust to new economic conditions but also an adequate training of human beings according to occupational requirements. Because it is better known and frequently commented upon, I shall pass over the difficult challenge which Latin American education faces to meet the demands of manpower requirements.

This brief reference to some of the functions of education in the integration of Latin American societies will be helpful in guiding our thinking about the role of the Christian community in education. In most of our countries there is an on-going, though terribly slow, process of transformation of the attitudes of Christians with regard to this role. We find that Christians engaged in educational activities are ceasing to consider education exclusively as an "instrument" for their religious objectives and are beginning to value it as a good in itself, worthwhile for its own sake.

Christians engaged in educational activities are no longer enclosing themselves in their own institutions and are beginning to consider all types of educational institutions as adequate media for their action. They are giving less importance to institutional ties with the hierarchy and are developing broader, more differentiated, forms of relationship to their bishops. They are less interested in the "triumphant" prestige of the Church as an institution and more preoccupied with giving humble service and authentic witness as individuals in a complex and secular society.

These and other transformations in the attitudes of Christians regarding education in general are results of the change of conscience brought about by the Second Vatican Council. But in most Latin American countries these transformations are still barely germinating. The agents for this change of mentality are to be found among certain groups of the younger clergy, of the younger members of religious orders, and of laymen. One does not find any demand for change among the masses of the faithful, or among the older clergy, or among the bishops (with the exception of some two dozen bishops who do have an extraordinary understanding of society's needs).

Public education presents problems of its own, with wide variations in different countries. But it can be stated in a general way that the attitude of the Latin requires a serious revision. Historical conflicts have resulted in prejudice, antagonism, and mistrust between public education and Christian educators. Especially in countries such as Uruguay, Ecuador, and Mexico, where a tradition of anti-Catholic secularism in public education is still alive it is not infrequent to find among Christians an attitude of antagonism, contempt, or, at best, indifference toward the public school. These attitudes have brought about a social and pastoral isolation of public education by many Christians. The Christian community must overcome such negative attitudes through an effort of charity and humility, so that the People of God will be effectively at the service of the world.

With regard to private education, and again with ample margin left for the peculiarities of each individual country, it can be affirmed that the Christian community is urgently in need of changing its attitudes in regard to private Catholic schools. Catholic education has enclosed itself too much, and the Catholic school has in a certain sense worked as a hindrance for the permeation of national culture with Christian values. The Latin American Catholic school has often been an exclusive fort for well-to-do children. I am well aware of the many and insuperable causes that have brought about this social selection in our Catholic schools, and also of the limits of this phenomenon, which is not as universal as many may imagine. But it is a fact that this situation prevents the Christian community from putting itself at the service of all men without distinction of social class. I would even dare to ask this question: Is this social selection of our Catholic schools not in fact turning the Church in Latin America into an agent of resistance to the process, eminently Christian, of attaining social equality?

Another attitude that requires revision among Catholic educators is the almost exclusive attention they give to the objectives of religious training in their Catholic schools. This frequently leads to neglect of other essential objectives of an integral education. Such an attitude has produced serious deficiencies in the pedagogical approach of many Latin American Catholic schools.

Yet another unsolved problem which confronts the Christian community in Latin America is the fact that its educational effort is almost entirely confined to private schools, while 90 percent of the baptized school population is attending public schools. All of us know the heated discussion that has developed in the last five years in many Western countries in regard to this dilemma. Should our efforts continue to develop mainly in private Catholic schools or should we better direct ourselves to the public schools?

Because they are well known, I shall pass over the two extreme positions that have been sustained in accordance with the freedom of opinion within the Christian community. But I do wish to emphasize the fact that the conditioning of this dilemma in our Latin American countries is fundamentally different from its conditioning in your country. Basic data of the problem in both contexts lead to a substantially different approach and, probably, to a substantially different solution. I believe that both extreme positions, the conservative defense of the private Catholic school as the chief means of Christian education, as well as the progressive call for abandoning the private schools altogether, suffer from a fundamental weakness. Both are "solutions" which lack a previous definition of the problem that they pretend to solve.

In the psychological, social, and ecclesiastical present of Latin America it seems to me a mistake to hold more than a temporary position subject to change at a later time. This transitory position would consist of three elements. There would be an open attitude toward change, rooted in sound ecclesiological principles, in the present-day conscience of a Church in transition and in the historical contemplation of the relations between the Church and education up to the present time. There would also be an effort of theological clarification in regard to the function which the Christian community should fulfill in national education, as well as in regard to the possible justifications of the present-day Catholic school. Finally, there would be extensive experimentation in search of new institutional formulas for Christian education. Only through this scientific approach, in virtue of controlled and evaluated experiments, will we be able to find those formulas that will guide us to reforms in an entire diocese or an entire nation.

Conclusion

I have tried in this paper to outline the principal functions of education in the integration of Latin America in order to suggest how the Christian community can fulfill its task in this respect. I have indicated also some of the problems which the Christian community faces in the present circumstances of our Latin American countries. This made us consider the necessary transformation of attitudes regarding education in general and the dilemma presented by the prevailing educational structures.

The Universities

RICARDO ARIAS CALDERON

The most profitable way to discuss the Latin American university and what it might do with respect to integration will be to analyze the historical periods through which the university has gone in the past fifty years. Half a century ago our institutions of higher learning were bureaucracies dependent on the government. They were considered part of the educational organization of the government to such an extent that many of them functioned as a kind of ministry of education, and were responsible for primary and secondary public schooling as well as their own university activities. The university not only was institutionally dependent but also considered that its main job was to produce those profes-sionals which society wanted because there was no way of determining the objective needs of society.

In this context, with a university institutionally and spiritually dependent on the existing social norms, the university students tended to act in a political manner, that is, in a manner that was related primarily to society's preoccupations rather than to the university's preoccupations. They acted in this political manner in either of two ways. One of them was very simple; they engaged in politics, but they did so in the same way as the politicians. They were just out to do better than the politicians. Or they were politically active in another way, an apparently academic way. They climbed the ladder of the professions so that by the time they reached the top, they might join the happy few. Such self-centered activity was just as much student politics as the other one, merely a little more subdued. So at the turn of the century you had a caricature of a university devoted to status-seeking and the status quo. And since status is a conservative factor, the university produced conservative lawyers and doctors. Student action within this context also tended to be conservative action. They might talk of reform or revolution, but not seriously. Their aim was personal advancement and careerism, not the reshaping of society.

The second stage of university development in Latin America began in 1918 at the end of World War I. At that date the University Reform Movement was started at the University of Cordoba, Argentina. This movement spread throughout Latin America, and even today is an example to all Latin American university movements. A major aspiration and achievement of the reform was to gain for the Latin American university its autonomy. This autonomy was designed to free the administration and students from government control and to make of the university an island or a fortress within society where none of the other general agents of order had any right to meddle.

This autonomous university also began to discover its own autonomous spiritual ends. It began to introduce careers which did not have direct relevance to established status in the society. Faculties of economics and schools of social sciences were established. It was at this time that many of the present-day research institutes were founded. But although the university widened its own consciousness and began to feel itself to be speaking as an institution with its own initiative, in effect it was still maintaining the old schema. Even though it was creating, for example, new careers like economics, it was not really teaching economics. It was preparing professionals to go into applied economics. It did not teach or do research in the basic sciences. It prepared laboratory technicians with the same attitudes and aspirations as before.

It was still just preparing professionals rather than developing science in the full sense of the word.

The university, as it acquired a wider consciousness and tried to become a renovating factor in society, also found that as an autonomous institution it had no way to affect society. By becoming autonomous it discovered its possibilities of renovating society, and not just reproducing it. But by being autonomous the university had tied its hands. It had no institutional connection with or insight into the society from which it had declared independence. This feeling, of wanting to be a factor of renovation but not being able to do it, generated cultural extension and social service programs. Professors sought to establish a bridge between the university and society because they felt isolated and separated. Because the university was not really connected to or concerned with society, it had to create a sort of lateral institution, a lateral organization. The intellectual elites realized that they could be innovators, but were not. And in order to overcome this ambiguous situation, they tried subsidiary ways of trying to relate to society, subsidiary ways which revealed the fact that they were not really preoccupied with society.

What were the students doing during this period? From political activity by which they just played the politicians' games, student movements began to acquire a definite revolutionary character. Students were now seeking to change society, not just fit into it. This political activity of the students, with its new revolutionary spirit, was at first not something rooted in their intellectual pursuits but rather parallel to them. A student might spend two or three years studying Roman law, and at the same time he would be a leader of a group advocating a total change in society. But there was little connection between that which he was studying and the action he was carrying out. University students became kind of schizophrenic.

At the present time there is a movement that suggests a new stage in the Latin American university. We have to have a great deal of faith in the university in order to see this movement, to discover the depth of its inmost spirit. This new stage is not just something you read about, not just something you study. You share in it when you live in the Latin American university milieu and are a part of it. Where does the movement seem to be trying to go? It is trying to reach a new situation, not that of dependency on the government or that of a distant autonomy with respect to society, but something I would like to call community integration of the university with society, integration as a community, not as an instrument, which seems to be the trend in the United States. Some universities in the United States are very much like corporations. They even are structured that way, so that I am not sure you yourselves have very much of a community. Last November, during the wonderful experience of visiting eight or nine American universities, I found a sense of frustration among North American university students. They felt that the university was not a community in which they could participate. So this problem that we are posing to ourselves may be of some interest to you also. We in Latin America are trying to integrate the university into society as a community, that is to say, as a group of people, all of whom participate in the power of decision in the institution and who join society, not to be instrumentalized by society, but to establish a relationship of mutual service. This problem of the instrumentalization of the universities seems also to be a problem which you might pose for yourselves. I read recently an article dealing with the implications of the contracts between the Departments of Defense and the social science departments in different universities. The author was asking himself to what extent the intellectual freedom of his department was or was not compromised. So here again, what we are trying to do might be of some relevance to you.

The community-integrated university would in my view have the following characteristics. It would function as a force of renovation, as a social force. The renovation would not be a function which would be added to the university but one which would be expressed in the very curriculum of the university, in research, in teaching. There is no institutional way to achieve this, but there is a kind of spiritual way of doing it. The university must be animated by a spirit of intellectual renovation, of a creative self-criticism that is relevant to society. It must have a sense of renovation and a social-mindedness in all that it does, not as something parallel to its intellectual pursuits. It would maintain its freedom from governmental structures, but it would also assume the responsibility that goes with that freedom. It would become part of the general educational plans of the nation and not become a kind of exotic flower within the nation. The university would continually feed renovating ideas and propositions to those planning for development. It would be free, but responsible.

We have to find adequate structural conditions that would make such a university possible. Economic support will be essential. And the student in this community-integrated university will not be disengaged from politics. Disengagement from politics is really, I think, an illusion. We are told that the university should not meddle in politics. If you mean by that electing a ward leader and that sort of thing, of course not. The university as such, we are all agreed, should not meddle in that sense. But if you define politics as the basic options which a society faces in its effort to govern itself, then I wonder on what principles the university should be disengaged from this. Take your own case. The people of your universities belong to all kinds of boards created by the Federal and state governments to study national problems. Many of your own departments are financed by contracts with all kinds of governmental agencies. When President Kennedy took office, his government took many people from the universities and gave them high places in government. These people then returned to the universities with all the knowledge and the experience of decisions which they had made in their policy-making position. The university should then demand reciprocity and have something to say with respect to the political options of the nation and of the world community. The students and the faculty members, in my opinion, should not avoid, they should perhaps even seek, political involvement understood as that involvement relating to the basic options of the society in its search for self-government.

The university's involvement, however, should be qualitatively conditioned. First, it should be a creative involvement. Latin American society needs conservative involvement, and it needs critical involvement, and it needs creative involvement. It is the whole gamut of these involvements which makes a society. The university as such is made for creative involvements which go beyond just criticism. Conservative involvement, I would say, is not the function of the university, of the student body.

The second qualitative condition that I would place on political involvement is that it be rooted in and express the intellectual activity of the university. It should not be something parallel and marginal to this activity, but should grow from the university's research and teaching. It should not be just one of those debating clubs you sometimes have in the universities, where students who spend part of their lives living in the eighteenth century go and debate twentieth-century issues.

This new university we are trying to envision is not coming forth. In a few places it is emerging; some groups are working toward it. But I must end on a pessimistic note. Professors and students in Latin America have not realized fully that the second stage is finished. The university is now passing through a crisis in Argentina, in Venezuela, in Peru, in Ecuador. I do not want to enter into a specific discussion of whether and in what case government intervention was and was not justified. There is no clear-cut rule about these things.

What is important is that in none of these countries, whatever the different justifications were, was there any public outcry against the military intervention. There was only silence. The society did not feel that something basic to it was in danger. It looked the other way; it did not care. That is the real crisis, not the intervention. And the crisis came because the autonomous university, knowing that it should be a renovating factor and realizing that it was not in a position to be a renovating factor, has not had yet the force and the vision to get out from that situation and to create a new university along the lines which I have suggested.

Cooperative Movements

CARLOS TALAVERA

Before we can apply the cooperative system to any society, we have to start with conditions as they exist in that society. In Europe, cooperatives have proved to be an economic benefit for a good part of the people. In the United States and Canada, besides bringing economic advantages, the cooperative movement fits in with the democratic ideals which are deeply rooted in the mentality of those peoples. In Latin America, however, the cooperative movement is a factor of development which must prepare its own ground in order to give the best results.

In Latin America there are 200 million people who have an average per capita income of 250 dollars a year. It is an economically unorganized continent where more than half the people work in agriculture but produce only one-quarter of the national product. The greatest proportion of economic activity by far is in commerce and services. Industry in many countries has barely begun to develop.

Latin America is a people lacking in education. Those who do go to school remain on an average no more than two years. Only one percent manage to complete a university course. Consequently the continent lacks technicians, educated administrators, and leaders.

Latin America, because of these conditions and because of its history, is made up of people who are in the habit of looking out for themselves and forgetting everyone else. In economic life, in politics, and in social relations the law of the jungle dominates: the strong grab from the weak.

A land like that is arid for planting something like the cooperative system, which needs good ground. So the idealists of the cooperative movement, people who have faith in man in spite of all his shortcomings, have to work very, very hard to give Latin Americans what they lack to become good cooperators. The ends and the means which the cooperative movement must use in Latin America have to take into account certain peculiar characteristics.

First, the movement must arouse the minds and the energy of us Latin Americans so we can begin social and economic integration. We Latin Americans cannot be satisfied with having our personal incomes increased by way of cooperative enterprise. A little more comfort and ease will not make us better men or create a better society. The majority of Latin Americans have not understood their problems or faced them as they should. We need to have the minds and imaginations of our people find the way to fulfillment of a new social order. We need at the same time to understand the importance of social living for our personal fulfillment.

The cooperative movement, therefore, must help us face our problems, furnish us incentives to solve them together, awaken us to a new attitude of realism and firm confidence in our mental powers. "Man can do ten times more than he thinks he can," Dr. M. M. Coady used to say when he guided the fishermen and farmers of Nova Scotia. He did this to make them feel the sense of accomplishment which would carry them on to development. Once this is understood, cooperation has a central role in the development of Latin America: to integrate man himself, to make him realize his own power.

Next, the movement must form in those awakened minds an attitude of cooperation. The principal cause, and the most important manifestation, of the underdevelopment of Latin America is an egocentric individualism which seeks the advancement of oneself regardless of everyone else. When Latin America has created in her people the spirit of open-mindedness to others and the sense of community manifested in an attitude of cooperation, we shall find ourselves on the way to freedom from poverty, ignorance, injustice, and humiliation.

This attitude of cooperation must be translated into the power to combine forces, to organize institutions, and to structure society. The material and cultural needs of 200 million Latin Americans cannot be met without the joint action of all of them. Whatever activity is carried on—whether by governments through international aid, or foreign investment, or community development work of private institutions—requires that Latin Americans be disposed to structure themselves into an order where each one takes his responsibility for the good of all.

If the masses of the people have become in a sense slaves [says Dr. Coady] it is because they have not taken the steps or expended the effort necessary to change society. The coal miner comes out of the pit, cleans up at the washhouse and calls it a day. The fisherman thinks he has done enough when he lands his catch on the wharf. The farmer puts in a day of drudgery and 'knocks off' until tomorrow. This is their great mistake. There is no standing still, and if the people do not take the means to advance themselves, they will slip surely backward. Let us take a lesson from the man in whose window a light burns late each night. He does not watch the clock or wait for a whistle. He is sufficiently interested in the advancement of his own affairs to work overtime without compulsion.

In addition to their daily occupations, the people must put in extra work on a program of study and enlightenment in order that they may create the institutions that will enable them to obtain control of the instruments of production. Building the new society is as much their business as digging coal, catching fish, or planting seed. If they do not bestir themselves to bring it about, no one else will. The only hope of democracy is that enough noble, independent, energetic souls may be found who are prepared to work overtime, without pay. Such a sacrifice is not necessary in a dictatorship— it is not even permitted. In a dictatorial system, all the directing energy comes from the top. In a democracy, it is the privilege of the people to work overtime in their own interests—the creation of a new society where all men are free.

Social integration requires from each individual the power to open his mind to others, the sincerity to recognize problems in their entire scope, the exercise of sufficient initiative. It requires the will to make decisions and to accept the decision of others; it requires responsible participation in the work of building society and the stability of mind and will to achieve the common good. We believe that the major task of the cooperative movement in Latin America is to bring about this result: social integration.

Another aim of the cooperative movement in Latin America is economic improvement. People generally think this is the only aim, perhaps because it is the most obvious. But it can never be considered apart from the others; it should never be considered superior or anterior to the others. It can only be understood within the frame of personal development and social integration. This is the only way material improvement can be of real benefit.

Experience in Latin America has demonstrated that many cooperatives fail when they are based on purely economic considerations. Cooperatives often suffer from functional problems when there has been a failure to arouse the spirit of their members with a clear attitude of cooperation. The cooperative movement functions upon a base of good understanding and requires men with a new vision of the world and of human relations, who use cooperative organization as an instrument to put into practice their new ideas.

Furthermore, the economic improvement which cooperatives produce cannot be reduced merely to the sum of the economic advantages they bring to their members. Solid economic well-being is based on a sound organization of society and on a full collaboration of all sectors of economic activity. "The regulative principle of economic life is the social end of economy, and this is identical with the principle of social justice." Cooperatives must therefore take their proper place within the national economy as a whole.

Cooperatives must help to improve the structures of Latin American economy in the productive sector. John Stuart Mill long ago pointed out two economic benefits of the cooperative form: that it would cut down the disproportionate number of people engaged in distribution and at the same time increase individual productivity. Another important role of the cooperative movement is in the consumers' sector: to make essential, everyday goods available to everyone, even those of low income.

Finally there are authors who teach that another aim of cooperative enterprise is moral development. This moral development is carried to other spheres of life. A society which thinks cooperatively can ordinarily find the right answers to problems of education, of politics, of culture. A vivid example of this exists in the town of Tacámbaro, with a population of twelve thousand, where cooperatives control 50 percent of the local economic activity and where the community, thanks to the habit of resolving problems cooperatively, is gradually freeing itself from bossism, from dishonest practices of politicians, and other problems like illiteracy and lack of technology.

As we have already seen, the cooperative movement in Latin America will have to prepare the very ground in which it can be planted and grow. To do this, three means are necessary: legislation, knowledge of principles and technology, and education. Along with amenable legislation and the necessary knowledge of operational techniques, the principal means to be used in planting the seed of cooperative enterprise is *education*.

Let us analyze these three means.

Legislation. Certainly a basic legal structure is a firm support for the existence of the cooperative movement. Laws pertaining to cooperatives have been on the books in different countries of Latin America for several decades. In some countries legislation was passed in 1903; in the majority, since the thirties. Cooperative legislation in Latin America lies along generally acceptable lines, and the different amendments of the basic law have improved it. Probably, though, it would be better to have a more daring, dynamic legislation to give a new impulse and encouragement to a movement which, as an important factor of development, could change the economic and cultural face of Latin America.

Knowledge. Like any cooperative development anywhere in the world, the Latin American movement must give its members a basic knowledge of cooperative principles, organization, administration, and financing. Though this may seem obvious and simple, experience teaches us that when the cooperative movement has tried to reach really deprived people, those at the economic and cultural fringes, it cannot be said too often and too strongly that these people must be brought to understand the implications of cooperation in their daily lives. It is not easy for a mentality which is culturally unaccustomed to pondering the implications of such knowledge to assimilate it quickly.

On the other hand, the cooperative movement, in order to be a positive factor in development, must offer a solid economic advantage to its members. It must also be an instrument of national economic integration. For this it must make abundant use of all available educational media in order to train its members, both professionally and technically. Agricultural cooperatives can offer advantages to the country only when their members have not only learned their cooperative principles but have also improved their farming technology. Marketing cooperatives can take part in the development of the country only when their members and especially their leaders have enough knowledge and experience in the field of marketing.

Education. Without any doubt this is the most important of all the means which the cooperative movement has to take in hand in order to establish itself. At the same time it is the most difficult part of the work to be carried out. Neither organization, nor financing, nor direction present so many difficulties as education of the members.

Cooperative education must induce social change. To do this, the members must be persuaded to accept into their lives the knowledge we just discussed. Latin American cooperative pioneers very early undertook the teaching of fundamental principles, and this they called education. The facts have shown that the work of education is directed not solely at the intelligence but also at moving the will toward cultural change. With that understanding of the problem, Latin American cooperative leaders in their technical meetings at the inter-American level have modified their concept of cooperative education.

The four fundamental points which were formulated at one of these latest meetings are these:

1. Cooperative education should be an instrument which fosters the process of social change and which stimulates the organizers of the corresponding movement to feel, think, and act in accordance with the norms of solidarity and social justice which animate the doctrine and the principles of cooperatives.

2. Cooperative education should adopt, with the necessary modifications, the format of the University of Antigonish, which fundamentally consists in a program of adult education, one of whose pedagogical principles is the study of social problems using the study club method, and whose economic arm consists of the cooperatives.

3. Cooperative education should help to mobilize the people so that by means of different types of cooperatives they can find a democratic solution to their basic problems, both those of home building and those of consumption of food and services, as well as the distribution of agricultural products.

4. Cooperative education should seek to make the movement one of the social forces which participate in the general process of development of the Latin American countries.

Fundamental to these four points is the concern for creating an attitude of cooperation which makes the cooperative movement possible, the necessary transformation of human beings which will allow development of the whole man and of all men.

The Antigonish movement in Nova Scotia, Canada, is in large part responsible for this new emphasis which Latin Americans give to cooperative education. The University of St. Francis Xavier of Antigonish set forth, through its extension department, a program of adult education whose aim was to attain the development of the people of the maritime provinces of Canada. The economic instrument for this educational work was the cooperatives. The success attained under this program and the conditions of underdevelopment which were very similar to conditions presently prevailing in Latin America have brought the present leaders of this movement to spread their experience in Latin America as well as in other parts of the world. The courses which they give on the international level have contributed greatly to the new search in Latin America for its own model of cooperative education. In fact, the principles of the Antigonish movement are an answer to the real situation there today, not only with respect to cultural and economic aspects but also concerning those ethical-moral aspirations peculiar to the Latin American character.

Here are the six Antigonish principles:

The first of these principles is the primacy of the individual. This principle is based on both religious and democratic teaching: religion emphasizes the dignity of man, created in the image and likeness of God; democracy stresses the value of the individual and the development of individual capacities as the aim of the social organization.

The primacy of the individual gives rise to the second principle: that social reform must come through education. Social progress in a democracy must come through the action of the citizens; it can only come if there is an improvement in the quality of the people themselves. That improvement, in turn, can come only through education.

The third principle is that education must begin with economic problems. People are most keenly interested in and concerned with economic needs, and it is good technique to suit the educational effort to the most intimate interests of the individual groups. Moreover, economic reform is the most immediate necessity because the economic problems of the world are the most pressing.

The fourth principle of the Antigonish movement is that education must be through group action. Group action is natural because man is a social being. Not only is man commonly organized in groups, but his problems are usually group problems. Any effective adult education program must, there-fore, fit into this basic group organization of society. Moreover, group action is essential to success under modern conditions; you cannot get results in business or civic affairs without organization.

The fifth principle is that effective social reform involves fundamental changes in social and economic institutions. It is necessary to face the fact that real reform will necessitate strong measures of change which may prove unpopular in certain quarters.

The final principle is that the ultimate objective of the movement is a full and abundant life for everyone in the community. Economic cooperation is the first step, but only the first, toward a society which will permit every individual to develop to the utmost limit of his capacities.

So much for general principles. What is the present situation with regard to cooperatives in Latin America? Statistics on the cooperative movement are so incomplete and so inaccurate that we can only look at the situation very generally.

The number of cooperatives in thirteen countries probably

comes to a few over twenty-five thousand. They are distributed more or less this way:

Twenty-five hundred in agriculture; thirty-two hundred in industry; thirty-three hundred in credit; thirty-five hundred consumer cooperatives; fifteen hundred service cooperatives; forty-five hundred school children's cooperatives; and less than five hundred housing cooperatives.

The membership of cooperatives in twelve countries totals a little under 8 million. Compare this with 214 million inhabitants, and you see how small and uninfluential the movement still is. And many of those 8 million are members in name only, without understanding what cooperation really means.

There are some thirty-five so-called second-level cooperatives consisting of groups of cooperative enterprises in twelve countries. These belong to seventy-seven federations, ten unions, and two confederations. These groupings are formed, with variations according to different laws of the various countries, to give mutual service and support to their member co-ops, and education to the cooperators.

It is easy to see from these general figures that the cooperative movement has up to now been quite insignificant, both economically and from the point of view of education. Nevertheless in a few countries it has some importance. For instance, 8 percent of the national product of Argentina flows through cooperatives. In Brazil 4 percent of the population belong to cooperatives. In Mexico cooperatives produce 33 percent of the fisheries' products. In Uruguay 25 percent of the farmers belong to co-ops. In El Salvador co-ops produce some 7 percent of the national product. There are some cooperatives of very great importance, such as the cooperative Goitia in southern Brazil, the agricultural cooperatives of Uruguay, and the cooperative network of Tacámbaro, Mexico.

In its approach to member education the Latin American movement has made mistakes in these first decades of its life. People have been taught how to form cooperatives, but no thought was given to how this knowledge would be accepted and used by the members. That is why there has been so little change, humanly speaking, in farmers and industrial workers who make up the bulk of co-op members, economically and socially depressed as they are. Studies show that as many as 83 percent of those who join co-ops do so for personal economic reasons and only 6 percent for reasons of solidarity with others. Fifty-five percent do not know that they themselves are the owners of their cooperative. Seventy-one percent do not know who is the president of the board of directors. Only one-third attend meetings, and only one-tenth take part in discussions. Eighty percent do not know the principles of cooperation.

The problem of education is therefore a very serious one in the cooperative movement. At the Ibero-American seminar on cooperatives held in Madrid last year practically every country emphasized this as the biggest problem in Latin American cooperatives. The various movements are making great efforts to remedy this situation. In thirteen countries there are in operation seventy institutions of all kinds promoting cooperatives. Serious work is being done within the framework of inter-American aid, which has been very effective in this area of cooperative education.

Another serious problem of the Latin American cooperative movement is financing. In spite of government institutions formed for the purpose of financing cooperatives, not enough credit is available. There is such a general lack of credit in Latin America that the amount available for cooperatives is very small. Large cooperatives do have access to private sources of credit, but those of medium size do not. To solve this problem, the Fund for International Cooperative Development, an affiliate of the Cooperative League of the United States, has promoted, with funds from the Alliance for Progress, the organization of a system of Inter-American Cooperative Finance.

We turn, finally, to the relationship between the Christian community and the cooperative movement. The fulfillment of man is not complete until it runs over into his will to realize the good of humanity. Our personal existence is reduced to nothing when it exists isolated, satisfied with achievements in its education, in its economic and its social life.

We men are linked together, and our faith makes us take a

new look at this bond. It is in Christ that we have the center of unity. Whether we like it or not, we humans are all united in Christ. In him we shall have the full development of humanity. But in the meanwhile we are making him share with us the underdevelopment in which two-thirds of the world is sunk.

The responsibility for self-realization implies the responsibility to realize humanity as a whole. The personal responsibility to be united in Christ implies the responsibility to build the Mystical Body of Christ. But the words "common good," "realization," "Mystical Body," "union of humanity" lack meaning when they are not translated into the search for the best and most abundant life possible now, at this moment, for all. These words mean health, adequate housing, a living wage, proper education, sound civic institutions and political organization, an enlightened religious life.

To carry out this task is a work of social justice. Only by keeping in mind these duties can we understand correctly the words of John XXIII which set the present task for Christians:

> Social norms of whatever kind are not only to be explained but also applied. This is especially true of the Church's teaching on social matters, which has truth as its guide, justice as its end, and love as its driving force.

The cooperative movement is founded on principles which are Christian. It demands respect for individual thinking and choices. It asks of us just treatment for all and places upon each the responsibility for the common good. It brings us to tie ourselves fast to each other in friendship. It is evident, therefore, that to promote cooperative principles is to promote humanity and to build the Mystical Body of Christ.

That is why cooperatives need the Christian community and the Christian community needs the cooperative movement. Cooperatives in Latin America need the Christian community because cooperative principles can only become active when they have the impulse that comes to us from our common life in Christ. The Christian community needs the cooperatives because they are a concrete instrument through which to make the life of the Mystical Body come true, in justice and love. Social justice means the will to make human good come true.

The Christian community has to work along these lines to develop itself. In Latin America Christians have worked in the promotion of cooperative movements. Lay leaders and priests without number have started cooperatives of all kinds, and in some countries have been the founders of the movement. In Latin America many Christians are giving their lives to the hard job of educating co-op members, because they have become aware that cooperation is one of the most Christian ways of economic life. Nevertheless, we cannot say that in Latin America the Christian community as a whole has taken a great interest in the promotion of cooperatives. The Latin American Christian community needs to acknowledge the integrating Christian value of the cooperative movement and summon its forces to promote it.

What is needed is an effort to build a hemisphere-wide Christian community. To do this we need to agree on four things. First, as members of a Christian community we cannot insulate ourselves from each other. The ignorance, misery, disorganization, and injustice of your neighbors to the south are your ignorance, misery, disorganization, and injustice. Development means development of all men, or there is no development. Second, we must agree that our first task is to build the men who will build a Christian community. Third, we must agree that cooperation is an attitude which we must create as a base for forming cooperatives. We should not look for economic success alone as the only aim of development, while we understand that even economic success can come only when there are enough good cooperators in Latin America. And we must agree, finally, that our forces must all be directed toward forming the minds that will bring social change.

Trade Union Movements

ADOLFO BONILLA

For better understanding of the role that the trade union movement must play in the development and integration of Latin America, it is necessary to take a look at the whole situation of society at the juncture in which we are living. Therefore, before touching what strictly concerns trade unionism, we will give a quick glance at the general economic, social, and cultural situation. We shall see that the integration of Latin America is no longer a vague idea or hope of some idealists. It is becoming a concrete thing through the creation of specific organisms with that exact aim. But it so happens that these worthy efforts are often diminished by the means utilized, since generally the planning of the development and the programs to be executed in order to achieve these goals are made and directed from the United States. There results an inadequacy, a weakening, and an inefficiency in the execution of the plans. We must remember that the North American economy is a capitalist economy, which is by definition a competitive economy. Hence it is impossible for the United States to help Latin America to be developed because nobody who is competitive can help another to become his competitor.

Latin American growth is currently being programmed by North American interests, together with the traditional oligarchies of our countries, and of course it is for their own benefit and not for the benefit of our peoples. In this scheme our peoples can only hope to receive the leftovers of the sumptuous banquet prepared by the minorities who are the only ones capable of developing. And these minorities are so small that in most of our countries we can count the number of families who control economic power as well as political power, and even education and the mass media.

Development is an internal, not external, process. Consequently there exists a development not for the people but with the people, and until we are capable of interpreting and applying this concept, our advance within the world society will be limited. That is why we consider that the Latin American economy must be developed personally and collectively. It must begin with men considered as human beings, not as objects of exploitation or a "human-resources" factor within the productive process, as some economists lately define us. They put us on a level with raw material or machinery because financial capital is what enjoys a superior category for them.

The Latin American Christian trade union movement realizes that in order to achieve a true integration on the continental level, it is necessary to give full responsibility to the peoples so that they can participate consciously and effectively in the process of development. It also realizes that in order for this development to be of real benefit to the great majorities, it must be channeled toward an integral change of the present structures which exist only for the maintenance of privileges for small groups in society. And the Church, acting within the field of its competence, should consider indispensable the formation of a Christian conscience so that this development leading to integration will assume a dynamic attitude of responsibility and participation.

In order to plan adequately it will be necessary to analyze the present situation because a prescription cannot be given without knowing the symptoms and diagnosing the illness of the patient. To begin with, Latin America is an economic reality of 237,500,-000 human beings, of whom 80 percent (190,000,000 people) are unable, to a lesser or greater degree, to satisfy their basic necessities, such as work, food, housing, education, health, and clothing.

The workers who are not able to assert a primary and elementary right, the right to a job, total more than 10 million. And if this is projected socially, it has an effect on 35 or 40 million people because for each worker there are three or four dependents. And this estimate, an official one, does not consider the peasants without land or work, or with temporary jobs of three to six months in the year, of whom there is no statistical record. If these are added to the figure of 10 million, unemployed people would be doubled or perhaps even tripled. In addition to this, it is estimated that by 1975 42 million new jobs will be needed, a demand that the present socioeconomic structures are not able to satisfy.

What predominates in our continent are the unproductive and anachronistic latifundium and minifundium. Our antiquated landholding system explains why vast tracts of land are not cultivated in most of our countries, even though the population is undernourished and it is necessary to import food. The oligarchies continue to monopolize the land, a condition which constitutes a source of political power and enables them to block progress. The salaries of the field workers, meanwhile, are so low that they have not the remotest possibility of some day acquiring a parcel of land which would constitute a productive economic unit.

Insofar as education is concerned, of the 130,600,000 persons who comprise the adult population of Latin America, 43 percent are illiterate, that is to say, more than 56 million. And this tragic figure does not take into account those persons who received less than four or five years of elementary schooling, which is the minimum required for functional literacy. In the urban areas, as a general rule, elementary education consists of six years, whereas in rural areas it varies from two to four years.

On a comparative basis, the average income per person in Latin America is equal to a seventh part of that in the United States, less than a third that of Europe, and inferior to the world average. Life expectancy is 43 and 49 years for men and women respectively, whereas in Europe it is 66 and 73, in North America 67 and 73, and in the Soviet Union 64 and 72 years. The average daily consumption of calories in Europe and North America is 3,200, whereas in Latin America it is around 2,500 calories. The child mortality rate is twice as high as in Europe and four times as high as in North America. The number of persons per room is twice as great as in North America, and less than half the homes have electricity. Recent statistics show that the housing shortage is increasing, as the construction of houses does not even keep up with population growth. In 1965 the total housing deficit in Latin America came to approximately 40 million units.

Medical care is as inadequate as food and housing. For each 10,000 inhabitants there are only 5.5 doctors; furthermore doctors concentrate excessively in the big cities so that there are regions where it is not possible to find a single doctor for hundreds of miles. Moreover, while in Latin America there is one nurse for every three doctors, in the developed countries the proportion is 2.3 nurses for each doctor, and 13 doctors for every 10,000 inhabitants.

Then we must point out the hospital situation, observing that there is a shortage of 700,000 beds in Latin America, and the amount spent per hospital bed is less than one dollar a day average, which means that in many cases the attendance is of ten cents daily per bed. By contrast, in the United States the daily average is thirty dollars per bed. This means that to the inadequate educational system, the chronic lack of homes, the undernourishment of great majorities that at the same time constitute a labor force vital to the development of our countries, we must add the health situation of the Latin American man and woman. These depressing statistics help explain the marginality in which four-fifths of the Latin American population is sunk.

Nor is the outlook for the next generation at all promising. We may note that education is obligatory only at the elementary level, and that even this condition does not mean much if it is not accompanied by the socioeconomic conditions to fulfill it. In many countries there exists the contradiction that while education is legally compulsory to fourteen years of age, the economically active population is considered to be from ten years of age and upwards. In some cases, especially in rural sectors, the labor force includes children six and eight years old. So we see that education in Latin America is not democratic and that its freedom is only formal. The poverty of the majority of the families prevents the effective attendance of their children at school, even at the elementary level. For these families, of course, secondary and superior levels are out of the question. The means of mass communication which might supplement the school system are poorly developed and almost always the object of commercial exploitation. Belonging and responding directly or indirectly to North American interests, the movies, press, radio, and television act as distorting rather than formative elements.

Having thus briefly outlined the economic, social, and cultural condition of Latin America, we can now deal with the trade union situation, which is, of course, closely linked to the sociopolitical, socioeconomic, and sociocultural development of the continent. That is why the Latin American trade union movement, like the continent as a whole, is going through a structural crisis which is to be observed especially in the maladjustment between the objectives desired and the means at hand for their achievement.

In the matter of organized workers Latin America is a continent requiring trade union promotion. Of the 90 million workers in the fields and the cities 76 million are not organized at all. And most of the 14 million workers who are in unions are organized in a loose and ineffective manner. On the other hand, the union movement in Latin America, especially those sectors inspired by North Americans and by Marxists, has its privileged groups of workers, organized in the key sectors of the monoproductive Latin American economy, bettering their own wages and conditions of life and at the same time withdrawing themselves completely from the rest of the laboring masses. Some of these sectors are in the oil, sugar, copper, and banana industries.

We can also observe that the Latin American trade union movement has not escaped from the intrigues and alienations produced by the Cold War. The struggle between Communism and anti-Communism, which is the external expression of the struggle of the imperialist blocs, has affected our trade union movement. Nobody can deny the continuous and increasing interference of

United States policy and interests in the internal affairs of the Latin American trade union movement by trying to control those forces to use them as factors of power within their strategy of predominance in Latin America. Nor can we deny the continuous and also increasing interference of international Communism in the internal affairs of the Latin American labor movement, which seeks to use the unions as "transmission belts" between the party and the popular masses. Communism works to attain world hegemony in its confrontation with occidental capitalism and imperialism, and substitute for it a supercapitalism and a new imperialism without precedent in the continent's history.

This reality has produced a union movement that looks outside our countries and away from our problems. It is incapable of centering itself on national and Latin American realities, incapable of becoming a loyal and effective instrument at the service of the development, the integration, and the revolution in our countries. Hence the trade union movement in Latin America finds itself isolated from the working and popular majorities; it finds itself politically castrated and ideologically alienated. And this may explain the confusion and distrust of the workers toward the present forms of union organizations. In spite of all this, however, the union movement must become one of the fundamental bases of the new society and a powerful instrument of social revolution in Latin America.

Sketching rapidly the history of the trade union movement, we find that the first attempts at continental organization of the Latin American workers were inspired by initiatives coming from outside Latin America. On the trade union level, as on the political and economic levels, there is the phenomenon of extraterritorial forces trying to control the unions with the idea of using them as tools for the benefit of interests and policies that do not correspond to the interests and policies that Latin America needs. These initiatives arise directly from North American trade unions and from United States policy in Latin America, as well as from Communism, with its double but monolithic international apparatus.

The Pan American Labor Confederation (COPA) was constituted in 1918, and this initiative, originating in the North American unions, was increased with time. In January, 1948, they organized the Inter-American Workers Confederation (CIT), which in 1951 was transformed into the Inter-American Regional Organization of Workers (ORIT). One of the "parallel" instruments that effectively contributes to the expansion, penetration, and control of the union organizations in Latin America for ORIT is the American Institute for Free Labor Development (AIFLD). It is directed by George Meany, with Peter Grace as second, the latter the principal person of the firm R. Grace & Co., which owns so many Latin American sugar plantations; steamship companies; soap, cosmetic, electric, and textile factories.

On the other side, we observe the influence of Communism at the continental level, which constituted in 1929 the Latin American Trade Union Confederation (CSLA). Then in 1938 Communists organized the Latin American Confederation of Workers (CTAL), with headquarters in Mexico. Later, after the Cuban revolution, the split between Peking and Moscow, and the increasing importance of the "guerrillas," the CTAL lost all its influence in Latin America because its basic orientation had always been Stalinist. All Soviet attempts to organize have failed, and they have only been able to establish a provisional organization called the Permanent Trade Union Congress of Latin America (CSPAL), with headquarters in Chile. After the Tri-Continental Conference of Havana, celebrated in January, 1966, a powerful new offensive of international Communism in the mass organizations may be expected.

It is pertinent to mention ATLAS, the Association of Latin American Union Workers, was established in Mexico in 1952 under the auspices of the General Labor Confederation of Argentina, dominated by Perón's followers and with the financial aid of Perón's government. This trade union central argued that there was need of a Latin American trade unionism independent of the Cold War. But it did not have any success among the masses of workers of the continent because of its identification and compromise with the Perón regime, and it disappeared when Perón's regime disintegrated.

Finally there appeared the Latin American Confederation of

Christian Trade Unionists (CLASC), organized in Santiago, Chile, in December, 1954. The doctrinal values which inspire its action and its presence in the Latin American labor movement arise from social Christianity as a universal and humanist doctrine. From the beginning and increasingly in recent years CLASC has been defining its trade union doctrine and policy adequately to the reality of Latin America. It is the regional organization of the International Federation of Christian Trade Unions (IFCTU) for this hemisphere, but it energetically insists on the need for an authentic Latin American unionism separated from the Cold War, which has no relevance to the real problems of Latin American workers.

CLASC promotes a democratic and unitary unionism at the national as well as the Latin American level, even though it must continue clarifying and deepening its union policy in certain countries. In March, 1964, at Rio de Janeiro, the Latin American Trade Union Front was established in order to promote the coordination and unification of all union forces willing to struggle for the true interests and genuine solutions that Latin America requires. CLASC stands for a revolutionary unionism because in Latin America the workers' interests are indissolubly tied to the transformation of the economic, social, political, and cultural structures, something that can be achieved only through a profound and radical social revolution.

It is for this reason that CLASC insists that a pragmatic and neutral unionism, based on collective bargaining over wages and hours, is not useful in Latin America. We believe that a unionism with a clear political content, allowing efficacious action in the revolutionary process, able to form consciences and mobilize the workers in complex and tremendous tasks, is necessary. Such unions must work for a change of structures and integral development to seek integration of the laboring masses in the global change of Latin American societies.

ORIT, on the other hand, while it claims to be neutral, in reality does take clear and definite political positions, such as its anti-Communist posture. It also gives backing, sometimes unconditional, to certain regimes or to political attitudes and actions;

we can mention, for instance, the support given to the military coup in Brazil in April, 1964. Also, while CLASC withdrew from a labor commission of the Organization of American States as an act of protest against that organization's refusal to discuss the political conflict in the Dominican Republic, ORIT remained, arguing that it could not touch political subjects. Yet at that moment ORIT was giving public support to the unilateral intervention of the Unites States in the Dominican Republic and was applauding the United States Marines' invasion of that Latin American country.

We see, then, that while the Latin American union movement has clear objectives toward which economic development should aim, it does not have the same clearness with respect to the means that must be employed for their attainment. Only some of the leaders understand the structural mechanism that must function in order to begin a process of socioeconomic development. And this situation is caused by faults in the system of union formation and education and in the limited sphere of action and comprehension that the majority of the trade union leaders have. An understanding of the means and resources that must be employed for development is an essential requisite for preparing a strategy of development.

Socioeconomic development will make possible a greater union development. But unionism must be converted into a dynamic factor of socioeconomic development and of change so that a dynamic interdependence between one and the other can be established. In order for this to happen it is necessary for Latin American unionism to go beyond the scope of the everyday claims to which it is limited at present and to assume the revolutionary role that corresponds to its position.

Sociocultural underdevelopment inevitably causes union underdevelopment in Latin America. As we mentioned before, 43 percent of the population is illiterate, which is the same as saying that there are more than 56 million illiterates. And the illiterate person fears and distrusts any type of organization because he does not understand it. When he does participate he does so in a passive manner. The high percentage of illiterate workers gives unions grave problems of solidarity and makes organization very difficult. Latin America's peasants, who represent 47 percent of the workers, are also largely illiterate, and the cultural and geographical isolation in which they live makes their organization and promotion even more difficult.

It can be observed, then, that even without having completed its organizational stage, unionism shows evident signs of stagnation and of bureaucratization. There is, nevertheless, a transition taking place which can be considered in terms of three general processes. These changes are from the unionism of small groups to the unionism of masses, from company unionism to unionism by trade, and from the unionism of negotiations to revolutionary unionism. These processes are sometimes seen with sufficient clarity at the leadership level. But the vision of union structure and of the crisis through which it is passing is sometimes distorted because it is seen at either a too global or too localized level.

CLASC's ideology finds itself in the stage of elaboration. General statements extracted from philosophical contexts in the period prior to World War II are replaced by an ideology elaborated from the Latin American workers' own values and needs. Away from a cold and intellectual doctrinairism there is evolving an ideology calling for change of the structures of society. However, there remains the grave danger of frustration on the part of union leaders and militants, who become exhausted by the disparity between the great objectives being stated and the precariousness of the material means at hand for their attainment.

Trade unionism's urgent need to expand continues to be hobbled by its deficient organization. The problem becomes acute in view of the growing need for action provoked by the demands of the revolutionary situation. So we find that between the proposed objectives and the requirements of action there exists a bottleneck called organization. And here we must remember that trade union legislation in most Latin American countries was elaborated from the top, by the governments and with the employers' influence. Therefore for unions the structures permitted, the form of organization, the types of action, and so on are very limited. Everything is spelled out in these regulations, and that is why the develop-

ment of the unions is so difficult. Neither the union leaders nor
the workers have participated in the writing of those laws. It has
become increasingly evident that in the task of changing the structure of Latin American society we must first change the union
structures themselves, for the present ones do not facilitate the
necessary growth and development.

In addition to the gloomy view of Latin American reality that
we have presented must also be added the political situation in
most of our countries, which obstructs union organization and
action. In most parts of our continent arise all kinds of oppressions,
vexations, threats, imprisonments, tortures, and even murders of
union leaders. Only last year a female peasant union leader was
brutally assassinated simply for exercising her right to perform
union activities. This murder was planned and executed by the
authorities of the place, known as Santa Rosa del Penon in Nicaragua. And it was a double crime because they not only ended
the life of the unfortunate Christian unionist by eight machete
blows but also finished the life of the child that she was carrying
in her womb. One of the two perpetrators of this murder is free,
since so-called justice in Nicaragua works that way.

And this is not the only case that could be mentioned. We have
a complete list of all those imprisoned, injured, and assassinated
in the different parts of Latin America, besides all the violations
of human rights and national laws involved in the suppression of
Christian trade unionism. We must face this pathetic situation
because CLASC strives for a radical, profound, urgent, and
definitive change of all the present structures which cause the
oppression and humiliation of the great majority of our people,
constituted fundamentally of workers.

We cannot refrain from mentioning the role that the Church
plays in this reality of Latin America. We must observe that in
many of our countries the clergy finds itself intimately linked to
regimes which, instead of representing and protecting the people,
exploit them and restrict their liberties. And we see that the clergy
too often remains silent before injustice. On those occasions when
a priest protests against these wrongs and takes the side of the
oppressed, he is criticized by the hierarchy, he is sanctioned,

exiled, or deprived of his authority, and this occurs even in cases of murder. Many a time, however, the Church's voice is raised to defend the government, which demonstrates that if the bishops fail to speak in defense of the most humble, it is not due to impartiality or to the belief that they are out of their range of action.

Facing these handicaps, Latin American unionism must learn to define its objectives clearly, to adopt firm decisions in its actions. Hence CLASC finds itself working to obtain the unity and solidarity of all the Latin American workers, to achieve consolidation of the masses, and to contribute positively and efficaciously to the development and integration of Latin America.

In the present plans of integration of Latin America there exists discrimination against CLASC. In such planning deference is generally given to ORIT, because this organization does not have as its goal the change of structures, which is the needed base for development and consequently for integration on the continental level. Many examples of this discrimination could be mentioned. Let us note, for example, the way the union movements are included in the Organization of American States (OAS), the Organization of Central American States (ODECA), and the Latin American Association for Free Commerce, where there exists a disproportion between the two main trade union centrals. At a meeting of the Labor and Social Provision Council of ODECA, held in Guatemala in October, 1965, the Nicaraguan Ministry of Labor typically introduced a proposal to accept only ORIT as a consultative organization of the commission. CLASC, at any rate, is searching, not for a passive participation, but for a real and effective one, that is to say, the right to a voice and vote in the deliberations and decisions of all the organizations of integration.

Christian trade unionism cannot, of course, be an end in itself. It is an instrument placed at the service of the workers, and therefore it must act realistically and take into account all the decisive elements of the Latin American situation. When unionism is looked upon as an end in itself, and slavishly begins to copy experiences that respond to other realities, it inevitably converts itself into a cartoon of trade unionism. It is absurd to try to utilize the exact patterns of trade unionism from the United States or Russia or Europe in Latin American nations which still have a good part of their transportation based on horses and ox-driven carts.

CLASC joins with other political and social forces in Latin America seeking to unify all the peoples of the continent to press for economic, social, and political development and to strive for justice, liberty, and peace. But one of the most formidable obstacles to building an independent unionism and unifying the Latin American peoples has been the systematic policy and interests of the United States. This policy and these interests continually interfere in the workers' movements of Latin America. It is well known that North American union forces comprise about 90 percent of ORIT, and it is from the United States that ORIT receives its money and its influence. This explains why ORIT cannot in any way respond to the interests of the workers and peoples of Latin America. It also explains why CLASC has always opposed ORIT and why the latter consistently betrays the interests of the workers and people of Latin America in favor of North American interests and policy.

It is for that same reason that CLASC does not agree with the so-called "inter-American" system, including naturally the union level. It is obviously negative to have the employer within a workers' union, for the employer will sooner or later dominate the organization. This is exactly what happens at present with ORIT, where the employer is the AFL-CIO, the powerful central organization which supplies the money. In the capitalist system, logically, he who puts up the money is the one who gives the orders. Consequently the North American workers' organization is the one that dictates the policy, the patterns, and the tactics to execute in the development of the unionism represented by ORIT.

This in no way means that CLASC is against the people of the United States. On the contrary, CLASC wants a dialogue with North Americans. But this will be possible only when the United States recognizes and respects the right that Latin Americans have to disagree and to have their own personality, their own autonomy, their own vision, and their own Latin American nationalism.

The United States should be in a position to understand the necessity and the right that Latin America has to take its destiny in its own hands. The North American people are a just, conscientious, well-intentioned people who have had their own revolution, which indeed was one of the most successful revolutions in the history of the world. And so the United States must understand that now it is Latin America's turn to make its own revolution, which implies an independence from North American economic and political interests, exactly as when the United States became independent from the British Empire.

These facts give us the guidelines of the climate in which Latin American unionism must develop. We come to the conclusion that the native enemies of unionism are the oligarchy and militarism, which, in alliance with imperialism, try by all means to detain the advance of the organization of the people.

The role that Christians must play within Latin American unionism is of crucial importance, and CLASC knows the serious responsibility that falls on it. That is why in its policy, program, tactics, and strategy it defends the unity of all the workers. It knows that all of them are within the same frame of misery, ignorance, and forlornness, whether they be members of any political party or of any religion or of any enterprise. It is precisely for the maintenance of this posture that CLASC is sometimes accused of being soft with Communism. But if the tactics employed by Christian unionism in some countries seem to be unwary and even collaborationist with the Communists, it is because we are living in a reality completely different from that of the United States. Christian unionism does not lie when adopting the adjective "Christian." It acts in good faith, with good will, preferring the individual and collective interests of the workers and demonstrating in action its unitary aim and its spirit of solidarity with the indigent and the exploited.

On the other hand, since the great majority of the workers in Latin America are not organized in unions, it would be commendable to abandon the unnecessary conflicts and struggles among union organizations, so that more time and resources could be employed objectively and dedicated to positive work. This is, however, often difficult due to unexpected situations that cannot be avoided. In spite of everything, it is never too late to start looking for understanding and harmony among sectors that have the same needs and hopes. And here perhaps we may hope for a change in the intentions and actions of the people and agencies of the United States toward Latin America, a change based on a true Christian spirit and human solidarity and involving a revision of their tactics and aid patterns. At present, for instance, there are investments of fabulous sums of money in a negative anti-Communism through institutions or organizations such as the CIA (Central Intelligence Agency). All of this expenditure does not have any effect other than being negative, confusing, and retrogressive in Latin America, and this money could well be used in a positive way in trying to build an alternative to stagnation or Communism. Then the people of Latin America would really appreciate it.

Finally, we must observe that the harmonious development of Latin America will be impossible without integration. And the trade union movement, as represented by CLASC more than any other union federation of the continent, must be in the vanguard of that movement. Its unity of principles, program, and goals which tend toward the creation of one great Latin American country, where respect for the dignity of the human being will prevail, makes it a fit instrument to help achieve authentic democracy at all levels of society.

The peoples of Latin America, who are becoming organized, who are acquiring consciousness of their own reality and of their own destiny, march, although not rapidly enough, toward a democratic unionism. When they achieve it, it will mean the end of imperialism, the oligarchies, and militarism. Christian unionism is the advance guard of this process, and that is the reason why we are sure that the future of trade unionism is to be the future of Latin America.

International Labor Organization

HENRY A. LANDSBERGER

I

Description

INTRODUCTION

The inclusion of this topic in the 1967 CICOP program is probably
due not merely to the laudable thoroughness of its planners and
their desire to approach the problem of Latin American integration from every conceivable angle. It is presumably also due to
the uncomfortable but undeniable fact that in some not-quite-
clear manner, the United States labor movement (or important
parts thereof), and perhaps the United States Government, are
in head-on collision with a Latin American labor group which,
in some equally unclear fashion, seems to be Catholic. Many of
those attending are no doubt uneasily aware of the much publicized feuding which has been going on for some time between,
on the one hand, the Latin American Confederation of Christian
Unions (CLASC—the Latin American regional affiliate of CISC,
the International Federation of Christian Trade Unions) and, on
the other hand, the Inter-American Regional Workers' Organization, ORIT, which bears the same formal relationship to the International Confederation of Free Trade Union (ICFTU) as CLASC
does to CISC. Of late, the AFL-CIO and the training institute
sponsored by it and by certain United States companies, and

financed largely by United States Government funds, have also been involved in the dispute.

In the second half of this paper we will analyze the causes of this dispute. But, before doing so, let me take some heat out of the dispute by that old and well-tried technique of providing facts about the history and structure of the chief *dramatis personae.* Few are familiar with these facts, and literature on the topic is scarce and not easily accessible. I have, therefore, thought it useful to provide concise factual summary as background to the present dispute.

A Brief Review of the History of the International Labor Movement

Profound differences as to ideologies, goals, tactics, organizational structure, and all other conceivable aspects of trade union life have been characteristic of the trade union movement from its inception in practically all parts of the world and at all levels of the movement. The quarrel is no fiercer in Latin America today than it is elsewhere, and it is no fiercer today than it has been in Latin America at other times or in other places at other times. It comes as a surprise only because most of us have not previously been aware of what went on in the house of labor. What is new is not factionalism in labor, but our consciousness of it.

The first attempt at international working class unity—the International Workingmen's Association, better know as the First International, founded in London in 1864—was in itself and without any formal rivals already an incredible melange of trade unions, cooperatives, revolutionaries, and politicians of very diverse orientations, which soon broke down precisely for that reason.[1] If we leave aside the establishment of the Second International in 1889, which was as much, or more, a union of socialist parties than of trade unions, it was not until 1903 that a purely trade union body was established at the international (inter-European) level: the International Secretariat of Trade Union Centers (ISTUC). The Secretariat left broader political issues to the Second International (with which it maintained friendly relations) and concentrated, relatively speaking, on matters pertinent to a trade union "pure and simple," especially the collection of relevant wage and membership statistics and provision of mutual support in industrial disputes. Separate from the Secretariat—indeed, considerably prior to it—unions from different countries, but in the same industry, had begun to form international trade secretariats of miners, typographers, and such. By 1900 there existed already seventeen of these.[2] Each of the three international trade union federations existing today has trade secretariats associated with it in parallel or subordinate form. These are from some points of view—in particular, from a strictly trade union point of view—the most effective sections of these international organizations, at least in the case of the ICFTU.

Nevertheless, despite this relative eschewing of political issues, the Secretariat and, even more, the national unions encompassed by it clearly were not acceptable by standards of Catholic social teaching, certainly not as the exclusive agents of a good Catholic. It will be recalled that in *Rerum Novarum* Leo XIII declared that "it were greatly to be desired that (workmen's associations) should multiply and become more effective." But it will also be recalled that he warned that many then existing unions were "in the hands of invisible leaders, and are managed on principles far from compatible with Christianity and the public well-being." For this reason he felt that no one would "hesitate to say" that Christian workmen must "unite their forces and courageously shake off the yoke of an unjust and intolerable oppression" (that of coercive labor leaders). Given Catholic suspicion of existing union movements not inspired by Catholic social teaching and often explicitly hostile to it or to the local church as institution, it is understandable that the early years of this century saw efforts by Catholics in various countries (notably, France, Germany, Belgium, and Holland) to establish unions of a confessional kind or at least ones having an interdenominational, religious basis and a Christian orientation. Nor is it surprising that the establishment in 1903 of the generally socialist-oriented International Secretariat of Trade Union Centers (ISTUC) to which we have already referred should be followed by the establishment in

1908 of a Secretariat of Christian Trade Unions. And just as the socialist-inspired ISTUC (renamed the International Federation of Trade Unions, IFTU, in 1913) re-established itself after World War I at a meeting in Amsterdam in 1919, so did the Christian Secretariat rename itself and re-establish itself as the International Federation of Christian Trade Unions (IFCTU-CISC) at a meeting in The Hague in 1920. And when the IFTU (in effect) once again reconstituted itself in 1945 after World War II (now renamed World Federation of Trade Unions, WFTU), the CISC likewise reconstituted itself after vain efforts to join forces with the WFTU.

From 1920 onwards, however, with the rise of international Communism as a force explicitly separate from the more moderate forms of socialism, and with its triumph in Russia, the trade union field likewise split into three, and not merely two, sectors. The Red International of Labor Unions (RILU), founded in the early twenties, became a rival of the IFTU and sought to undermine it and its affiliates whenever it could. Neither group, however, yet showed any major concern for what would now be called the developing countries. For a brief period in the 1940's, however, the rivalry between Communist and moderate socialist labor internationals temporarily ceased. Non-Communist and Communists, including the Soviet Trade Union Movement (AUCCTU), who had been apart and feuding for twenty years, collaborated briefly in the World Federation of Trade Unions established in 1945 in the euphoria of wartime cooperation and victory. But by 1948 the wartime honeymoon was over, and in 1949 the International Confederation of Free Trade Unions—the present ICFTU—was founded, to leave a Communist-dominated rump WFTU. CISC once again, as it had done in 1945, made overtures to join in the organization of the new federation and was once again rebuffed, with the legacy of bitterness that this might be expected to leave. Thus, by the early fifties the lines had been drawn at the international level: a Communist international, the WFTU; a Christian (mainly, but not exclusively, Catholic) international, CISC; and finally, the ICFTU—the largest of all—in part with a now even-more softened European socialist ideology, in part with less even than that, due to the membership and power of the

AFL-CIO, no proponent of socialism or even laborism.

But for our purposes it is Latin America which is of particular interest. And while the contours of the ideological struggle there have been somewhat different from those in Europe, ideological struggle there has always been, and the issues have in part been quite similar. We shall shortly address ourselves to this topic, but let us first look at the posture of the United States labor movement vis-à-vis the international trade union movement. For the United States labor movement has been an important factor both in the international movement and in the Latin American, or Inter-American, labor movement. Its behavior in the latter is more easily understood if we first understand its behavior in the former.

United States Labor in the International Labor Movement

Almost alone among the many, many labor movements which have sprung up all over the world the American labor movement established itself apart from radical left-wing parties and ideologies which, of course, did not exist on a massive scale in the United States. The American Federation of Labor (AFL) established in 1886, has never had any basic quarrel with a tamed capitalist and free enterprise system *qua* system, though this did not preclude vigorous attacks on the practices of employers and their greed as a group of individuals. The AFL therefore affiliated with the European socialist-dominated ISTUC only with considerable reservations in 1910. It left the reconstituted IFTU in 1921, partly because it feared that the IFTU constitution curbed its autonomy and partly for doctrinal reasons. It did affiliate with the IFTU later, in 1937, perhaps in part in order to preempt a place which might otherwise have gone to the rival group of unions who had formed the new Congress of Industrial Organizations. The CIO, though never socialist, was in general more to the left than the AFL, and it might have felt more at home in the IFTU than the AFL ever did.

In 1945 the AFL once again did not join the new WFTU, in part because the Soviet unions (and the CIO) were in it.[3] Moreover, from the early forties onwards the AFL had become thoroughly accustomed to run its own international activities, which were to become most important in the immediate postwar years in the resurrection of the French, Italian, and German trade union movements. Only when the West European moderates broke with the WFTU in 1949 to found the ICFTU did the AFL as well as the CIO affiliate. But while the CIO discontinued most of its independent international activities, the AFL did not, despite its membership in the ICFTU.

These historical facts, particularly the AFL's aloofness from international movements and its readiness to run its own international program, as well as the more flexible position of the CIO toward international and left-oriented movements, are all of critical importance in understanding the present. For when the AFL and the CIO merged in 1955, the new AFL-CIO Department of International Affairs fell into the hands of the AFL group accustomed to independent action and imbued with an activist, hard anti-Communist spirit. The CIO group, most particularly the Reuther brothers Walter and Victor, were then and continued to be unhappy over this fact, and their smoldering resentment has come out into the open in recent years. Among other issues, it did so over the role of the United States labor movement in Latin America and specifically over the activities of the American Institute for Free Labor Development, AIFLD.

With this background on the posture of the United States labor movement in relation to the international labor movement, we can take a brief look at Latin America. The very considerable interest of the United States labor movement in that region is not new. It antedates the struggle against Communism, and, in one of those ironic twists which history sometimes provides, it originated at least in part in order to restrain Washington policy and in opposition to United States big business interests, not in their support as is today's accusation about today's activities in Latin America by United States labor.

Western Hemisphere Regional Movements

Culturally, much of what has occurred in Latin America has been influenced by Western Europe, particularly by the Latin countries of Western Europe. Of few fields is this truer than that of labor. When French labor was riven by struggles between anarchosyndicalists and socialists in the late nineteenth and early twentieth centuries, so was Argentinian labor. Not long after Christian unions were established in Belgium and France, they were established in Chile, where Father Guillermo Viviani was instrumental in the establishment of unions of chauffeurs, railroad men, retail workers, and needle trade workers.

And so, too, it was at the level of regional organizations. Already the First International (the International Workingmen's Association) had affiliated groups in Latin America.[4] In 1907 the anarchosyndicalist trade union movement of Argentina—the *Federacion Obrera Regional Argentina* (FORA)—called a hemispheric meeting in Buenos Aires, to which were invited the United States IWW, the famous "Wobblies," the Industrial Workers of the World. They did not attend, nor did the projected hemispheric organization materialize. These events are nevertheless of prognostic importance. As in Europe, and influenced by Europe, attempts at regional unity would be made on the basis of ideological compatibility.

In 1918, however, the first serious and relatively effective inter-American organization was established: the Pan-American Federation of Labor (PAFL). It was the fruit of the joint efforts of Samuel Gompers, president of the AFL; Santiago Iglesias, a Puerto Rican socialist labor leader; and the leaders of the Mexican labor movement. The story of the founding of this organization is fascinating because it contains many different strands of much relevance today.[5] In part it represented the sympathy of Samuel Gompers, dominant figure on the American labor scene for over thirty years, for the struggle of Mexican labor and of the Mexican people in general, and his desire to prevent the United States Government from helping counterrevolutionary attempts. In part it represented a reaction to, an opposition to, the meeting of the Pan-American Financial and Trade Conference of 1915, which was regarded as a business threat to hemispheric labor. Yet in part the planning of the Federation from 1916 onwards also represented an attempt of a patriotic Gompers to help the United

States war effort against Germany. Money seems to have flowed from the United States Government to the organizers of the conference who were trying to create an appropriate climate for it, while information on German activities in Mexico flowed from Gompers to the United States Government.[6]

When the founding convention actually took place in Laredo, Texas, in mid-November, 1918, themes could be heard which are today major issues in the regional labor situation.

1. There was, on the part of some Latin Americans, e.g., Luis N. Morones, the Mexican labor leader, a pronounced fear that the United States labor movement would dominate the organization and expect others to obey it— *monroismo obrero*, as it came to be called.

2. There were implicit suggestions by some United States spokesmen (Secretary of Labor William B. Wilson, who made the keynote address in President Wilson's name) that the United States labor movement might well serve as a model and example to the labor movements of Latin America insofar as structure, policies, and methods were concerned.

3. Gompers, against bitter resistance from the Mexicans in particular, who did not want to get involved in larger political problems, convinced the convention to go along with a resolution supporting the United States Government on an issue of international politics outside the labor sphere as such; in this case, President Wilson's peace terms.[7]

4. Also as a harbinger of things to come, Gompers and his Latin American colleagues spent much time and effort in attempts to have representatives of PAFL incorporated in the growing number of organizations and committees dealing with inter-American affairs which were springing up under the auspices of the Pan American Union.[8] This is, of course, reminiscent of the vigorous activity of ORIT from the 1961 Punta del Este Conference onwards, to increase labor representation on all inter-American (that is, Alliance and OAS) bodies as well as on the national planning bodies stimulated by the Alliance.

5. PAFL is of interest because the United States labor movement—in effect, Gompers—was several times in the role of middleman and conveyed to the United State Government protests from labor groups in Latin American countries—for example, from those of Nicaragua and (shades of 1965!) the Dominican Republic—about their own dictatorial governments and/or the action of the United States Government and its military forces.[9] The impression one has is that Gompers, despite his closeness to the United States Government and to President Wilson in particular, was decidedly more ready than his counterparts in the 1960's to speak up on behalf of his Latin Ameri-

can brothers, and that he was less ready than his counterparts today to defend the actions of the United States Government. Indeed, resolutions severely condemning United States policies were passed at the Fifth Congress of PAFL in 1927.[10]

6. And finally, it was notable that some of the Latin groups (again, the Mexicans, but also the Argentinians) were restive over having their international contacts confined to the Western Hemisphere. They wanted more direct contact with Europe. The attempt to organize a Latin American federation excluding the United States and affiliating itself with the IFTU failed. But the effort is significant.

We have dwelt at some length on this early venture in inter-American labor organization because it is fascinating that forty and more years ago some of the issues argued with vehemence today were already visible. Almost all these issues involve the role of the North American colossus: its government and its labor movement, their relationship to each other and their relationship to their weaker southern colleagues. In part these issues were resolved differently then than now; in part they were resolved in very much the same way. When the AFL began to interest itself in Latin America in 1948 after a pause of almost twenty years (the PAFL expired in the late twenties), it was a very different group of men who did so. But the traditions of organizations and certain immanent policies live on beyond the men who made them. So do the problems, issues, and dilemmas external to these men and their organizations with which they are faced and which they have to try to resolve. These dilemmas are relived anew, therefore, and often resolved in the same way. The AFL gave early signs of strong leanings toward a robust, perhaps rather limited, patriotism on the basis of which it maintains the sympathy of a public easily aroused to suspicions of left radicalism. The AFL's posture also preserved, and still preserves, government goodwill and occasional support of a more tangible kind (for example, jobs in government) which are as important to its institutional well-being as is approval by the general public. This patriotic theme was adopted early in the life of the AFL. It is in crescendo today, but even when more muted during certain periods, it has never disappeared, and it is unlikely that it ever will.

We may review other efforts at regional labor movements more briefly, not because they were less important, but because their significance was so clear that little of our precious time and space needs to be spent elaborating on them. First, toward the end of the twenties there was founded not only an inter-American anarchosyndicalist organization (ACAT) but also a hard-line, purely Communist Latin American Labor Confederation (CSLA). It affiliated, of course, as did its national members, with the Red International of Labor Unions. This, too, we may regard as a permanent tendency in Latin America: the temporary congregation of sharply radical groups, soon to disintegrate as "openings to the right" are deemed expedient, and as isolation and loss of support lead to ineffectiveness.

Later, in the course of the thirties, when Communists everywhere rejoined other groups in a spirit of popular frontism, several of the newly enlarged major Latin American movements founded the *Confederacion de Trabajadores de America Latina* (CTAL). This occurred largely under the inspiration of the newly established Mexican Confederation of Labor (CTM) and its general-secretary, Vicente Lombardo Toledano, with the encouragement of President Cardenas. But it was vigorously supported by Argentina's CGT and Chile's CTCH. This effort, too, symbolizes much that is typical for Latin America: first, its restriction to Latin American to the exclusion of North American unions, and second, a confederation which, while radical, is broader by far than the extreme left. But this kind of regional confederation also is unstable. Before long it shrinks in effect into being little more than another extremist group. This occurs both because nonextremists tend to leave it and because extremists tend to win out in the internal struggle for power. That is exactly what happened to the WFTU in the late forties at the international level. That is exactly what happened in the late forties to CTAL at the Latin American level, though CTAL continued in formal existence until the early sixties.

Finally, in 1948, under stimulus from the AFL and its Latin American representative Serafino Romualdi, greatly concerned over the existence of CTAL as a radical regional organization excluding the United States but working closely with several Latin American movements which had eliminated Communist influence,[11] there was founded the *Confederacion Interamericana de Trabajadores* CIT. In 1951 this organization converted itself into ORIT, the Inter-American Regional Organization of the newly established ICFTU.

And is it to be wondered that at about the same time there should be founded the first Latin American Christian Regional Association (CLASC), affiliated, of course, with CISC?

I believe I have adequately illustrated that ideological rivalry is a permanent characteristic of the inter-American labor scene as it is of the international labor scene. We can now pass on to take stock of the present situation.

THE PRESENT SITUATION

1. *Nonaffiliated.*

Let it be recognized at the outset that as of May, 1964, over one-third of all workers south of the Rio Grande *who were in unions* were yet not affiliated with any of the three international organizations.[12] The members of several more unions might have belonged to the international trade secretariats of one or other of the world federations, particularly those of the ICFTU. However, Argentina, the country with perhaps the Southern Hemisphere's most powerful and well-developed labor movement, has none of its two and a half million members affiliated to an international or regional trade union federation. In Bolivia practically none of the unions or their members were affiliated; in Mexico almost 50 percent were not; in Uruguay 85 percent were not, and in Chile over 60 percent were not. As of the same date—1964—the only countries with important labor movements where the percentage of nonaffiliated was low were Brazil (5 percent), Colombia (27 percent), and Peru (12 percent). We note, therefore, that very important national labor movements may exist without affiliation to either regional or one of the three international trade union movements.

2. *The "radical" camp.*

There exists at present no regional confederation of radical orientation. A planning meeting was held in Santiago, Chile, in 1962, to plan for a further planning meeting in Brazil in 1964. The latter—during which CTAL was officially dissolved—met under difficult circumstances just prior to the fall of President Goulart. It decided to set up, in Santiago, Chile, a permanent commission to plan for a new Latin American confederation! It is doubtful that much will come of it.

Nor does the WFTU have many direct affiliates. Only in Ecuador, Venezuela, and in the tiny French Caribbean departments is a substantial sector of the unionized working population in unions affiliated with the WFTU.[13] Altogether the WFTU, which claims a worldwide membership of 138 million, actually has little strength outside the Communist-bloc countries, including Cuba, with the exception of France, Italy, and India.

Yet neither the failure to have a viable Latin American regional confederation nor the meager direct affiliation with the WFTU can be regarded as an accurate measure of the strength of radical ideologies and of radically oriented leaders in Latin American labor. Important sections of the Uruguayan and Chilean labor movements have strong radical leadership, and it is not far below the surface in the metal manufacturing industry in Brazil, as well as in Colombia and in the Dominican Republic. The failure to form an overt regional movement or to affiliate with the WFTU is, therefore, to be understood as a very sober and accurate assessment of the fact that at this particular juncture, with hostile governments almost everywhere, a Latin American confederation of openly radical orientation, or in the hands of radical elements, could achieve nothing except draw fire.

A temporizing policy may well be eminently sensible not only for these radical groups but also for others. It takes on added force when we recall, once again, how many of Latin America's organized workers—as well as, by definition, all its unorganized workers—are unaffiliated with any international labor organization.

3. *CISC and its Latin American affiliate, CLASC.*

At the Eleventh Congress of CISC, in '1951,[14] Latin American groups from five countries were admitted for the first time. But for lack of money they were unable to attend. At the Fifteenth Congress in Liège, in 1964, of the sixty-two nations represented, twenty-three—the largest single block—came from Latin America. Twenty African, thirteen European, and six Asian nations were also represented.

Nevertheless, CISC is not strong worldwide. It is generally estimated to have three or three and a half million affiliated members. And the numerical strength of CLASC, the Latin American affiliate, is not great, and it is certainly indeterminate. Only in the Dominican Republic is a major movement (the *Confederacion Autentico Sindical Cristiano* [CASC] with perhaps forty or fifty thousand members) affiliated to it. To this can be added certain nuclei in Venezuela[15] and an important segment of Chile's newly flourishing rural movement, as well as rural movements of indeterminate size in Peru, Ecuador, and Guatemala.

Painful for CLASC has always been the fact that the two most substantial Latin labor movements of Christian inspiration—the Colombian UTC and *Rerum Novarum* of Costa Rica—have been steadfast affiliates of ORIT, not of CLASC. More recently CLASC has felt compelled to expel the 200,000-member Brazilian Confederation of Christian Workers (CBTC) for its early support of the 1964 military coup (a support since rescinded). And finally it should be noted that Chile's Christian Democratic Party, while on record against ORIT, has not by virtue of that fact endorsed CLASC with any notable degree of enthusiasm.

However sound the policy positions taken by CLASC may or may not be, it cannot, in fact, speak for a large number of organized workers, nor even for a substantial sector of the Christian inspired unions of Latin America. On the matter of financing it is equally necessary to be frank and realistic about CLASC. While the sums at the disposal of CLASC may be far smaller than those of which "the ORIT complex" disposes, these funds are probably no more indigenous to Latin America than are those of its rival.

They come from CISC in Brussels and from other Western European, particularly German, sources.

4. *The ORIT complex.*

This is, therefore, by all odds the largest numerically, the best financed, and institutionally the most powerfully supported grouping. It consists of (1) ORIT itself, the Western Hemisphere regional organization of the ICFTU, in which the voice of the AFL-CIO is undoubtedly the dominant voice, and (2) various international trade secretariats active in the Western Hemisphere, such as the International Transport Workers Federation; the Metal Workers; the Postal, Telephone, and Telegraph Workers; and others. ORIT has by far and away the largest number of affiliates, among them some of Latin America's most firmly established national federations, such as Mexico's CTM; Venezuela's CTV; Peru's CTB; the two main Colombian federations, UTC and CTC; massive sectors of the Brazilian labor movement; and important sectors from many of the smaller countries where unions are, however, generally weak: El Salvador, Guatemala, and many of the Caribbean islands (where unions are strong). In 1964 ORIT may have had approximately 50 percent of all organized workers, and it may have had over 95 percent of all workers who were affiliated with an international labor organization.[16]

The most controversial member of the "ORIT complex" is, however, (3) the American Institute for Free Labor Development. This controversy is ironic because AIFLD was set up in part to permit the United States labor movement to deal more directly with Latin American labor movements without passing through a regional organization which, it was realized in the early sixties, was controversial and unattractive to many Latin American trade unionists. The Institute is sponsored directly by the AFL-CIO and in effect run by it. But its board also contains representatives of large United States companies operating in Latin America, such as Grace and Anaconda, and Latin Americans of the democratic moderate left, such as Romulo Betancourt and José Figueres. It has perhaps fourteen field offices in Latin America, over forty thousand students have passed through educational short courses sponsored by it in Latin America itself, over four thousand through longer resident courses, and over four hundred through longer training in Washington.[17] Apart from its educational program it has a social projects program under which housing, credit, and consumer cooperatives and the building of medical clinics are sponsored. The social projects department has a resident United States staff in Latin America which has been estimated at over sixty, and this number may be over two hundred if United States citizens servicing Latin America, but stationed at Washington headquarters, are included.[18] Through obtaining United States Government guarantees of loans extended by AFL-CIO unions to Latin American (trade union) borrowers, and through its contacts with the Agency for International Development (AID) in general, the Institute is involved in the channeling of tens, if not hundreds, of millions of dollars. Of its direct budget, probably 80 percent comes from United States Government sources, the remainder being approximately evenly distributed between business and unions.[19]

ORIT in general and the AFL-CIO more particularly are closely linked to various inter-American and Alliance for Progress bodies[20] as well as have easy access to United States Government agencies. Human nature being what it is, it is only to be expected that this influence and power as well as the immense resources for education, housing, and such which the ORIT complex disposes would be cause enough for feelings of envy and suspicion. These feelings are enormously reinforced by the ambiguous political role which the ORIT complex is seen as having played in recent critical events in Latin America. Despite its claim, sincerely meant and not really illogical, that its long-run aim is to foster trade unionism and the labor movement, some of its actions are highly political and interventionist. Key figures have stated proudly that they or their trainees played important roles in the toppling of the Bosch Government in the Dominican Republic and of President Goulart in Brazil. These acts, the support of strikes against Cheddi Jagan in Guyana, ORIT support of the Castillo Armas regime after it had ousted Arbenz, and the belated condemnation of Batista all seem to many to form a pattern of political support for right-wing regimes. In addition, accusations have been made of intimate connections between AIFLD personnel and United States intelligence services, accusations most recently voiced by Victor Reuther, brother of Walter Reuther, a long-time critic of the AFL-CIO's president, George Meany, particularly on foreign policy matters as well as other matters.[21]

The issues, then, are rather unpleasant ones. The "ORIT complex" is accused, first, of teaching to others a nonpolitical pure trade union approach to the solution of labor's problems in a setting where no such solutions are likely to be effective unless a substantial change in political power has first occurred. In short, it is accused of misunderstanding the nature of Latin American society. The participation of United States company representatives in an educational venture for Latin American trade unionists is regarded as symbolic of this lack of comprehension of Latin America's problems, or at least of its psychology. Second, the ORIT complex is accused of preaching a doctrine of nonpolitical unionism while actually engaging in political activity and even supporting or condoning right-wing violence. In particular, its fierce anti-Communism is regarded as sterile, a highly political act undermining its claim to be nonpolitical. Third, it is regarded as an instrumental part of United States Government policy, which may be good or bad, but means that it is not engaged in *bona fide* union activity. Fourth, there is a generalized fear that the immense wealth and power of the United States labor movement will have the practical effect of preventing the growth of strong local, autonomous labor movements. Fifth, there is a feeling that ORIT, in practice, utilizes as its standard bearers unionists in ill-repute with their fellows.

In the quarrel with CLASC, ORIT counterattacks by questioning for whom CLASC really speaks when voicing these fears, in view of its unknown representativeness, its numerical thinness, and its practical inexperience even at the top leadership level. CLASC's emphasis on the need for a genuine social revolution and changes in institutional structure are seen either as pure demagogy, empty phrases lacking any specific programmatic content, or as dangerously similar to Communist preachings of class warfare. In the latter connection, CLASC's strident anti-Yankee-ism and its failure to condemn the USSR and China with equal frequency are also noted (CLASC has condemned aspects of Cas-tro-Cuban policy). Finally, its foreign financing and its attempts to split and reaffiliate existing union movements are criticized.

Concerning the left tone of CLASC pronouncements coming from Santiago and, more recently, from its new headquarters in Caracas, as well as its lack of emphasis on religious matters, it is important to note that this is in line with CISC trends at the international level and is not confined to Latin America. The reformulated 1962 program of CISC has removed all references to God and Christianity and stated its goal to be a democratic rather than a Christian society. One of CISC's most important affiliates—the French CFTC—recently removed the final "C" (*chretiens*) from its title and substituted for it a "D" for *demo-cratique* (CFDT). CISC and its affiliates may be adopting a more flexible policy toward the WFTU and Communism in general than does the ICFTU. Rumored strains between CLASC and its par-ent body, CISC, may, therefore, be only partially true. On the whole, CLASC's policies with exception of its stress on political action may represent CISC policies quite well regardless of how many Latin Americans it represents.

II

Interpretation

How can we best understand what is going on today in Latin America at the level of regional and hemispheric labor organiza-tions? What functions are they really performing? Who controls them and for what ends? At what points are they succeeding and why? Where do they fail and why?

The interpretations which follow are unusual because their basic theme is that we are not dealing with ordinary trade union phenomena but with struggles for power, influence, and control between quite unusual contestants applying pressure at points not normally considered when thinking about the ways and means of trade unions. These interpretations may even appear cynical. But the aim is not that of seeking attention and notoriety by the crude device of shocking. The following interpretations are the result of much reflection, discussions with others who are more knowledgeable, and prolonged personal observation in at least one country, Chile.

Regional Organizations Cannot, on the Whole, Help Much in Day-to-Day Unionism.

A long-time student of international labor organizations has divided the goals and functions of these organizations into three: (1) representational, or "placing a generalized trade union point of view on current issues before intergovernmental agencies, such as the United Nations, the ILO, or regional bodies" (note the reference to regional bodies); (2) missionary goals: "the propagation of trade unionism, or rather of a particular brand of trade unionism, to areas where it does not yet exist or where its weakness requires external support"; and (3) servicing: "support of their affiliates, as through international strike support, research and welfare work, exchange of trade information, and assistance to migrating union members."[22] It is this latter which we have called "help in day-to-day unionism."

Both Windmuller and another long-time observer, George E. Lichtblau, agree that of the three functions, the missionary activity and not service in day-to-day union affairs has become the most important. "The 'cold war' remains the principal preoccupation of the international labor movements. . . . (and) consumes most of the energy and resources of the labor internationals."[23] Concentration of the cold war gives the missionary activity a peculiar twist. It means that as much or more energy may be spent in attempting to get already established unions to change their affiliation from one international organization to another, or to oust one group of leaders and replace them with ideologically more acceptable ones, as in organizing previously unorganized workers.

The day-to-day activities of a union at the local plant level, or at the company or industry level, may be divided into (1) its organization and establishment in the first place; (2) gaining recognition from the employer and the government; (3) negotiating agreements (this may include fewer or more steps, as appearing before mediation and arbitration boards, and organizing and executing strikes); (4) administering the agreement; (5) directing the internal life of the union, holding meetings, and the like; (6) educating members and especially those elected to be officials in the activities just outlined. These are the activities which most directly and immediately affect the individual worker.

When international organizations were first established, they were of some help in these activities. They could occasionally provide strike funds, stop employers from importing strikebreakers across European boundaries, refuse to handle his goods when exported, and such. The ICFTU international trade secretariats continue to be of some help in this general area of service in the day-to-day activities of unions, mostly in connection with initial organization and recognition or during critical negotiations. In particular, a visit by some senior (generally European) officer of the ITS's to a government official may be important in a critical labor dispute or if the very existence of a local union is threatened.[24]

But clearly it is not logical that regional organizations should address themselves to thousands of local situations. They do not have the financial or human resources to do so. Immersion in a local situation by an outsider is immensely difficult, and international organizations do not dispose of large quantities of such wise men, if, indeed, they exist at all. Nor does the problem usually lend itself to solution from the outside. The reaction of both the Chilean workers whom it is intended to help, and of the Chilean minister before whom representations are made, may be imagined if the spokesman for a regional labor organization happened to be, for example, a Bolivian or Argentinian. Regional organizations do not generally have sufficient time or resources to see a problem through to its solution. In the organization of new unions, for example, though the outsider is often gratified by his initial success in establishing one, he generally does not and cannot stay long enough to see it collapse a month, a year, or two years after the initiation ceremony.

By comparison with most national organizations, international organizations are as a rule poorly provided with those instruments that are essential to effective action, in particular, a well-functioning apparatus under authoritative leadership, adequate human and material resources, and certain devices for inducing or compelling adherence to their policies. In general their secretariats are weak, their resources scanty, and their coercive and persuasive powers exceedingly small.[25]

THE REAL GOAL OF INTERNATIONAL AND REGIONAL LABOR ORGANIZATIONS IN LATIN AMERICA IS THAT OF ORGANIZATIONAL CONQUEST.

We are doing little more than restating what has been said by the two experts we have cited above. The chief objective of international organizations is a missionary, not service, one. We would wish only to add one important clarifying footnote to that idea and to the term "missionary." It is our impression that the aim of these organizations is not really, in the first and most important instance, that of spreading their ideologies and thereby leading to different trade union practices and activities. Certainly this is not their aim in the short run or even the medium run. It is for this reason that not much space has been devoted to analyzing in what way the CISC-CLASC ideology concerning trade union aims differs from that of the ICFTU-ORIT or from that of the WFTU. As organizations, these entities are too weak, and local situational pressures too strong, for them to impose any philosophy of trade unionism on their affiliates even if they have any distinctive ones, which is not at all certain in the case of the CISC-CLASC and ICFTU-ORIT. In this sense they are not really missionaries.

International labor organizations in Latin America seem to be missionaries only in that less desirable sense which will be quite familiar to this audience: that of seeking formal converts, of increasing the numbers of those formally registered and affiliated, and, in particular, in ousting the representatives of rival groups. The anti-Communism of ORIT is, therefore, not so much or not only ideological. It is organizational. And the anti-Yankeeism and anti-ORITism of CLASC likewise represents in part a desire to remove persons whom it can never control and whose organizations it can never hope to capture while these persons are in charge.

This game of organizational raiding, of affiliating and reaffiliating, of plotting the ouster of one group of officers to install another because of their greater organizational loyalty, does not arouse this author to great heights of enthusiasm in favor of any of the contestants. It is an unending game which absorbs a great deal of energy and is of dubious advantage to the ordinary worker. Unfortunately, since the game is being played, it is impossible to ignore it.

THE CONTESTANTS AT THE REGIONAL AND INTERNATIONAL LEVEL ARE, TO AN IMPORTANT DEGREE, NOT LATIN AMERICAN

It is reasonably clear that without the administrative know-how and drive, and especially without the immense financial resources, of the United States labor movement (and, in part, that of the United States Government) ORIT would be but a shadow of itself. AIFLD and its manifold activities would, obviously, cease to exist. This is not to deny, let this be equally clear, that their help may not be welcomed in many cases by those who receive it. But it is not help by Latin Americans to Latin Americans. It is doubtful that the Mexican CTM, Venezuela's CTV, or Peru's CTP—the Latin American affiliates of ORIT which are strongest organizationally and financially—would band together without United States help in anything but the most perfunctory regional grouping. The reason is that there would not be—and there is not at present—very much "in it for them." It is not likely that they would get together to send teams of well-financed experts to the northeast of Brazil or that they would contribute to the financing of a well-appointed union hall in Ecuador.

The reason behind the intense interest of those leaders of the AFL-CIO who are interested in this organizational race is not fully clear to me. We might note that their number is small and that the goals they pursue are of little interest to their North

American members, though these clearly also do not oppose them. The easiest answers are ones which can be traced back historically. First, the AFL leadership has a long tradition of being fiercely anti-Communist. Second, like all organizations which have had to fight for their place in the sun, it is conscious of its power now that it has some and likes to exercise it in a variety of settings. These two motives, in combination, imply that the AFL-CIO's vigorous hunt of Communists in Latin America must not be seen as a simple, passive execution of United States Government policy. On the contrary, there is perhaps as much unhappiness as satisfaction with the massive and forceful activities of the "ORIT complex" among those government officials and policy makers who are aware of them but who cannot speak out for a variety of reasons. United States labor is leading, as much as following, the United States Government. In addition to anti-Communism and the desire to exercise power, the AFL leadership is genuinely patriotic, and this is certainly one motive for its action, however much one or another person may differ with it on what is appropriately patriotic at any given moment of time. The AFL-CIO leadership is also desirous of helping the Government because certain *quid pro quos* are involved, for example support for legislation which the AFL-CIO needs at home. And, finally, humanitarianism, of course, plays an important motivating role, that is, the desire to organize the unorganized and to help them toward a better life. But it must be remembered that there is much similar work to be done along these lines in the United States, and those leaders of the AFL-CIO who have been most concerned with overseas affairs have often given least indication of being motivated by this kind of drive at home.

The case of CLASC is basically not dissimilar. Its outside sponsors are, of course, also moved by humanitarian reasons, organizing the unorganized. But the classical religious motivation behind trade union activities, that of not abandoning the ground to capitalist or socialist-communist materialism, surely also plays a role. In this instance ideological motives are, we suspect, strongly reinforced by discomfort at the thought of organizationally abandoning Latin American workers to the North American colossus no matter what his ideology. And this discomfort exists not only in Latin America but in Western Europe. Once again the first step has to be to organize those who are threatened and to stop or eliminate rivals.

THE METHODS IN THIS STRUGGLE FOR ORGANIZATIONAL POWER ARE: (1) EDUCATION, (2) DISBURSEMENT OF RESOURCES, (3) REPRESENTATION IN DECISION-MAKING BODIES.

1. *Education.*

At all levels trade unions sponsor educational activities. But the further away, and the further up, that one moves from the grass-roots level, the more likely it is that the intent—and certainly the main effect—of this education is that of morale-lifting and, particularly, the building of loyalty rather than the building of specific organizational skills. Speaking as an educator and as someone who has participated in and observed the educational efforts of CLASC, ORIT, and of some more radical groups, I am dubious that much new skill or much information was learned, that it ever could be learned in the kind of setting in which it was offered, or that it was the chief purpose of the organizers that it be learned.

Administrative skills, skills in organizing and negotiating, and skills in conducting meetings and in otherwise communicating with union members, can be well learned, not in this kind of setting, but only over long periods of actual experience, perhaps in an apprentice relationship to an experienced man. Invariably courses run by regional organizations contain a good deal of general political, doctrinal, and so-called historical material, and this alone is sufficient to indicate its real intention.

Its efficacy in any direction is difficult to assess. That many trainees are "lost" in one way or another is quite apparent. But one or two trainees in the right spot at the right time may compensate for them. More information on the efficacy of educational programs is clearly needed, though each organization will undoubtedly wish to conduct its own study. Lacking more concrete information, we can only go by impressions, and these are strong that the purpose and the effect of training programs conducted by international labor organizations is primarily that of instilling organizational loyalty and giving a general boost to morale rather than equipping the student with specific skills.

2. *Disbursement of Resources.*

The giving and withholding of resources in order to get the right man elected or to achieve affiliation or reaffiliation of a particular union is probably a more powerful weapon than education. In fact, the disbursing of educational fellowships—a weekend or a week or four weeks at a training center, perhaps in another country or even another continent—is itself a resource which is used to make friends and win allegiance. More massive efforts are loans to housing or consumer cooperatives or the donation of a union hall. Less massive efforts are the supply of office equipment and jeeps. The price is the promise of affiliation or at least a good deal of publicity for the organization granting the benefit.

3. *Representation in decision-making bodies.*

There is here a parallel with European integration which in part is deceptive and misleading. Western Europe is, of course, in a relatively advanced stage of integration, and its union movement is relatively affluent and firmly established. Consequently, the union movements of the countries involved (West Germany, France, Belgium, and others) have been in a position to set up effective advisory committees to provide expert representation of worker interests. Thus, there is a European Trade Union Secretariat (established by ICFTU affiliates) which acts as an interest group vis-à-vis the European Economic Community. The European Free Trade Association and the Organization of Economic Cooperation and Development also have such trade union bodies attached to them.

The parallel is, of course, COSATE, the Trade Union Technical Advisory Committee to the Department of Social Affairs of the Organization of American States. Moreover, this group—from which CLASC has withdrawn as we have already mentioned—is pressing that trade unionists be involved in social and economic policy-making bodies at the national level in all countries participating in the Alliance for Progress. But the real question is whether the OAS, or the newly projected national planning entities, are in the foreseeable future likely to influence important policy-making bodies to the degree to which they are in Europe. Even if we assume that they are, there is a further question whether Latin American trade unions have the kind of personnel available, or trainable, who could effectively influence such important policies as are made. What seems much more certain is that positions on inter-American bodies and on national bodies can be important in the organizational fight to which we have drawn attention, even if they are not important in affecting major economic and social policies. It should be noted that in Europe, ICFTU and CISC unions have a reasonable *modus vivendi* at the continental level and at many national levels which CLASC and ORIT clearly do not have. The likelihood of using representation in inter-American or national bodies for organizational rather than policy purposes is, therefore, great. Thus, the parallel with Europe is partial, though it will become more real with the passage of time as Latin America becomes more integrated and as its labor movement has the resources to maintain staff experts who can participate in deliberations on problems such as continental social security systems, tariffs, prices, and other such issues. In the meantime, these European-looking forms have a different significance in Latin America.

* * * * * * * *

The total picture I have portrayed is clearly not a very bright one. Those who are concerned with helping the individual Latin American working man in this or that country or in this or that city and local region may well want to think carefully before becoming involved with the various international labor organizations. The latter are chiefly concerned with fighting each other and eliminating their organizational enemies, and that situation is unlikely to change in the near future. Nevertheless, they dispose of resources which may be indispensable, and they may slowly come to occupy a series of administrative positions which will make it difficult to ignore them and still survive. In any dealings with them it is good to look at the price tag, however, in order to know what is being offered in return for what. Dealing with these international organizations is difficult because the key figures are not in, but outside, Latin America. This requires unusual channels of communication. Yet accommodation may ultimately be impossible since local support is necessary to these international organizations, and they, too, are willing to pay a price for it. But it is *that* kind of a situation!

NOTES

1. This summary is based on John P. Windmuller, *American Labor and the International Labor Movement, 1940–1953,* Cornell International Industrial and Labor Relations Reports No. 2 (Ithaca: N.Y. State School of Industrial and Labor Relations, 1954), p. 2 *et seq.* For a fuller account, see Lewis Lorwin, *Labor and Internationalism* (New York: Macmillan, 1929), and *ibid., The International Labor Movement —History, Policies, Outlook* (New York: Harper, 1953). Another well-known source is John Price, *The International Labor Movement* (London: Oxford University Press, 1945).

2. John P. Windmuller, *ibid.,* citing Lewis Lorwin, *ibid.,* pp. 97–99.

3. John P. Windmuller, *op. cit.,* pp. 67 *et seq.*

4. Robert J. Alexander, *Organized Labor in Latin America* (New York: The Free Press, 1965), p. 242. The chapter devoted to international trade union organizations in Latin America (Chapter 18, pp. 242–261) is a very useful summary.

5. See Sinclair Snow, *The Pan-American Federation of Labor* (Durham: Duke University Press, 1964). The following material is based on Snow's book.

6. *Ibid.,* p. 41 *et seq.,* esp. pp. 43 and 45.

7. *Ibid.,* pp. 55–57.

8. *Ibid.,* pp. 67 *et seq.*

9. *Ibid.,* p. 74 *et seq.*

10. *Ibid.,* p. 136.

11. Cuba, Venezuela, Peru, the Catholic inspired *Union de Traba-jadores de Colombia,* Costa Rica's *Rerum Novarum.*

12. *Directory of Labor Organizations: Western Hemisphere,* rev. ed. (Washington, D. C.: Bureau of International Labor Affairs, U.S. Dept. of Labor, May, 1964), Vol. 1, p. xi.

13. *Ibid.* Fifty-three percent in Ecuador (where the extremists are bitterly divided among themselves); 15 percent, or 240,000, in Venezuela; and from 40 to 80 percent in the three French departments. While this source may appear to some as not unbiased, the facts are basically noncontrovertible: the WFTU has no major formal strength in the Western Hemisphere.

14. This, and much of the subsequent information on CISC, comes from an as-yet-unpublished manuscript of Professor Efren Cordova, currently completing graduate studies at the School of Industrial and Labor Relations, Cornell University.

15. *Confederacion de Sindicatos Autonomos* with perhaps 20,000 to 30,000 members. A coordinating entity, CUSIC (*Comité Unitario de Sindicalistas Cristanos*), relates CODESA to the *Federacion de Traba-jadores COPEIanos* (FTC), many of whose afflliates are, however, members of unions affiliated to the *Confederacion de Trabajadores de Venezuela* (CTV). The CTV is an ORIT affiliate.

16. *Directory of Labor Organizations,* p. xi.

17. William C. Doherty, Jr., Administrator, American Institute for Free Labor Development, "AIFLD and Latin Labor Building a Modern Society," *AFL-CIO Free Trade Union News,* Vol. 21, No. 7 (July, 1966), 3 and 6.

18. Sidney Lens, "American Labor Abroad: Lovestone Diplomacy," *The Nation,* July 5, 1965. Lens is clearly no friend of the AIFLD, but there is no reason to question these figures, which to my knowledge have not been challenged. The reference in the title is to J. Lovestone, since the early 1940's effectively in charge of the AFL's international affairs and, since the merger in 1955, in charge of the AFL-CIO's international program.

19. Lens, *op. cit.*

20. See, for example, the Report of the Fourth Meeting of the Trade Union Technical Advisory Committee (COSATE), Nov. 5, 1966, Department of Social Affairs, Pan American Union, General Secretariat of the Organization of American States, Washington, D.C. The establishment of COSATE was, in itself, the result of labor activity. The CLASC representative on it has withdrawn and/or the Committee has placed his position in doubt, since his vigorous statement criticizing the OAS and the Alliance.

21. See the statement issued by the United Automobile Workers as reported in the *New York Times*, December 30, 1966.

22. John P. Windmuller, "International Trade Union Organizations: Structure, Functions, Limitations," to be published in 1967 by the Industrial Relations Research Association and Harper and Row, New York, New York, in a special volume devoted to international labor.

23. Lichblau as cited in John P. Windmuller, *American Labor*.

24. See, for example, "Report on Activities for the Years 1962, 1963 and 1964," presented to the 28th Congress of the International Transport Workers' Federation, Copenhagen, Denmark, July 28–August 6, 1965. The section dealing with Latin America (pp. 88–101) contains interesting examples of both successes and failures.

25. John P. Windmuller, *American Labor*.

International Business

EDUARDO VALLARINO, JR.

When thinking of a contribution to make to this topic, I came to
the conclusion that it would be better to present my own experiences, however limited, rather than the results of a scholarly
investigation of the problems of Latin America. Most studies so far
have been plagued by the tendency to make generalizations about
a vast and diverse area, or to accept a set of concepts and myths
which are thereby perpetuated. By presenting my own experiences I hope to offer this group a useful basis for discussion and
to avoid falling into the same generalizations and cliches.

The importance of the policies of international corporations in
the integration of man into society can be summed up by Harvard
Professor Charles Savage's remark that "Business is the principal
arena in which social change is instituted." At the village level
or within the urban family it is not the political revolutions, or
the student speeches in the universities, or the diffusion of the
thoughts of Castro and Mao Tse-tung which is having an impact
on the values and traditions of the community, day-to-day family
life, and the personal aspirations and beliefs of the individual.
Rather it is such prosaic things as the construction of a road, the

installation of an industrial plant, a movie house, or a new production method, which cause deep and lasting changes for society and the individual. National and international enterprises have a special role to play in this process. By providing a job they can give a man the economic security that he needs to be able to develop his intellectual and spiritual faculties. Jobs also may provide women with a new economic independence that could have its effect upon the unity of marriage. And jobs may give young men the opportunity to leave home, to escape the influence of the family and radically transform their lives.

Within the structure of a modern corporation man can break away from the fatalism that haunts many of our rural people. The fact that a man believes that it is his "destiny" to be a farmhand or a domestic servant and that it will be his sons' destinies to be the same is a tremendous block to any kind of human development. Some people also come to believe that the level of development that they should or will attain is somehow magically arranged to coincide with their racial ancestry, that is, for example, the darker the skin of the person the less he can be expected to be or do in life. The extent to which international enterprises base their personnel practices on capability, potential, and performance instead of ethnic background will be an important factor in the liberation of man from this burden. Some international enterprises, unfortunately, have at one time or another established discriminating practices, originating perhaps from the personal prejudices of some of their executives.

Going a little further with the human problems involving susceptibilities and feelings, we find that they exist even in the higher echelons of management. This will influence the performance of many nationals within a foreign corporation as well as constitute an emotional problem for them. During a seminar on international business at the Harvard Business School in 1966, every one of the Latin American graduate students who had worked for a foreign enterprise in his own country declared that at one time or another he had a feeling of being handicapped within the company because of his nationality. As one of them put it, "I was being treated with a degree of amusement as an educated native." There is also the fact that there are large foreign agricultural enterprises, in Latin America for many years, with a majority of Latin employees but without a single Latin employee in a top position. Feelings of resentment, whether justifiable or just caused by oversensitivity, remain a problem.

It is true, on the other hand, that international corporations first brought industry to many parts of Latin America and triggered profound changes in areas that perhaps would otherwise have remained undeveloped. Mining companies in Bolivia, oil companies in Venezuela, banana companies in Central America, railroad companies all over South America, began development of those regions. More recently, companies such as Nestle in food processing, Sears Roebuck in distribution, Kaiser in automobile production, and products such as the Japanese transistor radio and modern drugs exert a revolutionary effect on people.

A colorful illustration of the effect of new technology on a community is the following observation made by a Harvard researcher in an Andean village. In this village the main economic activity formerly consisted of the women manufacturing some kind of coffee sacks in their homes and taking them to the local store to be bartered for food and other goods. The men were engaged in unproductive agricultural work and did not have much to do with the running of the household. The result was a matriarchal society in which the daughters would inherit the house of the mother.

The element that came in to disturb the ways of the village was a machine sent by the national government to increase the production of sacks in the village. Naturally, the government technicians chose the men to be trained to operate the machine and instituted a wage scale for the workers. When the new industry started and the men got hold of the money, the power structure within the household changed, and according to the women their husbands started drinking. The net result was that the women got together and destroyed the machines with sledgehammers, quickly bringing the village back to normality.

Most industries in Latin America are small and managed in a highly paternalistic fashion. It has been suggested by some researchers that these companies are not paternalistic because they are small but that the companies remain small in order to remain paternalistic. It is noted that when a company reaches forty employees, the paternalistic system starts to break down. So the tendency is toward the proliferation of small companies rather than the growth of fewer, larger firms. An indication that there is some truth in this analysis is the fact that the Latin American owner-manager develops a strong attachment to his workers, and vice versa. In his factory he plays the role of the boss, the patron, the father. Workers are expected to go to him even for the solution of personal problems which are quite unconnected with the enterprise. This system, taken over from the traditional rural order, reproduces the hacienda in an urban, industrial setting. It is a system that keeps people in dependence, does not give them an opportunity to develop their full potential or break away from their so-called destiny.

When an international enterprise is established, it usually takes the form of a highly impersonal, modern corporation. It is a large concern, and the foreign entrepreneurs are accustomed to dealing with their men indirectly through foremen and union leaders; they believe that paternalism is intrinsically wrong and inefficient. The worker who encounters this system for the first time may be bewildered and confused, and resentful at the lack of attention paid to him and his inability to tell his troubles to the patron. For his part, the manager may also be angered by what he considers the ingratitude of workers to whom he has brought opportunity, higher wages, and better working conditions. Mutual incomprehension of this kind may be prevalent even where the jobs are skilled ones, and the employees fairly well educated. I recall interviewing some high school- and college-trained employees of an American oil company who complained that the company was "unfair" to them because not enough attention was being paid: "father is neglecting us." Not even the fact that they were getting some of the highest wages in the country mollified them.

Exactly the opposite phenomenon was experienced by a large American retail chain operating in Panama. Although far from establishing a paternalistic system, this company did develop a more personal relationship with its employees and made a particular effort to show concern for them. One day during a very violent anti-American demonstration many of the employees of the store spontaneously volunteered to protect it physically.

The other side of this problem is the effect that the policies of a company will have upon the community and the individual. Other than the effect that was illustrated earlier with the anecdote of the sack-producing machine that was sent to the Andean village, the company needs to be aware of effects that it could cause in a community by even such desirable measures as introducing a new product, when and if this new product will replace others that were formerly made by less efficient means. This is usually the case with domestic shops and the modern clothing industry, the corner shoemaker and the modern shoe industry, the substitution of petroleum products for charcoal or firewood, the corner grocery store and the supermarkets, and many other cases. In most cases these changes are beneficial and should be encouraged. But they will have a disruptive effect on a sector of the community, and the agent causing this effect has the moral responsibility for avoiding or minimizing it.

The international corporation has come a long way in the recent past. From predominantly extractive industries of the past, which were seriously disruptive in spite of having a modernizing effect, which regarded labor only as a commodity, and which had the power and willingness to exert pressure on the government of both their home and host countries in pursuit of their interests, they have evolved into the modern manufacturing and distributing corporation, often smaller in size, making an effective contribution to the country both economically and in the education and development of their employees.

The management of these enterprises has also shown an impressive change. Not long ago, for example, an old-timer who used to manage a division of an American company in Central America said in a seminar in Boston that it would be in the best interest of everybody to close the universities of Central America because they were the breeding grounds of Communism. The higher management of this same organization, belonging to another and much more enlightened generation, is actively supporting higher education activities in Central America. The change in attitudes of foreign management is so apparent that little has to be said to describe it, though it must be added that there is of course much room for further development.

A trend which seems to be becoming stronger in Latin America is that of the international joint venture. Although a more complex way of doing business abroad, it is also a way to avoid many of the problems that international enterprises face, and it is certainly a better way to help the development of a country. The tendency toward decentralization of foreign subsidiaries, together with the increasing prevalence of local management in many of them, is another encouraging sign which points to a greater contribution in the development of the individuals involved and a greater degree of flexibility in adapting the corporation to a new business climate.

We should not finish without pointing out that we who call ourselves Christians have had in our hands for a long time very powerful tools to create a better society, and that in many cases, in the name of free enterprise, we have chosen to look almost exclusively to the economic aspect of our decisions. We have too often disregarded the effect of these decisions on our fellowmen, especially those who because of their needs and deficient education are not free to compete in a free economy. Even for selfish reasons we should recognize and live up to these responsibilities, or else we must expect that there will be new government regulations, more danger of nationalization or expropriations, and more people convinced that the only solution to the economic problems is state control of the economy.

We, the Catholic Church, both the hierarchy and lay members, having had *Rerum Novarum* before the Russian Revolution, and more recently *Quadragessimo Anno* and *Mater et Magistra,* have chosen to ignore them until pressured by the threat of Communism. These encyclicals and the works of other Christian thinkers do not provide the answers to all problems. But they do provide terms of reference from which to seek the solutions necessary within the context of each particular business situation. There is also the need for members of our hierarchy to be a little more forceful in exerting their influence in the social orientation of national and international enterprises in Latin America.

There is, I think, a parallel between the relationship of classes in industrial England at the beginning of the nineteenth century and the relationship of the developed and undeveloped nations today. Free enterprise meant increasing misery and injustice. And just as there had to be developed trade unions and factory legislation to equalize matters, so too I think there must be international legislation: price controls on basic commodities, perhaps, or preferential treatment, or the development of common markets as the equivalent of trade unions. There is a continual danger that American corporations will come in and destroy established local industries. As common markets develop, American companies may be able to force two countries to bid against each other for the location of industry, with unfortunate results. Foreign companies in general may be able to use their size and strength to monopolize scarce local resources: to absorb available capital; to buy up productive mines, farmland, and manufacturing facilities; to take over trained people, our scarcest and most valuable resource. Such a policy, a form of economic imperialism and colonialism, would be a short-sighted and ultimately self-defeating approach to the problem of assisting Latin America's development.

(During the discussion period a representative of the Creole Petroleum Corporation indicated that his company was very much aware of these problems and was attempting to find solutions to them:

We are the largest corporation in Venezuela, and very much aware of the impact of what we do there, both directly and as an example. The Creole Foundation, for example, sponsors about 130 students a year on scholarships that are in no way related to the company's commercial interests, in addition to the employees whom we are training to meet business needs. There are about 400 employees receiving full pay from us while they are studying full time to qualify themselves for technical positions at higher salaries.

As far as our impact on the national economy is concerned, we bring money into Venezuela rather than take it out (since the country is a producer rather than a consumer of oil). The industry of which we are such a large part provides 90 percent of Venezuela's foreign exchange, so that we feel we are making a definite contribution toward national development. We feel, simply, that it is good business to build up a country.

Surveys show that an overwhelming majority of people polled would prefer to work for private enterprise rather than for the government. And yet a majority of the same people say they think the government should take over the oil industry. They do not want to work for the government, but they believe the government should take over the leading industry.)

Mass Communications

MARINA BANDEIRA

As Christians, we believe that the measure of man is his dimension as made in the image of God and ordered by God to love other men with his whole soul and his whole mind, and to dominate the world through his work. This total man combines body and soul, heart and conscience, intelligence and will. Obedience to the law of his conscience is the origin of his dignity as a human being. Man has the capacity to distinguish one object or idea from another. From distinction comes choice, the origin of values. By the communication of these values to other men, their possibilities of choice are increased, and they are rendered capable of participating in the creation of a cultural world.

Man, in his inner self, is a social being. Without a link with other men he cannot develop his potentialities. In communication with other human beings he must not forget that true liberty is a sign of the divine origin of man, who therefore should not act from blind impulse or under external pressure. Man should act according to a conscious and free option, and be guided by personal conviction. Such communication is between persons having creative capacities that must be recognized. The residue of this

137

communication between human beings constitutes culture. As time passes, this residue grows, and men learn how to pass it on to other men in a systematic way.

What I have said so far concerns principles. The reality involves social, political, and economic aspects created by man which have led him to contradict these principles. The factory manager, for example, tends to look at human work only in its purely economic aspect. But the main factor of our Christian teaching is to consider man the basic unit of social institutions. When this fact is forgotten, society becomes deformed and accepts collective injustice and other dysfunctions. When a society is based on pressure, with elite groups acting as masters of the herd, men become thwarted, passive objects, marginalized from decisions which will affect their destinies. This sum of passive men constitutes the mass. The sum of normally developed men constitutes the people. Only the people are capable of forming public opinion, capable of accepting or rejecting the values they encounter. The mass, in the best of circumstances, can only constitute a market and accept any idea sold to them by more powerful groups. This mass, when transformed into a work force, is induced to produce goods, the profound meanings of which it does not grasp.

Once I have clarified the sense in which I am using these terms, I may say that communication is the acknowledgment of God in our self and in the self of another person. Mass communication, then, should be the communication of selves on a large scale.

In the development of large-scale communication we have advanced from the age of the small tribal community to the present day, when movies, radio, and television have brought us near to the age of interplanetary communication. The acceleration of history, the dizzying development of technology, the new intricacies of economics and other characteristics of our age, are in constant interplay with mass communication. Around the concept of mass communications has arisen what some specialists consider a specific branch of science connecting various disciplines such as psychology, sociology, anthropology, and other economic and technological breeds, with repercussions in the field of philosophy, political science, and even theology.

The rhythm of the acceleration of history shows itself, for instance, in the appetite of the public the world over for modern movies, science fiction, and comic strips, which with a massive impact are challenging traditional values and standards of behavior. New researches and experiments in the field of depth psychology reveal that these media can provide ample room for the manipulation of the mind of man. Vance Packard, the author of *The Hidden Persuaders,* is one of the most publicized of the writers concerned with this problem of the manipulation of men's minds through mass communications media. In the field of philosophy various schools have developed political ideologies which are behind the so-called doctrines of mass communication.

With regard to the administrative and economic aspects of mass media, the international trusts have ample room for maneuver. And on the national, and even local, level vested interests are present. On this subject Professor Jean Meynaud,[1] a political scientist from the universities of Montreal and Paris, and a specialist in the study of pressure groups, has described the influence of giant companies on the international level. He gives as a prototype the United Fruit Company, which owns lands, a chain of radio stations, a press service, and railway and shipping facilities in the Caribbean. Another important economic aspect of mass media is publicity. The prosperity of the media is connected with the advertisement contracts obtained from the largest companies of the world.

Governments, especially authoritarian ones and those which represent oligarchies, have learned to control the mechanism of information by regulating the activities of the instruments. Political expression of the policies of information is usually connected with the idea that influence is to be exerted on the public by the propagation of a given set of ideas or by the "doctoring" of other types of news.

Another element that enters the field is that of the international news agencies, which require large investments and a high level of efficiency. The underdeveloped countries, lacking capital and personnel, can hardly engage on the international level of mass communication with each other and with the more developed countries. The development of techniques which require ever-more costly equipment and larger and more powerful economic structures leads to the centralized control of mass media in the hands of a few. It would be antihuman to rail against the development of science and technology. The achievements of science are a proof of the success of the adventure of man, the cocreator. Besides, if science has done nothing else, it has taught man a greater reverence for truth and objectivity.

The truly important question here is, Should science serve man, for the benefit of all men, or should mankind be enslaved by a group of men who control the applied sciences? Socrates, in Periclean Athens, used to say that without liberty for the daily discussion of problems life was not worth living. In modern times the Declaration of Human Rights states that the highest aspiration of man is the advent of a world in which all human beings, freed from fear and from want, can benefit from freedom of expression.

Gaudium et Spes shows great concern for this problem and states that there is an imbalance between the demands of a specialized nature and the demands of a universal vision of all things created. This document proceeds to say that man not only can, but should, strengthen his domain over things created. *Gaudium et Spes* argues that it is the mission of man to establish political, social, and economic organizations which, with the aid of time, will better serve each single man, and each group of men, to assert his own dignity.

All this that has been so far said applies to the whole of mankind. Now let us have a brief look at the situation of mass communication in Latin America. In Lima, Peru, in September, 1966, a seminar was held to study the instruments of social communication in Latin America.[2] This seminar, which lasted nearly twenty days, enjoyed the participation of some of the best Catholic Latin American experts on instruments of social communication. I will quote some excerpts from the seminar's conclusions:

Latin American society may be described as traditional society in transit toward a modern society.

The masses have endured poverty for centuries with apparent indifference. Now, brusquely, they are awakening, and their demands surpass the social and economic rhythm of development.

The instruments of social communication contribute to awaken aspirations that cannot be satisfied and will increase discontent. This massive discontent favors a distributive and destructive revolution. But these same instruments may contribute to alter this process by favoring a creative revolution: preaching development instead of acceptance of underdevelopment, preaching the incorporation of the masses instead of acceptance of marginalization.

The expression "marginalization" is used to indicate a lack of participation, active or receptive, of a group. The marginalized group does not intervene in collective decisions, nor does it receive the material benefits and services of the community. In Latin America this situation applies to the majority of the population.

One of the characteristic traits of marginalization is the fact that the person, or community, is internally disintegrated. Internal cohesion is a necessary condition to overcome marginalization. For this reason, the problem of marginalization affects the national and even the world community.

A society whose economic and social structures admit the exploitation of human work cannot formulate, and much less live, a moral life which would be in accordance with Christian doctrine.

Promoción Popular, Popular Promotion, understood as the surpassing of marginalization and the transformation of society, can only be the task of the promoted ones themselves. It takes place as a consequence of their having reached "self-achievement" (*realizado a si mismos*) rendering them capable of participating in the removal of the obstacles that oppose their incorporation in the future society, which must condition itself for the organic participation of the ex-marginalized into the new global society.

These are some of the points from the conclusions of the Seminar of Lima that are closely related to our subject. But allow me to quote again, and this time from Bishop Candido Padim, head of the National Secretariat of Education of the Bishops' Conference of Brazil.[3]

We must admit that we are living in times that are carrying out a global renewal of institutions. Our times do not accept generous concessions from governments with paternalistic gestures. They demand the participation of all in the rethinking of the very sense and of the very form of the institutions, thus creating an original culture. Wherever the benefits of civilization arrive, they are received as the result of the conquest of each man's effort.

Fostering this rethinking and this re-creation is a lucid and constructive attitude. Among all, the educator is, without any doubt, the one who is more responsible for this aid that the new generations expect from the adults at this stage of social change.

This brings us to education and, in particular, to education for development in its relations with mass media. According to traditional concepts of education the responsibility of the teacher is to minister limited doses of cultural matter to the student, who receives what is delivered to him and is supposed to retain it. And this, in a caricature, is what mass media are doing in Latin America: transmitting materialistic values that have acceptance in developed countries.

Today, even in the developed countries the new generation does not accept this type of transmission of values. They feel the urge to discuss, reject, or accept values on a level of equality with the older generation. Persons, groups, and countries are beginning to refuse the classification of immature or dependent. And this brings us to one of the clues in this quest for development of an integrated society. Instead of teachers versus students, we are coming to the new concept of permanent education for all, young and old. And it is an education aiming at the formation of man and leading to a social progress which will, in turn, render the entire social context more just.

This education must make each student aware of the limits, obstacles, and possibilities to which he is subjected, and allow him to participate responsively. This participation will be rendered possible through a dynamic interpretation of the new values which will arise in the process of development, the reinterpretation of traditional values at the sociocultural level with reference to the personal and collective life. To this is added the need to train the person to undertake new forms of work and to participate in more complex situations in collective organizations that exist, or that will arise, in the process of development and in which the adult is inserted.

The aim of adult education for development toward an integrated society should then be to give the adult an awareness and capacity to criticize cultural values that have been unconsciously acquired, to criticize or adopt new cultural values, to create the habit of working in groups, and to stimulate attitudes of cooperation.

And it is here that the mass media can play a unique role by promoting a massive enhancement in aiding the mass to become the people. Radio, television, movies, and newspapers can participate in the integration of man and society. And this is not make-believe or idealistic dreams. I will mention one instance that I know from personal experience. I refer to the Movement for Education of the Base (MEB), the radio schools for the rural areas of Brazil, created and sponsored by the bishops of Brazil. MEB is working according to the lines described above; it does not consider itself a mastermind telling the people what is best for them. The secret of MEB is the feedback that it receives from the population from the underdeveloped areas, and the constant two-way communication on all levels. It is from this constant communication that MEB derives its guidelines, multiplied on a large scale through the motivation and support of the radio.

Through this participation in the work of MEB, the pupils, the teachers, the supervisors, and the coordinators are in a constant process of self-improvement. And the result is not just an awakening of conscience toward the responsibility in the individual, but the beginning of the progress of the whole people; not an individualistic advance, but a service to the community.

The synthesis of these concepts is expressed by the key word *concientizacao*, which can be translated roughly as the awakening of historical consciousness, the awareness of man's active role in the historical process. But this type of work—in Brazil as in other countries in Latin America—has to face the antagonism of the minorities that hold economic, political, and social power and favor the permanence of the status quo.

In conclusion, to integrate means the act of integrating, of completing, of giving cohesion to form a whole. Integration is not a synonym of uniformization. It seems evident that social, economic, and political structures in the whole world require re-evaluation and transformation. And in our own countries new creative use of the mass media is necessary if we are really interested in the integration of man and society in Latin America according to a Christian viewpoint.

(In response to questions from the audience Miss Bandeira made the following remarks about the work of the MEB.)

After MEB was organized by a group of Brazilian bishops, its operation was then turned over to laymen. Although partially financed by the government, MEB refuses to allow any interference with its work—something that is not always easy to avoid. Its method of operation is the following. Specialists in Rio, experts in pedagogy, methodology, and especially group dynamics, will travel to some area in Brazil—Manaus, for example, in the Amazon Valley. There they will select local leaders, ten or fifteen of them, and work with them, not by giving predetermined answers, but by asking questions. These people in turn go to as many communities and make contact with perhaps fifty villagers. They select people who can read and write and give them instructions in community development. Radio programs, usually on stations owned by the bishop of the diocese, provide reinforcement for what is done by the leader in each community, as well as lessons in literacy, arithmetic, and personal development.

The members of MEB were quite naive when they began their work, but they are learning all the time, learning from the participants in their program, getting feedback, and incorporating it into their future plans. The local people, after all, know what their problems are, what they need, what they want. MEB simply tries to show them how they can achieve goals which they set for themselves.

Commercial television and radio in Brazil are thoroughly involved in politics and in high finance and high-pressure advertising. They will preach hysterical anti-Communism, not because they are really afraid of Russia, but in order to change a minister, to get a lucrative government job. Our people listen uncritically and swallow it whole. Then also, by their massive advertising campaigns our broadcasters distort the sense of values of the Brazilian people by teaching them to hunger after nonessentials. There are Indians in the interior who have all at once become intensely materialistic, who suddenly feel that they *must* have a scooter, because the radio or television advertising has been hammering away at them. Those who own these stations are baptized and call themselves Christians, but their only aim is to exploit, to use their power to further the massification of our people. We have to change them, too, as well as the poor and the illiterate.

NOTES

1. Jean Meynaud, *Groupes de pression* (Paris: Ed. Armand Colin, p. 324).

2. Seminar of Lima, September/October, 1966, promoted by the Latin American secretariats of OCIC, UNDA, and ULAPC, with the approval of CELAM.

3. D. Candido Padim, *Educar para um mundo novo* (Rio de Janeiro: Ed. Vozes).

PART THREE

THE RELIGIOUS DIMENSION

Integration of Priests

JORGE MEJIA

Integration is not an easy task. It is particularly an uneasy and exacting task within the Christian community. This is clear when we consider that integration has, as terms to integrate, priests on one hand, bishops on the other, and the lay Christian in the face of both.

Integration, of course, does not mean just having the bishop sitting at the top of the diocesan pyramid; the priests, more or less interrelated, sitting considerably lower; and the common Christian staring up from earth as John does toward the heavenly vision in the famous description of God's court in Revelations. This situation, however smoothly it happens to work, is not integration, but rather, in a sense, disintegration. The point that I want to make here is this: integration, secularly speaking, means something quite specific, about which much has been previously said in this book, which of course enables me to take at least this meaning for granted.

If we are to apply this notion to our religious community, or its basic unity, the local church, the diocese, we will have to do a little thinking. We have known integration in the Church, mainly

149

at the level of the common faith, the common sacraments, the more or less common discipline. This is real integration, and the opposite situation is very justly called disintegration, either because it breaks the integrating bonds of faith (when it is called heresy) or because it cuts the bonds of participation in sacraments and discipline (when it is called schism). That this kind of integration in a given (local) church is always to be complied with, not just taken for granted, is something which should be borne in mind as the right frame for the rest of what is required.

Now, however, we are concerned with another type of integration, which presupposes this one but is not quite covered by its meaning. It is, if I may so describe it, a kind of personal integration, meaning that some persons or categories of persons in the local church are to enter a set of relations with each other so as to become a body. We are really a body, in a mystical way, but this bodyness is not translated into a real sociological unity while we are only connected—bishops, priests, and laymen—by formal or functional relations.

To make myself clear, I will try to describe the existing situation. Priests and laymen, although members of the same Christian community, have been so deeply drawn apart by historical circumstances that their connection as Christians rests mostly with their functions. Priests minister to the lay community; the laity receives ministrations from the priesthood. While this arrangement is in itself right enough, the rest of the lives of both priests and lay people are out of touch with one another. Priests function in a churchly sphere, where temporal concerns are alien; laymen function in a secular sphere, or a secularized one, where priests are completely and permanently absent. Can this be called a community?

Bishops and priests are naturally more closely related to each other. They belong to the same sphere, at least in principle. But besides the fact that bishops are even more remote from people than priests, they themselves have mostly administrative connections with their priests. These connections can be more or less permeated with a sense of paternal responsibility which draws the bishop to look after the spiritual and even the material well-being of his clergy, so as to become a good shepherd. Unfortunately, this is not enough to integrate either the bishop in his community, or the priests with the bishop, or the priests among themselves.

It is not strictly a question of feelings. Feelings may be hurt, and certainly, although the pain can remain unconscious, this kind of uneasiness can account for at least some of the disintegration we all have witnessed in the clergy in these last years. At times they find themselves quite suddenly as if they were hanging in the middle of space, between heaven and earth. When you become aware of being in such an awkward position, it is quite normal that vertigo overcomes you and you fall to the ground. Nobody is responsible for this or that particular fall, but the underlying situation must be carefully examined and eventually corrected.

It is also true that this situation is fast becoming problematic, and indeed dramatic, in Latin America and elsewhere. A sign of this is the distintegrating tendencies which have lately made their appearances in many local churches. Lay people tend to select a priest of their liking, with whom they make a kind of community with its own liturgy, a great amount of disciplinary autonomy, and a real involvement of the priest in the interests and concerns of the people. There are varying degrees of disintegration in such a pattern, and sometimes it can even be integrated if the participants can find the right moment (and the right bishop) to support them. But the phenomenon is on the whole an abnormal one, and if priests and laymen should be very careful not to fall into something like a gnostic schism, bishops and other authorities should be equally careful to remove the conditions from which these unecclesial movements spring.

Fortunately, needed reforms were encouraged by the Second Vatican Council, which seems to have rediscovered for a great part of the Church the meaning of the community of priests with bishops, priests among themselves, and priests and bishops with lay people. This community forms the People of God, a remarkable idea whose far-reaching implications are still largely unexplored. As this is not a theological discussion I shall avoid quotations and interpretations of conciliar texts. My aim is more modest. I wish only to indicate which are the paths that might be followed, and to a certain extent already are followed, in Latin America to obtain this deep, all-embracing ecclesial integration.

There can, to begin with, be no question of a partial integration of the People of God. Bishops cannot integrate among themselves while priests remain unintegrated and the common Christian simply remains aloof. Thus, while the Latin American hierarchy has in CELAM done something toward its own integration, the needs of priests and laymen should not be forgotten. Indeed, if something lasting is really to be done, integration should begin at the same time at all levels.

Bishops of the same nation are learning to work together in that almost new institution, the episcopal conference. But this is still only a foreshadowing of the real community among priests, bishops, and laymen that remains to be created. The true aim, the integration of the whole Christian community, should therefore not be left out of sight. What is the sense of building a beautiful episcopal preserve, or even a priestly one, if the laymen are left outside? I am not talking now about means, or even about priorities, but about ends. And this is the true end.

When we have said so much, we should add immediately that the building of a real integration in the hierarchical level of priests and bishops cannot but bring a similar effect in the basic Christian community. The sign and the example for this is certainly integration in Latin America, but this is somewhat outside my subject. Let us remember in any case that integration at all levels belongs together and can only be separated artificially.

I shall turn now to consider the problem of the integration of priests with their bishops. In principle, as the Council has stated, this integration is founded in common participation in the sacrament of orders and in common relation to the same portion of the people of God, the diocese. It is, therefore, something which goes very deeply into the reality of the priest's and the bishop's vocation. This community is what is called the *presbyterium*.

From this the presbyterial senate should be carefully distinguished. Most dioceses by now have created this legal institution, which represents and embodies the *presbyterium*. Latin America is no exception. Only this is in itself just a beginning. The institution is there, in the first place, to help priests and bishops discover that they belong together. Let us avoid all possible confusion. The presbyterial senate is not a different kind of diocesan chancery, organized to execute and transmit the bishop's wishes. This would be disintegration.

How then are priests and bishops to be integrated? The presbyterial senate will work in this sense only if the inheritance of centuries of estrangement is overcome on both sides. Bishops no more are feudal lords, and they have not been such in Latin America for a long time now. But they normally were parish priests or chancery officials and as such are accustomed to a certain type of exercise of authority which sees other priests mostly as executors, not as collaborators. This system used to work well, and it could even indicate the backing of obedience of a certain spirituality. So far so good. But what about considering priests as the natural counselors and cooperators (in the real sense of the word) of the bishop? The bare fact of having an elected presbyterial senate does not bring this consequence *ex opere operato* in Latin America or, I believe, anywhere else.

A conversion is required, to use a time-honored Christian expression. The bishop should try to see himself more as the center than as the top, as a "firstborn among many brothers," as sharing the same Christ's priesthood (although in a different way) as his priests. This means that his faith has to be constantly purified and deepened so as to overcome and counterbalance any superiority complex. Such a purification and deepening in the realm of faith is precisely what we mean by the word conversion.

In the same way the bishop should be aware of his limits. He does not know everything, nor has he all the data and the viewpoints on every problem. On the contrary, in the growing complexity of the present Christian life he is quite frequently behind his task. But he has to be humble enough to admit it. His *presbyterium* is there to enlarge and complete his contacts with reality. And if he is true to the meaning of this *presbyterium*, he will not only recognize its existence but try to build it in a more perfect way. Thus, integrating his priests means for the bishop to create in a certain sense his *presbyterium* around himself. To create, first, the climate which makes this cooperation possible and real. And, secondly, to create the plurality of functions and capacities within his *presbyterium* which will really answer to the situation of his particular portion of God's People. The eighth section of the conciliar decree on priests should be meditated in this connection. Latin America is no model from this point of view, although I could single out some bishops who have tried to build their *presbyteria* this way. Of course, in our situation it is almost impossible to do this alone. The integration of bishops is almost a necessary condition for the existence of a truly differentiated *presbyterium* where theologians and biblicists find their place alongside hospital chaplains and, if need be, workers.

I am not forgetting religious orders and congregations. The bishop should see to it that they are not left outside. For this he has to recognize their distinctive charisma and its importance for his part of God's People. In Latin America he will quite often be tempted to ignore some charismata for the benefit of efficiency. Bendictines and Trappists are monks in the first place, and this is their contribution to the local church, even to the priest-starved Church of Latin America. So let them be what they are for the benefit of all.

The position of priests is to be considered now. If they are to be integrated, they have at the same time and almost by the same movement to integrate themselves. This is not by any means an easy task. All kinds of obstacles militate from the side of priests themselves against true sacerdotal integration. They have been forgotten too long to be expected reasonably to find their place at the first trial. And then you have in Latin America the distances, the mutual estrangement, the tiredness of a very difficult and unrewarding life. Also in Latin America as elsewhere there is the problem of the conflict of generations or age groups, not so much biological as mental. There is a lack of confidence or outright difference on the part of the young and the rebellious, the "new breed" and those whom the bishop looks at with a wary eye. In some places where there are many priests there is, as elsewhere, the danger of faction, of parties, of division. Is the hope of integration unreal?

For the priests to build a *presbyterium* with their bishop is to begin by building one with themselves. I do not think this is possible without a conversion, to use that useful word again. They have to accept and assume each other in the mystery of Christ's priesthood, with a feeling of the diocesan character of the mission of each and all. It is not the little in which one happens to be working that is really important, but the common tasks to which all contribute, even the ill and the maimed. When you live hundreds of kilometers from your neighbor priest, or from the bishop, this can be terribly difficult. If faith is necessary, human experience is certainly required. Therefore the bishop should help to build his own *presbyterium* by rationalizing the distribution of his priests, by trying to bring them together as often as possible, by submitting to them according to the competence of each the common problems of the whole diocese. Here one should mention the benefits of priests living together for a common task involving different pastoral occupations, because here really begins the molecular building of greater unity. There are experiences of this kind outside the field of religious orders and congregations, especially in seminaries, some communities of working priests, and others. As long as they keep true to their essential purpose, which is to become centers of unification and integration, these kinds of groupings are precious. But they have to watch carefully to avoid the temptation of isolation and secession, which is so easy and so attractive.

I wish I could describe facts instead of talking about possibilities, but the truth is that everywhere we are still in the planting stage. There is not much fruit to be gathered yet. I do not know of any dioceses in Argentina where the *presbyterium* and its organ, the senate, function in an adult and developed way. It is a good thing to be aware of this. However, some dioceses have already gone far in that direction.

We turn now to the problem of the integration of the layman. A much more difficult question now confronts us. Priests and bishops at least belong, as indicated above, to the same category.

But men and women of this world: How are we to build a community with *them?* The problems here are fearful and unexplored. Latin America, I am afraid, has no solution to offer. If anything, there is even more distance between priests and people (not to say bishop) in a pampa parish in Argentina than in a suburban parish in New York. But at least we are becoming aware of the question. We believe we know that the solution is not to be found by the losing of a priest's identity. He is to remain a priest, in a true and sacramental sense. Otherwise it is not integration that we get, but another kind of disintegration, and the worst kind, because people will always look for the priest they lost and God knows where they will find him. But the priest's identity should not be equated with alienation from real life. He is at the same time to be, as Father Loew says, "Le temoin de l'invisible." Such demands make his present position particularly trying. This is another reason why we have, in Latin America as elsewhere, so many sacerdotal crises. And this is also why a solution is being tried, or studied, along the lines of the lay diaconate. But for the priest who wants to remain a priest the problem is a very difficult one.

But it is not without a solution. Liturgy has shown in certain parishes how deeply priests and laymen can become involved with each other by taking part in the same sacred action. This takes time to work out, but it goes very far. As the bishop is always involved in the liturgy, this relation also ties the faithful with him on all important points to avoid disintegration at this level.

The same is true of pastoral or apostolic responsibilities jointly assumed by priests and laymen with an equal share of planning and decision. This is what the Council implies with its call for mixed pastoral councils created at different levels. We favor these, not just to use the lay forces at our disposal, but to integrate the Christian community. What a long way we have to go yet to make this disposition a real and operating thing. Pastoral councils of the needed kind are being created in our countries. But I can imagine the obstacles to their functioning until a true conversion intervenes here also.

The problem, I must say, lies not only with the priest. He may have been educated to live in a world very different from the one he actually lives in. He may never have been taught to understand in depth the layman's problem precisely as it belongs to the layman, not as a kind of abstraction scarcely, if ever, founded in life. These negative dispositions are sometimes very difficult to overcome, and nothing will be really done about them, let me say in passing, till the whole pattern of priestly education has been examined under this particular light. All this is true and cannot be denied, although it is not necessarily more of a problem in Latin America than it is in the United States or in Germany, for that matter.

But what about the lay people? They themselves have never been taught properly how to relate to a priest or told precisely what to expect from him. Is he somebody who happens to be influential and can therefore obtain benefits from the people in power? This kind of connection between priest and laymen is rather frequent, I must say, in Latin America; is it not also elsewhere? Is the priest the real and effective leader of a community in all the dimensions modern life has given to it? Has he to provide the conditions for development, economic and cultural, or would this be another and more subtle kind of clericalism? I can see steadily growing upon the horizon a new kind of clericalism of the progressivist as there has been and still is a clericalism of the integralist. Shall the priest turn his back on all human problems and leave them to the secular powers which have the duty and the means to solve them? Or is he become a power factor himself in the developing society?

I know the questions. I do not know the answers. People in Latin America, and almost everywhere in less-developed circumstances, have been thought to depend on their priests for almost everything, exactly as, in more developed societies, people tend to look upon priests as merely religious functionaries. The truth lies somewhere in between. But where? There is a great deal of talk about the supplementary mission of the clergy in the Latin American circumstance. At least a part of it is fairly right. But this is expressly considered as circumstantial, and such a condition should not be forgotten. Otherwise there would be the danger of

creating another cleri-cracy. The priest is first and foremost the
man of the Word and of the sacraments, and he ought to integrate with the Christian people first and foremost alongside these
lines. Such an assertion may sound unconvincing and uncompro-
mising, but there is no way out of it if priests are to remain what
they are intended to be as part of the people of God. This is not
meant as an excuse for remoteness, for alienation, or for coward-
ice. It is meant, on the contrary, as a reason, and the chief reason,
for togetherness, for engagement, for courage. It all depends, of
course, of what we think when the Word of God is mentioned,
what kind of place we believe the sacraments must have in the
development of Christian life. Neither the sacraments nor the
Bible will in themselves build dams, transform agriculture, bring
about social reform, or help revolutions. Originally they were not
intended for this aim. They were intended to bring the heart and
mind of men in contact with the living God and hence transform the world. The priest is the minister of this encounter. He
may do a lot of other things to improve the real situation of his
people. But if he misses this central aim, he has simply failed
in his chief task.

The priest is in need of taking both sides into account: his own
vocation as a priest—to be found in prayer, sacrifice, and integration with Our Lord's death and Resurrection—and the real soul
of his people, whom he has to know in the profound Johannine
sense of this particular word. Only thus will he be integrated. He
may not feel integrated. He may even be despised or persecuted.
He may live all his life in a state of tension between what he
wants and believes to be true and what he is. But it is not feelings
which concern us now. It is reality, the reality of faith. It is a
teaching of faith that Our Lord was persecuted after having been
ignored by his own. His historical integration was a failure. But
this was the condition for the integration of us all in his Body.

There are monks and hermits in the Church. I believe the
priest, in the depth of his vocation, is always a solitary. This is
his greatness. He is not reducible to anything or anybody. Integration of the true kind will not suppress this condition, even, I
daresay, if priests get married. Moses had a wife, and he was

alone before God. Let the priest integrate what he is, the mystery and strangeness which seems attached to the priesthood, even the New Testament one. Because there are barriers which only love and service till death can overcome, even in Latin America. There, as everywhere, I believe we finally integrate as priests through the death and Resurrection of Our Lord, Jesus Christ, in whom and by whom all are to become one.

International Religious Cooperation

GUSTAVO PEREZ-RAMIREZ

We find everywhere in the documents of the Second Vatican Council a persistent appeal to human solidarity and cooperation among nations: "Among the signs of our times, the irresistibly increasing sense of solidarity among all peoples is especially noteworthy. It is a function of the lay apostolate to promote this awareness zealously and to transform it into a sincere and genuine sense of brotherhood. Furthermore, the laity should be informed about the international field and about the questions and solutions, theoretical as well as practical, which arise in this field, especially with respect to developing nations."[1]

The same idea is presented in the Declaration of Religious Freedom: "All nations are coming into even closer unity. Men of different cultures and religions are being brought together in closer relationships. There is a growing consciousness of the personal responsibility that weighs upon every man." (Section 15) I could quote dozens of conciliar texts to support this pledge for religious cooperation in favor of integration in Latin America. When speaking of international cooperation, we can say that "It is easier to receive than to give." Many traps challenge the giver.

I will not bother you with the already well-known and often-repeated list of mistakes and failures of international cooperation. Colonialism, paternalism, imperialism, and the like are facts, not empty words, although sometimes demagogues, appealing to the cupidity or the prejudice of the masses, mislead public opinion.

Let me, rather, discuss some other conditions to which international religious cooperation has to adapt in order to help rather than prevent cooperation in favor of integration in Latin America. There must be, first of all, recognition and respect for cultural variety. Culture is what makes man human. While men everywhere are essentially the same in terms of their physiological and biological makeup, they differ greatly from one society to another and from one group or class to another within a particular society because of culture.

Culture, according to the classic definition, is that complex whole which includes knowledge, belief, art, morals, law, custom, and any other capabilities and habits acquired by man as a member of society.[2] Or, more sociologically, culture is "socially shared and transmitted knowledge, both existential and normative, symbolized in act and artifact."[3] Culture is a central concept in anthropology as well as in sociology, for it embodies the rules that define the roles which make the relationships that make the group. No wonder then that we insist on it as the Council does.

Every culture is a vehicle for a better understanding of Divine Revelation. Every culture promotes certain ideas or values which, of course, differ according to the particular culture. Therefore, there is a relativity of each culture, as well as a relativity of the various ecclesiastical forms in relation to other cultures. The Constitution on the Sacred Liturgy recognizes this reality:

Even in the liturgy, the Church has no wish to impose a rigid uniformity in matters which do not involve the faith or the good of the whole community. Rather she respects and fosters the spiritual adornments and gifts of the various races and peoples. (Section 37)

Acculturation is then a basic process for missionaries, technicians, and volunteers as a prerequisite to a valuable and effective cooperation within the society in which they are to work. Their role is not to import their own culture, but to assimilate the new one in which they work. From a religious point of view there is the exigency of incarnating the faith within the new culture. The Church would impoverish itself by destroying a culture to impose its faith. Thus, cooperation with other cultures is an exigency of faith.

Of course, respect for the culture of the societies to which cooperation is offered should not act as an excuse for a static position:

> With the excuse of respecting fully the independence of the underdeveloped countries, it is not proper to abandon them to autarchy in misery. In the name of human solidarity, the rich countries have the rigorous duty of assisting the poor countries. The prosperous countries, when they come to aid the poor countries, must not think they are giving a gift; they must think they are only fulfilling an elementary moral duty.[4]

Foreign aid and international cooperation should help make underdeveloped societies dynamic. But by no means should aid reinforce the obsolete structures of the establishment. I would say that this dynamic position is a direct consequence of the doctrine on collegiality as well as the doctrine of the unity of the People of God. This doctrine gives us the guidelines for change when renewal is a condition for betterment. Nevertheless, there is a tendency in religious cooperation to give more help to the most conservative structures within the Church or to support traditional institutions in societies at a different state of development and with different culture needs. There is a need to find new patterns and systems of aid, to reorient traditional forms. It is a serious strategic error to direct aid mainly or only to traditional obsolete sectors. Such a policy will make transition and renewal even slower or impossible.

It is difficult, almost impossible, to imagine an effective international cooperation in favor of Latin American integration without conceiving it as aid to a revolutionary change of attitudes and behavior based on the reality of what is occurring today in Latin America. A fear of revolutionary change would result in reinforcing the obsolete structures which are responsible for the backwardness and dejection of these countries. Large sums of money could be invested, armies of technicians and groups of volunteers could be sent, yet if the focus of the whole effort is only a simple repetition of traditional schemes and formulas, more harm than good would result. The traditional structure, reinforced by foreign aid, would hinder the necessary changes for progress to which integration is oriented.

Integration, in fact, is part of the process in which all mankind will be committed as social classes become free and all oppressed countries acquire their independence. As Teilhard de Chardin describes the phenomenon, unification will be imposed as a result of the harmonization which will counterbalance the individual and collective forces of dispersion in the world. This process, which Teilhard called planetization, is the result of the two equations which he put side by side:

Evolution is equal to the rise of consciousness.

The rise of consciousness is equal to effect of union.

"All this becomes intelligible from top to bottom as soon as we perceive the natural culmination of a cosmic process of organization which has never varied since those remote ages when our planet was young."[5]

If it is to be meaningful, integration will be a revolutionary process which develops in relation to needs which demand satisfaction. It is a process that comes from inside, pushing from the bottom of a system, and acts against the obsolete schemes which the dominant classes wish to preserve. This sociological process of segregation-integration today claims the attention previously given to competition-cooperation, conflict-accommodation, immigration-assimilation.

The cooperation which we seek is aimed precisely toward integration in the true sense. That is cooperation inspired by the unity and solidarity of the People of God and as an exigency of the community of faith, hope, and charity. Such nonpaternalistic and noncolonialistic cooperation implies a real commitment with all its consequences, a commitment to cooperate in the solution of basic problems by going directly to their roots.

In Latin America, as in all the countries of the Third World, the situation seems to be more desperate every day, as the rich countries become wealthier and the poor, even poorer. The Council describes this situation as "truly monstrous." The fact is that the products of the Third World, basically raw materials of agricultural origin, are worth less day by day in the international market. Prices are fixed in the world market through an implacable law of supply and demand, without any possible influence from the countries of the Third World, precisely because they are underdeveloped and therefore unilaterally dependent. In Colombia, for example, the price of coffee is subject to continuous variations. In 1954 we received 93 cents a pound. Prices came down progressively to 52 cents in 1958, and to 43 cents at the present time.

This disastrous decline has very serious consequences for our economy. It means that we have received 50 million dollars less in 1966 than what we expected from the sale of coffee we were allowed to sell by international regulations. This means that in one year alone we have lost an amount of money equal to what German Catholics have been able to collect in a decade, with great generosity, through MISEREOR, a campaign against hunger and disease in the world.

The possibilities of industrialization, meanwhile, become even more difficult. Because of the low prices paid for our raw material exports we do not have enough funds to buy the necessary capital goods for industrialization and the diversification of our economies. According to the data presented by the Colombian delegate to the Assembly of the International Monetary Fund, for example, "in Colombia it cost 14 sacks of coffee in 1954 to buy a jeep, but in 1962, we had to give 39 sacks for the same jeep." Today we are giving close to 80 sacks of coffee for the same jeep. Does this really represent the cooperation urged by the Gospel and by the principles of international solidarity?

You might argue that this is the result of an economic process, since the market is regulated by the law of supply and demand. I would answer with the words of the Council Fathers, who insist that economic development must be under human control:

Economic development must be kept under the control of mankind. It must not be left to the sole judgment of a few men or groups possessing excessive economic power, or of the political community alone, or of certain especially powerful nations. It is proper, on the contrary, that at every level the largest possible number of people have an active share in directing that development. (Pastoral Constitution on the Church in the Modern World, Section 65)

Or perhaps you might argue that besides grants and loans in money there are donations of different kinds, food supplies, construction of hospitals and schools, housing projects, and the like. But this is like a drop of water in the desert because of the growing needs of an ever-increasing population and its legitimate expectations for a better life. These donations would have to be duplicated and multiplied indefinitely to be meaningful.

I do not, in fact, see any way to overcome Latin American backwardness except by the creation of revolutionary changes in mentality, attitudes, behavior, obsolete structures. No cooperation program which does not start from this premise can be effective. As the Council declared:

Not only the effects but also the causes of these ills must be removed, and the help should be given in such a way that the recipients may gradually be freed from dependence on outsiders and become self-sufficient.

Or, in the words of Professor Scheyven, in his course on international cooperation and technical assistance at the University of Louvain,

Of all the questions which concern the developing countries, the first that must be resolved is the stabilization of the prices of their basic products. The solution for this problem represents, therefore, an essential element within the totality of the solutions of the problems of the developing countries. A rise of prices of the raw materials would have the great advantage of bettering perceptibly the Third World's situation, without causing the industrialized nations to feel the burden and the vexations of a fiscalization, and without inflicting on the assisted countries the humiliating feeling of being supported.[6]

A well-known moralist has argued that

The exploitation of a country by another one is as immoral as the exploitation of a man by another. To force underdeveloped countries, as it happens today, to sell, at a very low price, the raw materials taken from their soil or subsoil as well as food products which they produce and, at the same time, to sell to these underdeveloped countries, at a high price, the manufactured products which are offered in exchange, is undisputably immoral. [Equally immoral is] this kind of blackmail mendicity that some leaders of the under-developed countries are practicing more or less successfully with the large rival powers.[7]

We Catholics have countless organizations of assistance and charity: hospitals, leper homes, insane asylums, orphanages, nur-series, institutions for deaf and dumb, fallen women, old people, abandoned children, and all kinds of charity-inspired social works. Most of these institutions date from earlier times, when the exi-gencies of charity were realized in this way. Charity has always been present in the Church, though it has been shown in different ways according to the century's proper needs. Today this charity aspires to the name of justice and requires new forms of institu-tions to make itself present.

The highest form of charity [says Tresmontant] is justice. But it must be practiced in accordance with the nature of the problems of today, in the manner which will bring about their solution, that is in a political manner. What we need is a politician St. Francis, an economist St. Vincent de Paul.

Following this idea, I would propose the creation or rededica-tion of an inter-American body designed to promote justice in international relations, with a staff of members from North and Latin America. This organization should be sponsored by all the Christian communities in line with the Decree on Ecumenism of the Second Vatican Council, and in closest cooperation with our Jewish friends and with all men of good will. It could be conceived as the counterpart in this hemisphere of the Secretariat for the Promotion of Peace and Justice in the World which is being founded in Rome.

Special attention should be given by such a body to the crucial problem of marketing the products of underdeveloped nations and to all other problems by which justice is challenged. The morali-zation of international relations would be one of its primary func-tions, as well as vigilance over assistance given to the Third World to ensure that it does not turn into another expression of domination and create rivalries among the developed countries and blackmailing among the underdeveloped ones.

There is a growing consensus to support such a program. Not long ago in France, Mr. Leopold Sedar Senghor, president of the Republic of Senegal, faced a challenging interview. In what way, he was asked, is cooperation with Africa useful? How were the millions of dollars of foreign aid actually employed in Africa? Mr. Senghor, pioneer of African integration and federalism as well as promoter of the reunion of African French-speaking countries, took the opportunity to explain what the deterioration of the terms of exchange means for the African peasant.

The Great Powers [he said] do not agree and do not commit themselves to sustain on the world markets the current exchange of African products. Their value becomes less and less and therefore the black workers receive less and less for their labor, while the prices of foreign manufactured products sold to Africa are rising more and more. The best aid to the Third World would be, along with the training of technicians, the moralization of the prices of the basic products.

Let me insist that Catholics and Christians in general must be present in the organizations of international markets, financing, banking, and the like to restructure the patterns of world trade, credit, investments, and finance in order to ensure justice, which is the basis for cooperation. Failure to provide international justice will result in increasing irritation of the deprived masses, already tired of alms and of unaccomplished promises. Cooperation should base itself upon truth and justice. These seem to be the two major guarantees for the survival of Christianity. Providing them is the greatest challenge Christianity faces today. It is fair to acknowledge that they have been neglected in recent years.

Among the various fields of the apostolate, and the more important fields of action presented in Chapter III of the Decree on the Apostolate of the Laity, it is clearly stated: "Catholics should try to cooperate with all men and women of good will to promote whatever is true and just, . . ." (Section 14) This is one of the major religious tasks to be accomplished in Latin America. We Latin Americans are also guilty of causing the backwardness of our own countries. We have corruption and disorganization in administration, bureaucracy, inefficiency, lack of responsibility, lack of a sense of justice, and so on. What is being said in general seems to be very true in Latin America, namely, that "Catholics sometimes give the impression of not having any other virtue than obedience and no other vice than impurity." This lack of concern for justice and truth may explain the selfishness of many people and why they fail to heed the teachings of their faith. A proof of this is the exodus of capital to developed countries when it is so badly needed in Latin America to be invested in industrialization and to give employment. Another proof is the exaggerated waste of financial resources on luxury houses, conspicuous consumption, and other expenditures for display proper to the "peculiar culture" imported by alienated elites.

As People of God and members of a community of unity in faith, hope, and charity we must pledge to fulfill the various tasks of international cooperation. This is truly a participation in the mission of salvation, which seeks to reincorporate all things in Christ. May God teach us, as St. Paul says, "to reject irreligion and earthly ambitions, in order to live on earth with soberness, justice, and love of God. . . . in order to free ourselves of all sin and make of us a purified flock, people who are consecrated to do good" (Titus 2:11–15).

Let me suggest that you read again in its entirety the Pastoral Constitution on the Church in the Modern World. I did so myself recently; coming here, I must confess that I was tempted to rewrite this paper in order to emphasize in a stronger way my plea for unity and cooperation. Let us ask ourselves honestly if the opening words of the Constitution are true for us: "The joys and the hopes, the griefs and the anxieties of the men of this age, especially those who are poor or in any way afflicted, these too are the joys and hopes, the griefs and the anxieties of the followers of Christ."

NOTES

1. Decree on the Apostolate of the Laity, Section 14. Cfr. John XXIII, *Mater et Magistra*, May 15, 1961, ASS 53, pp. 448–450.
2. E. B. Taylor, *Primitive Culture* (New York: Holt and Co., 1889).

3. E. K. Wilson, *Sociology* (Homewood, Ill.: Dorsey Press, 1966), p. 51.

4. Ignace Lepp, *La Nueva Moral* (Buenos Aires: Ed. Lohle, 1964), p. 158.

5. Teilhard de Chardin, *The Phenomenon of Man* (New York: Harper Torchbooks, 1961), p. 243.

6. Raymond Scheyven, "L'Aide aux pays en Voie de development," lecture at the University of Louvain.

7. Ignace Lepp, *La Nueva Moral* (Buenos Aires: Ed. Lohle, 1964), p. 158.

Historical Perspectives
of Protestantism

JOHN MACKAY

At no time in my life have I felt so deeply moved in rising to address an audience as I find myself this evening. There are two reasons for the special emotion that grips me. There is, first, the fact that I, a Protestant, should be addressing an audience of Roman Catholic brothers and sisters in Christ from across the United States and from many Latin American lands. Second, it stirs me to the depths that the theme upon which I have been asked to speak should be one that has been a major concern of my life and thought for half a century and more.

In the fall of 1916 your speaker, following a period of study in the United States and in Spain, left his Scottish homeland, along with his young bride, for Lima, Peru. We were sent as pioneer missionaries of a Presbyterian denomination to the ancient land of the Incas. From the time of our arrival in that beloved country, things Hispanic, both Iberian and Latin American, have been a major source of inspiration and concern to me. I have said on more than one occasion that I owe more to the great Hispanic tradition, to personalities and ideas, to issues and developments in its religion and its culture, than lips can tell or life repay.

With this allusion to the historical and psychological factors that have influenced your speaker let me turn to the subject which the distinguished committee that organized this conference has presented to me, the historical perspectives of Protestantism in Latin America.

In dealing with this topic I propose to take seriously what is involved in providing "perspectives," "historical perspectives," of Latin American Protestantism. I will not set out to provide a multiplicity of factual data regarding the coming of Reformation Christianity to Hispanic America and its unusual developments in the Southern Hemisphere. I will give precedence to setting in high relief representative personalities, crucial events, spiritual principles, psychological factors, and theological ideas that have produced, or been related to, an event, one of the most significant episodes in modern religious history, and which might be designated the Evangelical Epic in the Hispanic world.

The Protestant Presence in Latin America

The question arises, What is Protestantism? Protestantism is the designation given to the Christian movement, involving theological ideas, forms of life, and Church structures, which began to come into being in the sixteenth century as the fruit of what is historically known as the Reformation. That movement came to birth through the rediscovery of Christian truths that had been rejected, neglected, or demoted by the official Christian Church, the Church of Rome.

Protestants in Latin America, because of associations attached to the term Protestantism in the Hispanic cultural tradition, have preferred to call the diversified religious reality to which they belong "Evangelical Christianity," their churches "Evangelical Churches" (*Iglesias Evangelicas*), and themselves "Evangelicals" (*Evangelicos*). That is to say, they have stressed and continue to stress their doctrinal and ecclesiastical identification with the Evangel, the Gospel, which is the indisputable, unsectarian core of the Christian religion. Jesus Christ, we are told, began his public ministry "preaching the gospel of God" (Mark 1:14); he brought his earthly ministry to a close by enjoining his disciples to "Go into all the world to preach the Gospel to the whole creation" (Mark 16:15). In this respect Protestantism in Latin America has sought to represent Christianity at its truest and best.

Let me now proceed to present some of the salient features of Latin American Protestantism considered as an historical, sociological, and religious reality.

During the entire Colonial period in Latin American history it was illegal, and could be fatal, for Protestants of any race to propagate their faith or to assemble for worship in the territory controlled by Spain and Portugal in the Western Hemisphere. With the movement toward political independence initiated and achieved in the second decade of the nineteenth century, it became possible for the Bible in the Spanish vernacular, a book formerly banned and damned, to be circulated in the lands that were liberated from Spain. The historic coming of the Holy Scriptures, whose rediscovery in the sixteenth century had produced the Protestant Reformation, into the life and thought of the new republics of Latin America is associated with a Scotsman, James Thomson, a representative of the British and Foreign Bible Society. A personal friend of San Martin, the Liberator, who encouraged him in his work, Thomson became a pioneer of Bible dissemination and popular education from Argentina and Uruguay, through Chile, Peru, Ecuador, Colombia, and Mexico. In Colombia, with the support of eminent nationals, he founded the Colombian Bible Society, which later was dissolved following papal intervention.

Because of the restoration of Vatican influence in the new Latin American republics, an influence which was very slight in the epoch immediately following the Wars of Independence, it was not until the fifties of the last century that Protestantism began to take on a congregational or church dimension. Its advent in the form of organized communities began in 1855, when a missionary from Great Britain, a medical doctor, Robert Kalley, arrived in Brazil from Madeira and soon thereafter established an evangelical congregation in Rio de Janeiro. That congregation became the precursor of the establishment of Protestantism as a sociological fact and a potent Christian reality in the twenty republics of Latin America. The contact of North American Protestantism with Latin America began with the arrival in Chile in 1845 of Rev. David Trumbull, and the coming to Brazil in 1859 of a young Presbyterian missionary from Pennsylvania, Rev. Ashbel Green Simonton.

In Brazil today there are more than five million Protestant Christians, and in the Southern Hemisphere as a whole more than ten million. According to demographers the population of Latin America is growing faster than the population in any other region of the world. Church statisticians, Roman Catholic and Protestant, provide evidence that the Protestant community in Latin American lands is growing even faster than the general population. In a word, it would seem to participate in that "boundless ness" which is a native trait of the Hispanic spirit, a spirit in which, according to the Spanish poet-philosopher Unamuno, "The normal is the abnormal."

With these historical facts in the background let us move on to consider the fact of Protestantism on the Latin American scene today.

That great Roman Catholic layman Baron Von Hügel, a leading authority on Christian mysticism, once said, "Christianity taught us to care, caring matters most." When the Christian religion is true to its founder, Jesus Christ, it produces a "caring" spirit, concern for people in every facet of their lives. Christians in the great missionary tradition of their faith, whether acting as Catholics or as Protestants, have done precisely this: they have *cared* for people.

The Protestant record in Latin America has given concrete expression for more than a century to what it means for Christians to care for others in the spirit of Christ and his Apostles. Concern in this sense has manifested itself through the years as *evangelistic endeavor*. This has involved the proclamation of the Gospel, the creation of "new men and women in Christ," and the upbuilding of the Christian Church. Unique expressions of Christian evangelism in Latin America have been responsible for the Church growth already referred to. A remarkable effort called "Evangelism in Depth," which was born a few years ago in Costa Rica, had uprecedented success in Venezuela, and is now under way in Peru. It is inspiring similar evangelistic effort in other parts of the world.

The twentieth-century Pentecostal movement, in which Roman Catholic bishops and cardinals are showing increasing interest, has had extraordinary success in Latin America. Evangelism, as carried on by Latin American Pentecostals in the past few decades, has had far-reaching consequences in the expansion of the evangelical community and in the production of better social conditions for the common people. At the present moment there is being erected, by Pentecostal Christians in the city of São Paulo, an edifice designed to seat 25,000 people. This building when completed will be the world's and history's largest church auditorium. Another example of Hispanic boundlessness! In 1959, when Chilean Pentecostals celebrated the fiftieth anniversary of their movement, representatives of the government and universities of Chile were present. They expressed their appreciation of what the movement had contributed to social betterment in their country.

Other marks of the Protestant presence in Latin America that are closely related to the proclamation of the Gospel are the phenomenal distribution of the Scriptures in Spanish and Portuguese, the development of national Bible societies, the translation of the Bible or portions of it into indigenous tongues, and the proliferation of book stores which contain both religious and secular literature. Epoch-making was the establishment, several decades ago, by a North American named Clarence Jones, of a Protestant radio station in Quito, Ecuador. This station, in addition to putting on the air evangelical discourses and providing news of the world, was made available to the Ecuadorian government, which had sanctioned its founding and expressed gratitude for its service. Today there are many other radio stations in Latin American countries which are operated by Protestants and which render invaluable service in the religious and secular order.

No less epoch-making, and of world significance, was the oranization of the Wycliffe Bible Translators by a creative evangelical visionary from the United States, Cameron Townsend, who became a close friend of Mexico's revolutionary president Lazaro Cardenas. Townsend rallied around him a group of young American Protestants, men and women of missionary zeal and brilliant intellect, who dedicated themselves to learning Indian languages which had never before been reduced to writing. This they did with a view to making literate the aboriginal natives through the reading of portions of the Bible which their warmhearted American friends had translated.

Evidence of the far-reaching significance of the work of the Wycliffe Translators is the resounding world echo that followed a tragic incident some years ago, in which some members of their group were slain by Auca Indians in the remote jungles of Ecuador. The loving response of fellow translators, following this event, won the tribe, two of whose members were present at the recent World Conference on Evangelism in Berlin. Equally significant is the fact that in the new building erected in Lima by the Peruvian Ministry of Education a whole floor has been given to the Institute of Linguistics of the Wycliffe Translators to serve as their headquarters in the Republic.

No less illustrative of the impact of Protestantism upon Latin America on all levels of life is the magnitude and influence of the educational and philanthropic enterprises that have been carried on by mission boards and national churches for very many years. Presbyterians, Methodists, Episcopalians, and later Lutheran and diverse Baptist churches supplemented their evangelistic efforts and the establishment of churches by developing a wide variety of schools, colleges, hospitals, and orphanages.

For many years leading private schools in great Latin American cities, schools which were founded by Protestant missionary societies and which continue to function in the spirit of their founders, have exercised and continue to exercise a decisive influence upon the lives of young men and women and upon the culture of their native country. Representative of such institutions at the highest educational level are the Agricultural College in Lavras, Brazil, Mackenzie University in São Paulo, and the newly founded evangelical university in Guatemala City, which is called by the name of an eminent Guatemalan, Dr. Mariano Galvez.

As regards educational facilities for the cultural development

of Church leaders, Bible schools and Protestant theological seminaries abound throughout Hispanic America. The increasing number of Protestant missionaries who move into those lands receive
first-class training in the Spanish language in San Juan, Puerto
Rico, and equally good instruction in Portuguese in the city of
Campinas, Brazil. It is striking and significant that in those language schools the missionary student body is an ecumenical
microcosm of world Protestantism. Those who study there with
linguistic zeal and in true Christian fellowship run the ecclesiastical gamut from Quakers, Southern Baptists, and Pentecostals to
Methodists, Presbyterians, Episcopalians, and Lutherans.

I will conclude this introduction to the Protestant presence in
Latin America by alluding to the man who, in my judgment,
is the noblest and most representative symbol of this presence.
His name was William Morris. He was an Anglican missionary
from England to Argentina, who, when he died in the early 1930's,
was described by a leading Buenos Aires newspaper as "The
Argentine Saint" (*El Santo Argentino*). In his memory, two years
ago, a statue seven meters high was erected in Palermo, an
important district of the Argentine capital. William Morris, whom
I knew personally, and to whose spirit and influence I have owed
much, was in his lifetime the incarnation of the evangelical missionary spirit, across all ecclesiastical boundaries, both Roman
Catholic and Protestant. That spirit has been present in the Christian Church, in different degrees and in diverse forms, from the
first to the twentieth century.

Christian pastor, theological scholar, religious editor, founder
of the orphanage "El Alba" (the Dawn), founder, director, and
sustainer of the famous Philanthropic Schools of Argentina in
which hundreds of thousands of Argentines have been educated,
and which now belong to the Argentine government, this man,
William Morris, in the last days of his life left behind for his
friends a little poem addressed to Jesus Christ. The last stanza
of that poem runs thus:

> I cannot hold Thee fast, though Thou art mine.
> Hold Thou me fast.
> So earth shall know at last and heaven at last
> That I am Thine.

It was Jesus Christ, whom William Morris loved with an ardent passion, that made him the man he was and inspired him to "care" for others in every facet of their lives. This "Argentine Saint" reproduced in his life and thought the spirit of the Spanish saint and scholar Raymond Lull, a thirteenth-century missionary to the Moslems. Lull's devotion to the Man of Galilee and Golgotha led him to exclaim, "I have one passion in life and it is He."

The Protestant Advent in Latin America as the Fulfillment of Evangelical Yearnings in Hispanic Catholicism

In 1932, after sixteen years in Latin America, I published a book entitled *The Other Spanish Christ*. It was a distillation of my thinking on the spiritual history of Spain and Latin America. The basic thesis of that book could be stated thus: In the religious tradition of Spain there were personalities whose Christian thought and devotion ran counter to the official thinking and policy of the Hispanic Catholic Church to which they belonged, the Church which was destined to become the decisive and only Christian influence in Latin America for more than three centuries.

This thesis I reaffirm. In doing so let me give evidence that the viewpoints and aspirations of many Iberian Christians in Spain's Golden Age have been given vital expression in Latin American Protestantism. They have also been accorded contemporary acclaim by Hispanic Catholics in this new ecumenical era.

It is a recognized historical fact that the influence of Erasmus, Luther, and Calvin was so potent among Spanish intellectuals and churchmen in the first half of the sixteenth century that, had it not been for the Inquisition, the Council of Trent, and King Philip II, Spain might have gone the way of Germany, Holland, England, and Scotland. Two things are indisputably certain and are being affirmed today by eminent Catholics, both clergy and laymen, in the Hispanic world and beyond its borders. First, it is being acknowledged with sorrow that the Hispanic Catholic Church was the most highly institutionalized church in Christian history, that it tended to function as Christ's patron and not as his servant, and that in Latin America it imposed its structure, its ideas, and its ritual upon the people instead of winning the people to faith in Christ and allegiance to him. For Jesus Christ in ecclesiastical circles was not a living, transforming, contemporary reality.

Second, there were men and women, loyal Catholics, in the Hispanic Church of that period for whom Christ was a potent, living presence, relevant to their personal problems and with whom they could enjoy fellowship apart from any ecclesiastical mandate or ritualistic observance.

For those early Spanish "evangelicals" Christ as revealed in the Bible was more than an image, more than a denizen of Paradise who, following his Ascension, left his followers in loneliness and could be found as a real presence only in the Eucharist. Members of this group, though mostly unknown to one another, were the eminent Valdes brothers, Juan and Alfonso, and also the great Spanish mystics, Theresa of Avila, John of the Cross, and Luis de Leon. Juan de Valdes had to flee to Italy because of the centrality he gave to the Bible and to Christ in his theological writing. John of the Cross wrote his great mystic poems, *The Ascent of Mount Carmel* and *The Dark Night of the Soul,* in a prison of the Inquisition. Theresa of Avila passed through a profound experience of conversion while a nun in a Carmelite convent. The living Christ became both seraphically and practically real to her. Later, when young sisters in a convent which she founded complained to Theresa of the very drab and routine nature of their work, the Saint of Avila replied to them, "My daughters, the Lord moves among pots and pans." For having dared to translate one of the books of the Bible, the "Song of Songs," into the Spanish vernacular, Fray Luis de Leon, the rector of the University of Salamanca, was imprisoned for four years. In his prison cell in Valladolid he wrote one of the great classics of Spanish literature, *The Names of Christ.* This outstanding Augustinian friar is the author of the famous saying, so meaningful to a rural population, and to people who fail to find in a Church sanctuary what they long for: "Christ lives in the fields."

The last chapter of the famous volume to which I have just referred defines in evangelical terms the basic significance of

Christ. "Christ is 'Salud,'" he writes. In Spanish the word *Salud* has a double meaning. It means "salvation" in the deepest Christian sense, that is, the deliverance of a man from his sinful self-centeredness to God-centeredness. It also means "health," that is, the complete harmonious development of human selfhood when redeemed by Christ so that the "new man" becomes like Christ.

Among the clergy who accompanied the Spanish conqueror to the New World and exercised the role of missionaries to the indigenous people were some whose Christian approach to the Incas, Aztecs, Mayans, and jungle dwellers was not impositional but incarnational, not Church-centered but Christ-centered, in the great evangelical tradition of the Spanish reformers and mystics. Outstanding among these was Bartolomé de las Casas, who came to the Western world with Columbus on his second voyage with the intention of becoming a pioneer landlord. Passing, however, through a profound experience of Christian conversion in the tradition of Augustine, Luther, and Theresa of Avila, Las Casas became one of the greatest missionary personalities of all time. His incarnational approach to the human situation is enshrined in a book entitled *How to Attract all Peoples to the True Religion*. How is this to be achieved? When in their concern for others and in their desire to communicate the Christian faith to them Christians become literally incarnate among the objects of their concern, they will thus win a right to be listened to because of what people have found them to be.

What I am saying is this: The Protestant advent in Latin America gave expression to yearnings and experiences and ideas which were present centuries earlier in the Spanish reformers and mystics, and in missionary personalities such as Bartolomé de las Casas. Today this revolutionary fact is being recognized. There has begun to emerge in Roman Catholic circles a new "evangelicalism" and in Protestant circles a new "Catholicism," as members of both groups become dedicated to exploring in Biblical perspective the eternal dimension and the contemporary relevancy of Christ and the Church. This gathering itself is a symbol of my hope—that the Christian tradition represented by Juan de Valdes, Theresa of Avila, Luis de Leon, and Bartolomé de las Casas will cooperate with the present-day successors of James Thompson, Robert Kalley, Ashbel Green Simonton, and William Morris for the expansion of Christ's Kingdom in Hispanic America and the world.

Historic Challenges to the Protestant Presence in Latin America

Fifty years after Protestantism had begun to be established in Latin America, the propriety of its presence and missionary activity in that continent was challenged by a world Protestant gathering, the missionary conference which convened in Edinburgh in 1910. That epoch-making gathering refused to recognize the validity of Protestant missionary action in Latin American lands and forbade membership in the conference to representatives of the evangelical churches in Latin American countries and to missionaries who labored there. The theory was that lands where Roman Catholicism was the official religion were an illegitimate sphere for Protestant action, which in such a case could be regarded only as proselytizing activity. And such activity the Edinburgh conference would not sanction.

In the light of the sociological fact that Latin America was rapidly becoming the most highly secularized area in the world and that Catholicism in those countries was becoming increasingly nominal, the action of the Edinburgh conference can only be regarded as ironic, shortsighted, and insensitive to human reality. But in the decades that followed, the attitude of world Protestantism changed, and Protestant development in Latin America was destined to become one of history's most creative Christian efforts, to be hailed both by secular leaders and by evangelically minded Roman Catholic churchmen.

Let me state with the utmost brevity what happened in the wake of Edinburgh, 1910. Concerned Protestants, men and women from North and South America, profoundly ecumenical in spirit, realistically aware of the spiritual situation in Latin America, organized the Congress on Christian Work in Latin America, which met in Panama City in February, 1916. Several hundred Protestant leaders from North America and Latin America came together after a careful survey of the facts. The group was composed of mission board executives, missionaries, and Latin American clergymen and laymen. Studies of the Latin American reality and of the Protestant presence and task in Central and South America were published in three large volumes. The Panama gathering was followed by several others throughout the Southern Hemisphere. In April, 1925, there was convened in Montevideo a second continental assembly, called by the same name as its predecessor, Congress on Christian Work in South America. Among the speakers were several eminent South American intellectuals, not themselves Protestants, who gave expression to their personal viewpoints about Latin American lands and the issue of religion and culture in their spiritual heritage.

When the heirs of the Edinburgh conference met in Jerusalem in 1928 under the same chairman, John R. Mott, two hundred delegates from around the world recognized, and in no sectarian spirit, the legitimacy and importance of the Protestant presence in Latin America. It was my privilege at one of the sessions of this gathering to give an address on this subject: "The Power of Evangelism in South America." Ten years later, at the third world gathering of mission-minded Protestants, which convened in Madras, India, a considerable group of Protestant Christians from Latin American countries were seated as regular members of the assembly.

A comment is in order regarding the historic significance of the Panama and Montevideo conferences which were organized by the Committee on Cooperation in Latin America. This was the first regional organization ever established by Protestants anywhere in the world. Founded under the leadership of a great Latin Americanist, Samuel Guy Inman, a new era began in Protestant cooperative effort. National federations and local committees were formed throughout Latin America.

Cultural significance was given to this new movement by the publication of a review called *La Nueve Democracia*. It functioned for many years under the editorship of a former Spanish priest, Juan Ortiz Gonzalez, who was succeeded by a distin-

guished Mexican intellectual, Alberto Rembao. Contributions to
this magazine were frequently made by leaders of the cultural
community in Latin America, including the Chilean poetess Ga-
briela Mistral, who won the Nobel Prize for Literature, because
of their respect and affection for its great editors.

By the close of the 1940's Latin American nationals undertook
the direction of Protestant cooperation in Latin America, so far
at least as the older churches and missions were concerned. This
was symbolized by a conference held in Buenos Aires in 1949,
followed by a similar gathering held in Lima in 1961. However,
it became evident at the Lima conference that sectarian forces
were at work to divide Latin American Protestantism into two
segments: those in favor of the ecumenical movement, as represented by the World Council of Churches, and those opposed
to that movement. This situation continues, and constitutes a very
live issue in the Protestant community in Latin American countries today, as it does also in the United States and in other
countries of the world. There is everywhere an "ecumenical"
dichotomy in contemporary Protestantism, and it is in Latin
America that the issue is most crucial.

Protestant division was accompanied by Catholic opposition.
In the fall of 1942, Protestants in the United States were startled
by a public pronouncement of the archbishops of the Roman Catholic Church at their annual meeting in Washington, D. C. The
pronouncement charged that the success of the "Good Neighbor
Policy," sponsored by the Roosevelt government in the interests
of better inter-American relations, was placed in jeopardy by
the presence of Protestant missions and missionaries in Latin
American countries. This presence was regarded as the chief
obstacle to the establishment and maintenance of friendly relations in the Americas. This unprecedented declaration came as a
shock to the American public and to the Protestant churches in
this country.

A few weeks later, however, the viewpoint of the hierarchy was
dramatically and effectively rebutted by the Federal Council of
the Churches of Christ in America at its biennial meeting in
Cleveland. In a document entitled *Our Heritage of Religious*

Freedom, which received wide publicity throughout the Hemisphere, the Federal Council said:

Among the citizens of the United States who have contributed to spiritual and cultural advancement in the United States are names of men and women of Christlike spirit, who, unashamed of the name of missionary, devoted their lives and talents to those lands. The memory of many of these is today preserved in the countries which they served, while institutions which they founded continue to be popular centers of cultural influence, and patterns of humanitarian endeavor. Through the work of these men and women and their successors elements of supreme worth in the religious and cultural heritage of our country have been shared with Hispanic America; while innumerable links of understanding and mutual confidence have been forged between the Americas.

It is with deep concern, therefore, that we have witnessed an effort, now publically endorsed in the United States by the archbishops and bishops of a sister communion, which constitutes a religious minority in this country, to set the relation of Protestant Christianity to Hispanic America in a perspective which does violence to historical truth and contemporary fact.

Following this statement a new era began. Eminent Roman Catholic scholars like John J. Considine of the Maryknoll Fathers and Peter Mastin Dunne, S.J., chairman of the Department of History of the Catholic University of San Francisco, paid visits to Latin America. Following their visits, those distinguished men wrote books which have become classics. Fathers Considine and Dunne, because of their realistic analysis of the situation that confronts the Christian religions in Latin America today, their awareness of the nominalism and indifference that have marked the traditional Church, their appreciation of the Protestant presence, and their penetrating understanding of the total scene, became the harbingers of a longed-for dawn.

Here are some of the events that have made history in recent years. They are related to the new approach being made by the Roman Catholic Church to the current situation in Latin America and to the dramatic change in the realm of Catholic-Protestant relations. This represents a new historical perspective for Protestantism and also for the future of the Christian religion in the Americas.

In the town of Chimbote, Peru, there was held in 1953 a unique

conference of Roman Catholic clergy and laity from most of the
countries in the Western Hemisphere. Its significant theme was
"Latin American Catholicism: A Self-Evaluation." The historic
Church had become self-critical. In the course of the last two decades Latin America has become the chief mission field in the
world for American Catholicsm. Today more than 5,000 Catholic
missionaries from this country are engaged in work in the lands
south of the Rio Grande. Moreover, some of the most penetrating studies published in recent years on Protestantism in Latin
America have been the work of Latin American Catholic authors
in such lands, for example, as Chile and Mexico. Also there is now
warm Christian fellowship between many Protestants and Roman
Catholics in Latin America, a sharing of ideas and concerns, a participation in enterprises for the public good, and in certain places
and at certain times a meeting together for common worship.

But, of all that has taken place in recent times in the sphere
of inter-American relations in a Christian context, nothing, in
my judgment, is more significant than this gathering in the New
England city of Boston. Protestants with a Latin American background are appearing as guest speakers under the auspices of the
Catholic Inter-American Cooperation Program. Is it too much to
say that in the ballroom and corridors of this hotel there has been
moving around in these days the Living Christ of Theresa of Avila
and Luis de Leon, of Bartolomé de las Casas and William Morris?

Latin American Protestantism in the Perspective of Tomorrow

I come now to the historical perspective that looks toward the
days ahead. What is the future of Protestant churches and missions in Latin America? That, of course, is in the hands of God
and in the lap of history. But one thing is certain: If Evangelical
Christianity is to be loyal to its true nature, and equipped to
fulfill the task which such loyalty entails, in one of the world's
vastest and most crucial areas, and in history's most revolutionary hour, there are certain imperatives to which it must give
unswerving allegiance.

First, *evangelism should be given priority status by Protestants in Latin America.* Churches, missions, and individual Protestants must take seriously the reality of Jesus Christ as "Salud," that is, as man's Redeemer and the Pattern for the true human living. They must pursue the goal of spiritual change and create through the Holy Spirit "new men and women in Christ." In this dedicated effort clergy and laity must cooperate. They must be careful at all times that in their approach to people who are objects of their evangelical concern they shall not impose themselves, their ideas, or their customs upon them, or be merely condescending toward them. They must, rather, become incarnate among them to a right to be heard by them concerning Christ and the Gospel. Evangelism carried on in this spirit should be conducted cooperatively across all ecclesiastical boundaries. Those engaged in it should learn all they can from the movement called "Evangelism in Depth." They should also be inspired by, and give creative expression to, the new acclaim that is being given to the Bible in Protestant, Roman Catholic, and secular circles in Latin America.

Second, *the current surge of clericalism which has become manifest in some Protestant communities in Latin America should be confronted as a serious menace to the Christian cause.*

I have in mind a phenomenon in which Church leaders lose their evangelical zeal and love of people. Idolatrously bound to outworn scholastic concepts and clichés, they interpret their vocation as a call to purge the Church of fellow ministers and theological students whose ideas challenge the established order in Church and society because they show concern for the welfare of the common people and crave a true understanding of the Christian faith. The attitude of those clerics recalls the Spanish Inquisition. But the new inquisitors, though temporarily potent in a country like Brazil, for example, where an unscrupulous dictatorial regime controls the nation, will not, I am convinced, prevail. Nevertheless, this new menace must be taken seriously and must be wisely and decisively met by the Protestant community in Latin America.

Third, *Protestants in Latin America should pursue ecumenical fellowship.*

The Hispanic spirit is natively ecumenical. The Christian Church, when true to its nature and its Lord, gives expression to the reality of oneness in Christ. It must learn to transcend certain differences in doctrine, organization, and forms of worship which do not belong to the Christian essence. But to be "ecumenical" in the deepest Christian sense does not mean the pursuit of monolithic institutional structures or even of church union in an organizational, ecclesiastical sense. Ecumenical fellowship means private and public manifestations of Christian love, a holy togetherness in Christ, and a visible cooperation with one another in the service of Christ for the world as members of the one Church which is Christ's body.

Because of the very unique Christian situation in Latin America, in which Pentecostals and so-called "sects" predominate numerically in the Protestant community, and where an unprecedented change of mood and outlook has taken place in the Roman Catholic communion from cardinals to members of the laity, the possibilities for Christian unity and cooperative effort in the religious and secular order are without parallel in history. In such a context ecumenical unity and cooperation can be, and should be, pursued. It must be conducted in such a way that we will learn from one another, while being at the same time utterly frank with one another in the affirmation of what is believed. In this way Christians will promote together the Kingdom of Christ and make it possible for people outside the Church, or those who are only nominally Christian, to believe that Jesus Christ came from God and that he is relevant to every need of the human individual and of the society in which he lives.

Fourth, *concern for social justice should mark the thought and life of all Protestants in Latin America.*

Christians worthy of the name are called upon to "care" for people, not only for their souls but also for their bodies and, in a special sense, for the conditions under which they live. It is a tragic fact that an overwhelming proportion of the inhabitants of Latin America live in a state of human dereliction. This is true not only of the millions of Indians and peasant folk who dwell in the continental interior but of other millions who inhabit shacks in the environs of great cities. Responsible for this situation are traditional feudalistic ideas and attitudes, men and women of wealth and prestige insensitive to human right, governments that represent the wealthy and not the common people, and great economic forces, national and foreign, that put into power, and thereafter subtly control, not a few Latin American governments.

What should be the Christian approach to a situation like this? What should Protestants do at a time when a new revolutionary mood is gripping the Latin American masses, when a large proportion of the younger intellectuals in Latin American lands are becoming social radicals, when the traditional peasant spirit of fatalistic resignation is giving way to a mood of revolutionary expectation, and when the influence of Marxist ideology is becoming increasingly potent, both in university patios and in rural hamlets?

In such a time it is incumbent upon all concerned Christians and church bodies in Latin America and in North America to remember John Calvin's prophetic concept of the role of the state in relation to human society. This father of a large segment of world Protestantism defined the state in these terms: "The state," he said, "is God's vice-regent to maintain humanity among men." Here is a norm by which Christians should judge organized government in their native land. Does a government make it possible for all citizens to live lives that are truly human? Are its policies directed toward the humanization of men and opposed to groups and structures that in their own selfish interests seek to maintain masses of human beings in a dehumanized condition? If it is true, to use another of Calvin's prophetic insights, that the Christian Church is the "instrument of God's Glory," that is, the medium through which he shall manifest his Character and Will to men, then the Church, and all who call themselves Christians, are obliged to seek the social welfare of their fellow men. In the name of God they must challenge people, systems, and policies that thwart, or are indifferent to, God's concern for his creation and the world for which Christ dies.

It is a thrilling fact that in both Protestant and Roman Catholic circles in Latin America today a new dawn is breaking in the realm of social concern. Let me mention three representative examples of this new Christian spirit.

Outstanding, and an augury of things to come, is the action of a young Roman Catholic Colombian priest Camilo Torres. Torres, concerned about the welfare of the peasant masses in his country and disillusioned by the insensitivity of the Colombian hierarchy on this social issue, joined the guerrilla bands and soon thereafter was killed by government forces.

In political circles two devout Roman Catholic laymen, President Frei of Chile and President Belaunde of Peru, are giving creative leadership in the confrontation of social issues that involve the welfare of the common people. In a book entitled *The Conquest of Peru by the Peruvians* Fernando Belaunde Terry presents the thesis that the government of his country should pursue the policy of picking up where the Incas left off by giving, as did the Incan rulers, a sense of personal dignity to every individual member of Peruvian society.

As regards Protestant concern for social justice, dynamic leadership is being given to this cause by a group of Latin American clergy and laymen with headquarters in Montevideo, Uruguay. These men issue a publication called *Iglesia y Sociedad* (Church and Society), which is the successor of *La Neuva Democracia.* The group in question, to which a distinguished Uruguayan layman, Luis E. Odell, has given dynamic leadership, has held important continental gatherings in Peru and Chile. Those attending have grappled with the problem of Christian responsibility in an area in which the rich are becoming richer and the poor are becoming poorer. Important publications are also being issued by the *Iglesia y Sociedad* fellowship. This literature is designed to arouse fellow Protestants to confront the current dehumanization of man in the light of Jesus Christ and the Church's mission in the world.

Fifth, *Protestants in Latin America must pursue the development of theological education in such a way that students in seminaries and Bible schools shall be given an intelligent understanding of the Christian faith. Students must also be equipped to present that faith in such a way as shall take cognizance of cultural and sociological conditions in their environment and create Church communities that shall be creatively relevant to their surroundings.*

Two attitudes which have marked centers of learning and also intellectuals in the Hispanic cultural tradition must be avoided. Let the impression never be given in centers of theological learning that the goal of seminary education is simply to make students theologically sophisticated so that while they come to know all that has been thought or said about important truths, they themselves become committed to no one truth in particular. Let teachers and students beware of what Miguel de Unamuno called "intellectual libertinism." He had in mind people who become infatuated with one idea after another but who never make any one idea their lifelong companion. In such a case theological professors and students would become what many contemporary teachers and thinkers have tended to become, devotees of the current cult of the *uncommitted,* never entering into honest, abiding wedlock with a great Christian centrality. They would be simply theological "Juan Tenorios," cultural disciples of the classical Spanish libertine.

Equally to be avoided is what a Peruvian author, Luis Alberto Sanchez, has called "Hispanic Arielism." One of the books that profoundly influenced young Latin American intellectuals in the early years of the present century was the small literary masterpiece entitled *Ariel,* whose author was the famous Uruguayan writer José Enrique Rodo. Taking as his symbol for the Latin American intellectual and for every Latin American the angelic sprite who appears in Shakespeare's famous drama *The Tempest,* Rodo advocated a winged intellectualism that keeps ever-soaring above the sordid world of the dragon "Caliban."

But reaction has set in among concerned Latin American thinkers against "Arielistic" detachment from human reality. They want no more a mere flighty intellectual restlessness or an Astheticism that lives detached from the real world. They repudiate the Ariel ideal, that is, the thinker who glories in mere hopping around with "library dust on his wings."

Let theological professors, students, and the Church leaders in Latin America take note of both these perils. Let them be aware at the same time of the peril of a rigid dogmatism, of that scholastic spirit where ideas become idols and thereby take the place of the dynamic Christian reality they were designed to define. In a word, let all who are interested in Christian truth become possessed by him who is himself the Truth, whose influence as *Salud* produces God-centeredness and man-concernedness in every dimension of human thinking and human living, and who can become known only through the Scriptures.

In saying this I cannot refrain from a closing allusion to a theological seminary which I visited during a recent trip to Latin America. Taking seriously the classical Christian tradition in its full ecumenical dimension and the importance of understanding and communicating essential truth, this institution, founded by Presbyterians in San Felipe, Guatemala, makes a revolutionary approach to contemporary reality in that country.

Members of the seminary faculty arrange from time to time to encounter men and women who crave a true understanding of the Christian faith and desire academic preparation in order to be of service to the Christian Church. Among those people are businessmen and professional people who, in addition to attending theological courses arranged for them in the area where they live, devote a period of study on the seminary campus. With the passage of the years many of those part-time students graduate with a degree in theology.

When it was my privilege in October, 1966, to give the graduation address on the occasion in which a number of those dedicated people received their theological diplomas in the mountain city of Quezaltenango, there came to me this conviction. The future of the Christian Church in Latin America, whether in the Protestant or Roman Catholic tradition, is inseparably bound to the equipment of the laity for a luminous and dynamic role in the promotion of the one Faith. This Faith centers in Jesus Christ, Son of God and Son of man, the Savior and Lord of life, who is also the Head of his Body, the Church.

Main Currents of Protestantism

JOSÉ MIGUEZ-BONINO

In his study of Protestantism in Chile, Father Ignacio Vergara remarks: "Although Chilean Protestantism is not given to intellectual speculation and does not give birth to a strictly doctrinal stream, its thought is oriented by common Protestant ideas."[1] This statement rightly portrays the theological face of Latin American Protestantism. It has not created anything theologically; it simply reflects what happens elsewhere. It is, nevertheless, important to focus our attention on those particular aspects of Protestant thought it does reflect and the way it does so.

A few sentences will be enough to sketch the historical background of the theological ideas which have shaped Latin American Protestantism. As it is commonly known, three different currents make up its composition. The first two date back to the time of our national emancipation. It was a time of ideological ferment, of rebellion against the social-economic-political order of the colonial regime, and consequently also a revolt against the ecclesiastical order which was seen as part of this structure. Liberal ideas, coming directly or indirectly from the British or French Enlightenment, provided the ideological support of the move-

191

ment. It was at this point that Protestantism entered the scene.

It was established originally through immigration from Europe, mostly in the form of German, Swiss, and Scandinavian communities which settled down as closed cultural entities, keeping the language and religion of origin. Descendants of these settlers now constitute approximately a third of Latin American Protestants. These groups brought their clergy with them from Europe. Their theology was simply a reflection of confessional thinking at home except for the fact that these expatriated groups tended to become more strictly orthodox and conservative.

A second source of Protestantism was the evangelistic work of Protestant denominations—mostly Baptist, Methodist, and Presbyterian—and "Free churches" and missionary societies related to them. There were two kinds of approaches in these groups. First, a "liberal-culturalist" tendency, strongly interested in education, the creation of schools and hospitals, and devoted to the ideals of human dignity, democracy, and freedom.[2] Second, a revivalist tendency, centered in the idea of personal salvation, a joyful experience of inner freedom and a visible change of life. This latter is certainly the most representative stream of Latin American Protestantism. Since the beginning of the present century, and particularly in the period between the two world wars, Latin America has entered a time of rapid social change. The demographic explosion, ever-increasing urbanization and internal migration, the beginnings of industrial development are the basic elements of this change. Among the displaced masses put in motion by this process arose a new form of Protestantism: the Pentecostals. Sometimes begun by foreign missionaries, sometimes originating as splinters from more traditional Protestant churches, these groups grew rapidly and now, particularly in Chile, Brazil, and Central America, outnumber the older churches. In some countries they constitute as much as 75 percent of Latin American Protestantism (exact figures being unavailable because Pentecostals are inimical to statistics).[3]

This movement from unbelief to faith among Pentecostals is expected to take place as a dramatic experience, sudden and overwhelming, frequently accompanied by impressive emotional manifestations. There is often crying and public confession, which gives place to peace, joy, and confidence. Conversion and the new birth are commonly identified with this experience; infant baptism (whether practiced or not, and almost irrespective of the official doctrine of the churches) is seldom seen in conjunction with regeneration.

Even when the emotional side of the experience receives great emphasis, the ethical side is never lost sight of and in certain churches tends to become central. Conversion, which turns the sinner into a believer, must result in a visibly new and different life. In a clear and decisive break with the old patterns of behavior, usually identified with drunkenness, sexual license, and dishonesty, the convert is expected to enter a new pattern characterized by a strong puritanism. This moralism, nevertheless, must not be mistaken for a purely formal, rigid, pharisaical legalism. It is often a joyous manifestation of the inner power of the new life, a consecration of the whole of life to the Lord of their faith. On the sociological level, at the same time, it is the zest of poor, but not the poorest, people seeking the kind of life which will help them to move up in the social ladder.

Evangelicalism has certain characteristics which become pronounced in Latin America in virtue of the minority character of the movement and the Roman Catholic milieu in which it grows. The first is biblicism. Wesley defined himself as a man of one book, and evangelicalism has always been strongly and consciously biblicist. But in Latin America the Bible was not simply a book of doctrine or a devotional guide. It was the basic tool for evangelism, the seed of the Church. Again and again a missionary traveled from place to place, leaving Bibles, New Testaments, and single books, and evangelical congregations sprang up in his trail and gathered around the Word of God.[4] Lay preachers, many times without theological or even secular education, became powerful evangelists, resting their authority solely on the Bible. The strong biblicism which characterizes Latin American Protestantism today traces its roots back, not so much to intellectual considerations as to this fundamental role of the Bible in the expansion of Protestantism.

A second trait is otherworldliness. Again, this has a theological root in the tradition of revivalism and a sociological root in the fact that the first Latin American Protestants belonged to the incipient urban or semiurban proletariat. The converts were people uprooted from the rural milieu or immigrants from Europe who had not yet found a place in the emerging social structures. They found a home in the fellowship of believers, and this community was foreign to the Roman Catholic environment. Conversion, moreover, meant a break with the past, not only with the realm of sin, immorality, and dishonesty but also with the poverty, dependence, and rejection in which they had lived. Heavenly otherworldliness was easily embraced by people who experienced earthly otherworldliness every day.

Finally, the polemic element latent in evangelicalism, with its nonconformist, antiestablishment, nonliturgical character, became a central feature of Latin American Protestantism. The particular type of Roman Catholicism which the early Protestants found in our continent, with its counter-reformation imprint, its inherited identification of religion and nationality, its frequently unenlightened and formalistic character and superstitious practices of the masses, gave impetus to a polemic trend which at the same time provided a ready-made target for controversy. Rejection, opposition, and sometimes persecution developed on one side; violent, indiscriminate denunciation, intolerance, and prejudice on the other. Controversial literature, preaching, and teaching made up a good portion of the Protestant output. Sometimes it was more sophisticated and focused on doctrinal issues like salvation by grace, transubstantiation and the sacrifice of the Mass, the doctrine of the clergy, or the superstitious practices of the faithful. As a significant by-product of this polemical attitude, many early Protestants received relatively full doctrinal instruction, buttressed by a thorough, if literal, knowledge of the Bible. Protestants were thus frequently able to present and defend their beliefs in a cogent and articulate way.

In our historical sketch we pointed out a "culturalist" wing in the early Protestant missions. It is through the missionaries of this orientation that the impact of theological liberalism was felt in Latin American Protestantism. Critical biblical and historical studies reached some of the seminaries. But more than that, the ethically oriented Ritschlian theology of the Kingdom of God, mainly in the American form of the Social Gospel, strongly influenced the preaching and teaching of some denominations (Methodists, Disciples of Christ, Presbyterians), particularly in the River Plate area and, less thoroughly, Chile, Brazil, and Cuba). It never went to the extremes of Modernism in Europe or the United States because it was controlled by and amalgamated with the evangelical churches.

This liberalism tended, nevertheless, to identify the Christian message and missions with political and cultural liberalism. Some of the concerns of the liberals, in the Latin American sense of the word, were education, freedom of thought and expression, and democracy. These seemed to Protestants the natural expression of the values of the Gospel, conceived in the famous phrase of Harnack as the universal fatherhood of God, the universal brotherhood of man, and the infinite dignity of the human person. These ideals appealed to them, both because of their inherent theological value and because they were the only protection they had in the Latin American society.

Liberalism took over the polemical bent of Latin American Protestantism but gave it a different emphasis. The ethical character of the Protestant religion was stressed as against the so-called formal, ritualistic piety of Catholicism. Free enquiry and judgment were opposed to so-called Catholic dogmatism and obscurantism. Autonomous decision and democracy were contrasted to Catholic authoritarianism and hierarchical structure; personal faith and commitment were extolled against a merely gregarious and inherited religion.

It would, nevertheless, be a mistake to think of the "evangelical" and the "culturalist" wings as two separate or clearly distinguishable movements. They were trends and tendencies which mixed in different proportions in churches, missionaries, and the faithful, sometimes without any consciousness of the contradictions involved in this mixture. But this did not last long. In Europe, and even more in the United States, the reaction against liberalism crystalized in the churches in a conservative stance which in the United States took the name of "fundamentalism." And this antiliberal struggle was transplanted to Latin America in the 1920's. It took first the form of a doctrinal battle against biblical criticism and the watering down of Christological and soteriological doctrine. It found a strong response, not because of its theological value, but for other reasons. It appealed to some of the roots of Latin American Protestantism: love of the Bible, the centrality of Christ the Savior, the experience of salvation, and the rejection of the world. Some of the churches, almost wholly dependent on their American or British origins, reflected the trends and fashions prevalent in them; it is interesting to note that fundamentalism is more intransigent in the less independent or indigenous churches. In the last two decades fundamentalism has appealed to anti-Communist sentiments, an approach quite effective in some middle-class groups. In this last connection we must remark that the fight against doctrinal liberalism tends to give place to the denunciation of political and theological liberalism (in the American sense of the word).

This fundamentalist-liberal conflict is the most conspicuous and damaging thing that is taking place in the theological realm in Latin American Protestantism. It is, in my judgment, a sterile and misguided debate. Fundamentalism fights, rightly in my view, against a naturalization of Christianity, against the progressive elimination of transcendence, miracle, divine sovereignty. Unfortunately it tries to carry on this struggle at the level of a literalistic biblicism which is not even specifically Christian. It has lost the sense of the relation of the Word with the living, active God whose Word fundamentalists try to defend. Liberalism fights, rightly in my view, against the narrowing of the Christian faith to the purely individual realm and to the afterlife. It calls for an active participation in society, for the abandonment of the pietistic ghetto, for the proclamation and realization of the social dimension of Christian redemption. Unfortunately (at least in its Social Gospel form) it tends to do this not in the name of what is central in the Gospel, namely, the person and work of Jesus Christ, but in the name of cultural and political liberalism or, lately, of a so-called "humanization," only thinly veiled by the appeal to certain teachings of Christ and the prophets, or to a fuzzy application of the doctrine of the Incarnation torn from the theological context of the Gospel.

This debate feeds on slogans and receives its impulse from centers of ecclesiastical—and even political and economic—power outside Latin America. It threatens to split not only the evangelical movement but the churches themselves into irreconcilable camps. It attempts to draw the strongest and most promising sector of Latin American Protestantism, the Pentecostals, into a theological debate which is neither relevant nor genuine. It prevents the birth of an indigenous theological activity, really biblical and evangelical in character, and relevant and vital for the Latin American churches and society. It limits the theological perspectives to a few subjects, and even these in a distorted way, and thus robs theology of its catholic amplitude. Very much depends, therefore, on whether Protestantism will be able, theologically, and ecclesiastically, to come out of this false liberal-fundamentalist dilemma into which it has been forced, mainly by outside forces.

I have already, in the last paragraphs, stepped out of my role as objective reporter and given a value judgment on the fundamentalist-liberal debate. I shall now engage myself even further by daring to speak of "signs of renewal" in the theological activity of Latin American Protestantism. I do not think we can as yet speak of "renewal" but only of influence and beginnings, the forerunners of what may become a meaningful vitalization of theological thought.

A first positive stimulus to theological renewal is the ever-increasing encounter of the different streams which constitute Latin American Protestantism and which had hitherto run parallel and independent courses. The traditional European communities of immigration and the more indigenous churches of the Anglo-Saxon evangelization are discovering each other as fellow Christians and partners in mission. In this encounter the former contribute the confessional emphasis, a more mature and catholic theological perspective, a more stable tradition, a fuller understanding of the Church, and a more positive relation to culture. The latter contribute their sense of missionary urgency, of a personal and militant faith, their freedom to experiment with new ways and forms. The encounter takes place in councils of churches, in the production of literature, in theological education through united seminaries or communities and associations of seminaries.

A second important form of meeting is to be found in the increasing contacts between the more traditional churches and the Pentecostal movements. The churches which used to look down upon and make efforts to disassociate themselves from these so-called "pentecostal sects" are beginning to show an interest in them and to make an effort to study and understand them in order to establish relations which may be fruitful to both. The studies begun in Chile, and the efforts of the theological community there, are a sign of this tendency. On the other hand, the Pentecostals, now reaching the second and third generation, are becoming aware of the need for a more articulate theological understanding of themselves. This encounter is again a promising sign for a theological renewal.

The ecumenical movement—whether under the aegis of the World Council of Churches or of the specialized ecumenical agencies, the Student Christian Movement, the YMCA and YWCA—has not always been welcome, particularly among the more conservative groups. But it exercises an undeniable influence and undoubtedly will have a more and more decisive impact. These new trends put Latin American Protestants in contact with currents of thought in other countries through representation in congresses and conferences. They offer a wealth of literature and a new vision of the responsibility and mission of the Church. These contacts provide a reservoir of ideas and materials to the young generation of Latin American Protestants and liberate them from a slavish dependence on the peculiarities of the missionary movement to which they happen to owe their existence.

Partly as a consequence of the influences mentioned above and partly through other channels, European theologians (particularly Barth and Brunner but also Bonhoeffer, Cullmann, Tillich, and Bultmann) are having a marked influence on the younger gen-

erations of Protestants in Latin America. It helps them to overcome the false dilemma of fundamentalism-liberalism and to
discover a theological perspective which is radically biblical and
open to scientific study, profoundly Christocentric and interested
in culture, thoroughly eschatological and conscious of the need
for concrete engagement in the area of social, economic, and
political thought and action. This theology offers a relation to
tradition, while it does not stifle freedom and creative adventure.
While it has not yet reached beyond the seminaries and some
small lay circles, it is growing in influence.

The birth of a neo-fundamenatalism in the United States will
undoubtedly bear fruit in the Latin American churches related
to these circles. While it is conscious of its orthodox tenets, this
new fundamentalism (represented by theologians like Bernhard
Ramm, Carnell, Hendry, and others) is theologically articulate
and alert, anxious to open and maintain a dialogue with other
theological tendencies, aware of the social dimension of the Gospel, and careful to maintain high academic standards in the
pursuit of theological studies. Again, some of the seminaries in
Latin America are bringing this revitalizing current to the
churches. Inasmuch as it becomes influential it will actively integrate the more conservative churches in the search for a theological understanding of the place and mission of Protestantism
in our continent.

Protestantism itself is reaching a new maturity at the level of
the third and fourth generations. At this point young people have
a sense of belonging to the life of the nation and culture in
which they have been born, while a longer tradition in the Protestant faith gives them a certain stability and a stronger sense of
security which makes it possible for them to venture upon new
ideas and experiments. The higher cultural and social status they
have achieved has destroyed some of their traditional prejudices
and given them a greater poise. If ecumenism has enhanced their
theological perspective, cultural belonging has opened the range
of questions and concerns to which they must and can apply
theological understanding.

Last, but not least, there is the Roman Catholic renewal. The existence of Protestantism in Latin America is conditioned by the Roman Catholic reality. In a certain sense Protestantism is, and must be, in Latin America a commentary, a footnote, to the Roman Catholic Church, a supplementary, explanatory, or a corrective footnote, but inevitably related to the text which it thus qualifies. Historical circumstances which we must acknowledge have made our relation one of mutual reaction. The possibility arises now of redeeming this relation and transforming it into a source of renewal, both for Roman Catholic and Protestant theology and action. It is still too early to know how this can be worked out. But contacts are multiplying very rapidly, and the possibility of a theology of dialogue, and not of simple confrontation, is now within view in Latin America. This new relation to Roman Catholicism will force Protestantism to face squarely some of the basic issues for a theological self-understanding. We will have to reconsider the nature of the Church and baptism, the diversity and unity of Protestantism, the relation of proclamation and proselytism, the nature and mission of a minority group, and many other questions to which some of the traditional answers now seem obsolete and irrelevant in the face of Roman Catholic renewal.

I should like to close by trying to point out what I understand to be the basic direction of Protestant theology in Latin America. I think the basic task, not only theological and not only Protestant, may be defined as the need for a "conversion to the world." Latin America is seeking the road to self-understanding and self-realization in all areas. It is not the task of Christianity to define the ways or to direct the process. But it is definitely its responsibility to contribute to it modestly through a theological reflection on the meaning of life, development, crisis, change, revolution, justice, freedom, peace, man, and society. It must reconsider all the elements and structures of the situation, not in the abstract but in the living conjunction of the message and experience of the Church and the given facts of the situation. Protestantism has a long way to go in order to be able to participate actively and responsibly in this task. And this is its first theological duty.

In order to fulfill this basic task responsibly it has to develop a rigorous academic and scientific discipline; it is not out of mere good will and enthusiasm that such a theological reflection can take place. It is necessary for Latin American Protestantism to overcome its anti-intellectualism, its mistrust of academic rigor, its distrust of specialists, its worship of mere numbers and immediately provable success.

If "conversion to the world" is the basic task, and scientific discipline is the presupposition, "ecumenical dialogue" is the method for the development of this theology. No true theology can be developed in isolation. This is especially true today in Latin America where, against the background of centuries of isolation or conflict, and in the presence of tragic problems of communication between groups and sectors of society, the "ecumenical dialogue," more than an instrument of theology, is a theological fact in itself, a first proclamation of the message of reconciliation, a way open to the world for the understanding and the acceptance of him in whom "all things are integrated."

NOTES

1. Ignacio Vergara, *El Protestantismo en Chile* (Santiago de Chile: Ediciones del Pacifico, 1962), p. 206.

2. Interesting evidences of this approach and its positive reception in the Latin American liberal milieu is gathered in George P. Howard, *Religious Liberty in Latin America?* (Philadelphia: Westminster Press, 1944).

3. A very reliable and careful study of Pentecostalism has been prepared as a doctoral dissertation in Basel by Prof. Hollenweger under the title *Handbuch de Pfingsterbewegung.* One volume of the seven-volume work is devoted to Latin America and will be published in Spanish and English in the near future.

4. The story of the distribution of the Bible and its influence in the formation of Latin American Protestantism is told in two books by the former secretary of the American Bible Society, Charles Turner, *La Biblia construye en America Latina* (Buenos Aires: "La Aurora," 1954) and *La Biblia en America Latina* (Buenos Aires: "La Aurora," 1950).

Indigenous Expressions
of Protestantism

KEY YUASA

It is my task and privilege to speak about more recent and popular forms of Protestantism in Latin America today. They may be referred to as indigenous expressions of Protestantism because

They have no relationships to missions abroad.

If they have relationships, they are of a fraternal nature, and not of dependence or subordination. They are autonomous and govern themselves.

They are self-supporting.

They expand rather spontaneously with their own resources in funds and in personnel.

Culturally, the expression of Christian Faith and corporate life seem to be not foreign, but close to people's ways. Their singing, musical instruments, and rituals have certain kinship with their folkways.

These churches, especially strong in Chile, Mexico, and Brazil, are noteworthy for their phenomenal growth, which by far surpasses the prevalent demographic explosion, and also for the terms of comparison which they represent to other Protestant groups.[1]

How Do These Churches Get Started?

Let me tell a story which is very illustrative. In a small, traditionally Roman Catholic village in São Paulo, Brazil, there has been for a long time a chapel where the priest of the neighboring church comes for monthly Mass and pastoral work. Major problems on the personal and family level had been a lack of regular work, drunkenness, and fights. Religious festivals, pilgrimages, and the like very often ended in fights and drunkenness. The people were in great need, and the priest was too busy in this parish to give sufficient attention to them.

One of the women of this place, whose husband José used to beat her after drinking, in desperation bought a book which was not particularly evangelical, but which she thought might bring her some light, some orientation. She never read it, but one day her husband found it in a drawer and looked through it. The only thing he remembered reading was: "In the last days there shall come a people which shall announce the Gospel of God." This man said to himself, "I shall wait for this people to come." Time passed and the next religious propagandist to come along was a Pentecostal evangelist. He visited the houses, prayed for the sick, and announced the Word after reading the Bible. An old woman who had been sick for a long time was healed in these days, and the fame of the evangelist grew. People started to come more to his meetings.

The man who was in expectation of something to come listened, too, and was converted to Jesus Christ. He understood his sins were forgiven on account of the Sacrifice of the Cross. Later on he wrote: "The Unknown God was revealed to me at the Cross. Glory, glory, Jesus has saved me!" He stopped drinking and fighting at home, and eventually asked to be baptized again. Ten or fifteen more people were converted, and a small worshipping community was started in that place.

One day the people discovered that the evangelist who announced the Gospel to them was not very honest about his Christian life. He preached but did not practice what he said. And worse, one day he disappeared, never to be seen again, and with him went all the money that the people had gathered. What happened then? The people were distressed, but not defeated. Their faith had been put in Jesus Christ, not in the visiting evangelist. The group of laymen decided that they would continue the worship. One of them, a natural leader, became the pastor, the lay pastor, and re-established contact with the church that had sent the evangelist. The community prospered, and about half of the village, where some eighty families live, became members of the church.

In the neighboring town it was amazing to find what a positive assessment the Catholic storekeepers, teachers, and police had of the *creentes* in that area. They were punctual in their payments; they were eager to send their children to school; they collaborated with the government when there was an increase in taxes. According to a politician they were a little naive politically. And his wife, owner of the pharmacy, was somewhat worried because the priest himself of the town used to pay compliments to the honesty, discipline, and good will of these converts to the evangelical faith. The local sheriff said: "I consider them my best collaborators, for 90 percent of my problems here are related to people who drink a lot. And the '*creentes*' do not drink and help people to get rid of the vice."

After the service in the chapel that evening we went home to the house of the lay pastor. As he sat, he asked his wife to bring him the guitar and the notebooks. He had written, in shaky script, songs and unpublished hymns which he sang to a tune he had devised.

José had become not only the lay pastor of the church but also administrator of the local government's forest and supervisor of eighty workers in the reforestation plant. In that position he was teaching his workers to read and write because he was becoming aware of the power of the vote. The church had already branched out in five different directions in neighboring towns and villages, where regular meetings were held.

I hope this story is illustrative enough to show the way the message of the Gospel, brought to this place by such imperfect means, has been able to give vision of a new life, a new community life, and an interior discipline necessary for work and life in society. This sort of example might be multiplied hundreds and perhaps thousands of times.

But is not Pentecostal understanding of the Gospel and of the Church very elementary, and even heretical? Are not they too sectarian minded? Dr. Eugene Nids, secretary of the American Bible Society, has noted how by and large the indigenous churches in Latin America tend to be of the Pentecostal type. Bishop L. Newbigin of the Church of South India, for a long time officer of the World Council of Churches, has noted how the Pentecostal view of the Church is indicative of one aspect of the nature of the Church, alongside the Protestant and the Catholic, and how it has many good biblical groundings.[2] As the name indicates, these churches believe that the event of Pentecost, the outpouring of the Spirit on the Apostles which gave birth to the Christian Church, is not only a past phenomenon. The receiving of the Holy Spirit is not only for Jews but also for Gentiles, not only for the Jew and Gentile of apostolic times but also for Christians everywhere and in all times. The Holy Spirit shall lead them into all Truth, shall illumine their hearts and minds in order to understand the words of the Bible. He will also give Christians the gifts of the Spirit, which are the word of science, wisdom, faith, healing, wonders, prophecy, discernment of spirits, the gift of tongues, and interpretation of tongues. The Spirit shall also give the Church the fruits of the Spirit, which are love, joy, peace, long-suffering, gentleness, good faith, meekness, temperance (Gal. 5:22).[3]

In certain Bible institutes of the Pentecostal Church in Latin America, systematic theology is taught. The whole system of biblical teaching is organized in order to give prominence to the doctrine of the Holy Spirit and his active presence in the Church's worship, in corporate prayer, in singing, and in evangelization. Very often Pentecostal ministers do not have degrees from schools of theology. They do not have volumes of Bible commentary, and they do not have a long tradition to defend them. But they live in the confidence that the Holy Spirit is guiding them and shall teach and reveal anything they really need to know. The definition of what the Church is in conceptual terms is less important for them than is the experience which with overwhelming joy they have had of forgiveness of their sins, of belonging to a living Christian community which announces the Word, convinces the sinner, and goes forth with enthusiasm and power to the streets of the villages, praying for the sick, expelling bad spirits, and baptizing.

The Church in the state of mission has an intuition that is part of the Church of the Living Christ, where Christ is not only present through the minister, the Word, and the sacraments but is also present in members to make them alive and to give them words of prophecy, thanksgiving, and praise. The minister who directs the service is not necessarily the main depository of the Holy Spirit, but he is the one sensitive to the presence of the Spirit and leads the service so that the manifestation of the Spirit may be orderly.

It is common to say that one cannot understand the religious situation in Latin America without taking into account the influences of African and Indian gods, myths, and magic which are often present in a syncretistic way in popular Catholicism, in spiritism, and so on. On the other hand, some relationships between Pentecostalism and African religiosity have been noted by different authors, in its origin in the United States as well as in developments in Africa and Latin America.[4]

Can we say, then, that Pentecostalism is well equipped to face the world of a more primitive sort of religiosity? My observations tend to indicate that the more traditional Protestants rebuke these beliefs and practices as superstitions. The Pentecostalists, because of their belief in bad spirits and angels (they take literally the words of the Gospels without looking for more sophisticated psychological or sociological rationalizations), seem to be just in the midst of the turmoil in order to fight against the bad spirits, face to face, with the Spirit. The best example of this I have seen, in the Apostolic Church, is the fact that an important part of the service consists in prayer for the sick and exorcisms.

If enough time and attention were given to this subject, we

might arrive at the conclusion that the way in which Pentecostalists live with and deal with the Spirit is a sort of demythologizing of the world of spirits. It is a world feared by people because it is uncontrollable. It is a world which pushes them to look for any sort of remedy if there is some hope of solution. Perhaps this explains why Pentecostalism has become an indigenous movement in Latin America, and how indigenous forms of Protestantism tend to take the Pentecostal form.

In the northwestern part of Mexico City there is a community which has built a whole *colonia* close to the city. The land in this area, consisting of some twenty blocks, was purchased by them. Here they have built a community of *hermanos*. Everybody is supposed to work and produce, but if someone is in need, the community will take care of him. Many are starting to work in the city on regular jobs. People who come from rural areas can learn and adapt themselves to urban life first in this community. The group has become politically minded because the local politicians have discovered the importance of gaining the votes of these 5,000 citizens who vote like one man.

The 25 congregations of a Pentecostal church in Santiago de Chile have 150 lay preachers and one pastor who trains them in Bible classes every week. In a church in the São Paulo area, which has no paid ministers, there are 200 congregations with only 26 lay-consecrated "elders" who are entitled to baptize. These 200 congregations have a belief which bring the people together for baptisms, for social relief programs, and for weekly Wednesday worship services. The rest of the week is planned so that neighboring congregations avoid having services on the same day. It is as if one saw in 200 congregations just one rhythm of gathering and scattering in all parts of the city. The central congregation is regularly packed with 5,000 to 7,000 people three times a week.

By and large the indigenous type of churches in Latin America tend to look at the things of this world as vanities. They sense the imminence of the second coming of Our Lord Jesus Christ and therefore tend to avoid political questions and involvement in social issues. Despite this, and perhaps because they are forced many times by circumstances, they are becoming aware of political realities. Some of their church members, and even pastors, are starting to be elected to public office. In other cases we see many entering trade unions, and slowly the second and third generations of Christians of these churches are starting to attend secondary schools and universities. Changes are to be expected.

NOTES

1. Pe. Ignacio Vergara, *El Protestantismo en Chile* (Santiago, many ed.) and William R. Read, *New Patterns of Church Growth in Brazil* (Grand Rapids, Mich.: Eerdmans, 1965).

2. L. Newbigin, *The Household of God* (London, SCM Press).

3. About glossolalia Morton T. Lelsey, *Tongue Speaking, An Experiment in Spiritual Experience* (Garden City, New York: Doubleday, 1964) with excellent bibliography, and Carl Brumback, *What Meaneth This?* (Springfield, Mass.: Gospel Publishing House, 1946).

4. Jan-Heinz Jahn, *Muntu* (London: Faber & Faber, Ltd., 1961).

Protestants and the Process
of Integration

JORGE LARA-BRAUD

For the typical Protestant in Latin America the central reality of
his life is conversion. By that he understands a turning away
from a "worldly" to an "evangelical" existence. The language he
uses to denote the experience is highly significant. A Latin American Protestant seldom or never speaks of conversion to Protestantism or to any of its varieties. It is rather conversion to the
Gospel, to the Evangel ("Cuando me converti al Evangelio").
Strange as it may sound to a Catholic audience, such language
implies the absence of the Gospel in one's previous religious
experience. It also implies the convert's intention to live hence-
forth with other believers in conformity to the Gospel. For that
reason he prefers to be known as an *evangelico* rather than as
a *protestante*.

Becoming or remaining an *evangelico* is of necessity the repudiation of the old order. The language of evangelism, catechesis,
preaching, and pastoral care abounds in biblical references to the
distinction between believers and unbelievers, the Church and
the world, light and darkness, holiness and sinfulness. It also
abounds in graphic contemporary illustrations of the consequences

of living under the sway of the world. The allusions are almost always to personal vices and immorality: smoking, dancing, drinking, gambling, philandering, cheating, quarreling, and so on. The appeal is, in any case, to legitimize one's conversion by a life free from these sins and adorned by the fruits of the Spirit. Where this understanding of the new life prevails, the result is an extraordinary personal transformation, but also a great renunciation of the world.

Most converts to Latin American Protestantism have come and continue to come from the poorer classes, where the inequalities of society are felt in their most oppressive form. In the evangelical communities they have found an egalitarian fellowship in which they matter, in which spiritual endowment, a disciplined life, and evangelistic zeal are put above one's position in the world. It is not surprising to find today, especially in the older churches, a substantial number in professional and managerial occupations who trace their remarkable upward mobility to such humble but liberating beginnings one, two, or three generations back. Protestant apologists insist, naturally, that there is a causal relationship between conversion to the Gospel and personal accomplishment, between renunciation of the world and success in the world.

It will come as no surprise to many of you that many of us loyal Latin American *evangelicos* view this success with mixed feelings. For one thing it sanctifies a simplistic scheme of "life in the Gospel" versus "life in the world" which fails to see the social dimension of God's Good News for the world, and which creates a pharisaical separatism from the very ones whom the Gospel calls us to serve. It is simply not true that conversion to the Gospel, genuine though it may be, puts an end to man's sin or to his solidarity with the world. Indeed, because of the Gospel there is a new sensitivity to one's own sin and a corresponding tolerance of the sin of others. Luther's description of the Christian is far more accurate: *simul peccator et justus*. Moreover the business of the Gospel is reconciliation, not alienation. To be sure, the Bible speaks of the saints, the separated ones, but as those set aside and equipped to be God's servants in the world.

Holiness is not a display of virtues to shame one's neighbor into repentance; it is rather a new life pressed into his service.

One of the most tragic consequences of Protestant separatism has been its rejection of the Roman Catholic Church as a major symbol and ally of that traditional order repudiated in the experience of conversion. Protestantism, particularly the United States variety, arrived in Latin America deeply colored by anti-Catholicism. The arrival of the first missionaries in the mid-nineteenth century coincided with the virulent Protestant American nativism which resorted even to acts of violence to stem the so-called popish tide from southern and eastern Europe in an attempt to keep the United States predominantly white, Anglo-Saxon, and Protestant. What we now regard as historic denominations framed at the time doctrinal statements to prove the apostasy of the Roman Church. As early as 1835, and again in 1845, the General Assembly of the Presbyterian Church, the most theologically sophisticated denomination at that time, declared the Roman Catholic Church apostate, and as such without valid sacraments. (To the credit of the Presbyterians, their most prestigious theologian, Charles Hodge of Princeton, vigorously criticized the statement of the kind of sectarianism which Luther and Calvin would most assuredly condemn.)

The first, and most subsequent, Protestant conversions took place within the framework of this forbidding theological prejudice exported by well-meaning missionaries. Repudiation of the Roman Catholic Church was further justified by its glaring contradictions and by the endless acts of hostility against Protestants instigated or permitted by Church authorities. Survival, and even growth, in this life and death struggle strengthened Protestants in the conviction of God's vindication of them as his true people. It is ironic that the very same historic churches which taught anti-Catholicism to their Latin American converts have been among the leading advocates today of a rapprochement with Rome through the ecumenical movement, a praiseworthy initiative which their Latin American sister churches are understandably slow to grasp or to emulate.

If by integration we mean full participation in the shaping of a national and even a hemispheric order, and if our attention is drawn to the possibilities of such participation by Latin American Protestants, it is essential that we look further into the past and at its remnants in the present. It may well be that the key to Protestant participation in the process of integration in Latin America may lie with the progressive initiatives of the reforming sector of the Roman Catholic Church.

The pluralistic nature of Latin American society is strikingly recognized at this Conference by your kind invitation to four of us as speakers representing Latin American Protestantism, and by the presence as active participants here of many other Protestant brethren in some way related to Latin America. The vast majority of Protestants south of the Rio Grande, however, still adhere to the misconception that the Roman Catholic Church claims Latin America as its exclusive domain, repudiating, as always, though less openly now, the presence of Protestant churches and missions. Perhaps the traumas of the past, and unimaginative ecumenical approaches, account for continuing distrust. It is deplorable to discover how many Latin American Protestants, especially those with relatively fresh memories of religious harassment, dismiss talk of Roman Catholic renewal as a clever smoke screen to disguise the same old, irreformable stand against them. Before we write them off as incurable fanatics, a question is in order: What tangible evidence have they seen that a new day, a true *aggiornamento*, has arrived? We Protestants who are here have seen those evidences and gratefully acknowledge them. With Roman Catholic prelates, priests, and laymen we have opened the pages of Scripture, have prayed together, have exchanged petitions for mutual forgiveness, have been thrilled together to read those magnificent, truly evangelical declarations of the Second Vatican Council on the Church, on ecumenism, on religious freedom, and have dared to plan together for the transformation of our societies in the light of the Gospel. It is far less difficult to talk about the process of integration in Latin America when we begin with the previous powerful experience of integration in Christ.

Protestants do not have to continue to be marginal to Latin

American life to be true to their proverbial conversion to the Gospel, nor must they confine the powers of the converted life to personal fulfillment. Perhaps their beleaguered history has robbed them of that openness toward the world where a genuinely free decision can be made between the keeping of life which is death and the losing of it for the sake of Christ and the Gospel which is the true gaining of life. As long as they are forced by theology or circumstances to live their life in isolation from a world clamoring for newness, their major contribution will continue to be kidnapping of converts in a tacit disengagement from the solidarity of less virtuous Christians and men of good will who struggle to bring about a new order for all.

Recent signs are encouraging. Take for instance the declaration of the Presbyterian Church of Colombia, with a long history of persecution and suffering. At its July, 1966, meeting it publicly declined to take any part in a forthcoming Eucharistic Congress to be held in Columbia to which, according to the press, Protestants were being invited. It went on record, however, declaring that

. . . the Presbyterian Church of Colombia expresses its good will and prompt decision to work together with all Christians in our country, and especially with the Roman Catholic Church, in all efforts aimed at putting into practice the spirit and letter of Christianity in the social, political, and economic spheres where misery and suffering is caused for the great majority of our Columbian neighbors. In all these forms of practical Christianity, we believe that the cooperation of all Christians is not only convenient but required in the moment in which we are living. (Quoted in the *Reformed and Presbyterian World*, Vol. XXIX, No. 4, December, 1966, p. 181.)

Only those of us acquainted with the appalling animosity prevailing until recently between Protestants and Catholics in Colombia can begin to fathom the significance of this statement. It is in effect a call to integration in terms of responding to urgent national needs, apart from being also a tacit recognition that without the mobilization of the Roman Catholic Church the efforts of Protestants are severely limited.

A similar sign of the right kind of integration is the attitude of Protestants in northeast Brazil as Dom Hélder Cámara, Archbishop of Recife, faced recently the irresponsible charges of communism leveled at him by the army commander of that region. Note the ardent statement of solidarity signed by some 120 Protestant laymen and clergymen, many of whom had formerly been rabidly anti-Roman Catholic:

Faithful to the Biblical Spirit, and in accordance with the imperatives of a Christian conscience, we wish to affirm our solidarity with Father Hélder Cámara and the other Roman Catholic representatives for their stand . . . in the struggle against oppression and for the sake of justice toward those who are oppressed and persecuted. We call upon all Christians to close ranks for a watchful resistance against the dictatorial acts which disrupt the life of our country. (*Carta Latinoamericana,* Vol. II, No. 7, P.R.)

Let me close upon a note of hope. Any convincing initiative expressive of the commitment to a new and more humane order, especially if it is inspired by the Gospel's concern for the dispossessed, strikes a responsive chord in the heart of all true *evangelicos.* In personal and congregational life they have aimed to make good the words of the Apostle: "Whoever is in Christ, he is a new creation. The old has passed away. Behold all has become new." No sincere Christian—Protestant, Roman Catholic, or Orthodox—can be expected to integrate himself into an order obviously in contradiction with Christ's love for the "least of His brethren." There is a sense in which the integration of Christians to society must always be marked by that certain eccentricity which allows for commitment but also for detachment. Latin America desperately needs Christians committed as much to full participation in national life as to courageous condemnation of its injustices. I have the impression that history has peculiarly prepared the majority of the ten million or more Latin American Protestants to play precisely this dialectic role in integration. They wait upon the encouragement of their more influential brethren of the Roman Catholic Church.

Justice, Development, and Peace: Our Joint Christian Concern

ROBERT BILHEIMER

My colleagues in the National Council of Churches and I deeply appreciate the opportunity to participate in this important inquiry. We note with gratitude the reference to "our joint Christian concern" in the title that was given to this discussion, a phrase surrounded with overtones suggesting that "our joint Christian concern" about Latin America may be assumed as an axiom. I assure you that we shall do everything we can to put power and reality into the fine assumption that our concern for Latin America is one that we hold together as Christians.

If we are to move forward with our joint Christian concern for inter-American justice, development, and peace, what shall we do? The suggestions I have to offer for consideration are based upon three fundamental factors. It is my view that whatever practical work we may as Christians do together, it will have to arise out of the point where these three basic, given factors intersect.

The first concerns Latin America, the continent, the countries, and the peoples in it. In this vast continent there is a desperate need for rapid social change. The concentration of wealth and power in the hands of a very few, the prevalence of poverty and a marginal social and political situation among the many, have produced a situation in which human beings cannot live with dignity. The dependence of Latin American economies upon circumstances and powers external to themselves means that significant changes within Latin America will be delayed unless there is change in the relationship between the Latin American countries and those outside, notably the United States. A human being cannot live with dignity unless he possesses the resources and power to do so. Men who do not have the resources and power to achieve dignity, who live in a hopeless and powerless dependence upon the few, are trapped. Their state of dependence denies them spiritual power, and poverty, with all its evils, debilitates both mind and body. The same is true of nations. Interdependence is a good thing; dependence is a bad thing for the dignity of the human person. That is why the overriding need in Latin America is for rapid social change.

There is more than need. There is also the fact of rapid social change in Latin America. If structures in many Latin American countries have not changed as rapidly or as radically as is required, there is nearly everywhere the movement of change. It is in the minds of people. Social change is the objective of specific movements and organizations found both outside and within traditional institutions. Some voices call stridently for revolution at any cost. Others work with an extraordinary combination of passion and "coolness" to achieve the fundamental technological, industrial, and political conditions of which open, dynamic societies are made. There is need for rapid social change in Latin America, but rapid social change is also a fact.

The second fundamental factor concerns the United States as the participant in a situation which is intolerable from the viewpoint of Christian conscience. The best tradition of our country, the tradition of which as Christians we are most proud, stands for "freedom and justice for all." Our country was built by men who longed for freedom and who established it here. We have worked and struggled to achieve a tolerable justice. We have proclaimed to the world that we stand for freedom and for justice. The best of the United States tradition is not imperialistic. Yet today, in 1967, three situations cause men around the world to wonder. One of these is the race situation at home. Our national laws proclaim racial freedom and justice. But the present situation forces many to ask whether the white American has any intention of creating the integrated society which justice and the civil rights laws require. The racial situation has always been a contradiction of our claims about liberty and justice. Today the contradition is even sharper precisely because the more we try, the more the hardness of the white heart is revealed.

A second situation is in Vietnam. We fight there in the name of freedom, and many men and governments accept this. Yet many other men, even in the friendly countries of Asia, begin to wonder whether this massive military operation reveals a devotion to freedom or a determination to enforce our national will in Asia at a moral and human cost which is too high? Third is our relation to Latin America. The fact is that nowhere in our history has the best in the American tradition been so distorted, ignored, and corrupted over so long a period as in the case of our relations with Latin Americans. In view of our military, political, economic, and even ecclesiastical practices in Latin America—not merely in the present or recent past, but over a long period—it is little wonder that Latin Americans find themselves confronted with a credibility gap when they hear us speak of liberty and justice. Our wealth in a world of poverty presents our joint Christian concern, our common Christian conscience, with a profound issue. As we face Latin America, we are not confronted with the mere adjustment of our relationships with them. We are confronted with a long institutionalized history of relationships in which the prevailing pattern profoundly contradicts the best of our own national tradition. This is the more serious because Latin American relations are not the only place today in which these contradictions are apparent.

A third given factor in our joint concern for Latin America is of a different sort. It concerns the Church. We might proceed to ask at once how the churches should respond to the need for rapid social change in Latin America and to the need for a changed relationship between the United States and Latin America. If we were to answer that question now, without reference to this third factor that I have in mind, I fear that there would be—humanly speaking—little hope. In all probability the churches would respond as they have before, divided among themselves and, on the whole, supporters of the status quo in Latin America. But there is now a new dimension, a new reality in the life of Christians and their churches. And in our concern about Latin America this is the third basic factor in the situation.

In our time the general community of believing Christians throughout the world—the Church in this great, broad sense—has been blessed by a fresh movement of the Spirit of God. This is a movement in which the divine purpose of the Father for the history of his human family has broken afresh into our narrow ecclesiastical purposes. It is a movement in which we see in a new way the radical distinction between the Son of God and the sin of the world—the utter devastating and saving difference between God-in-Christ and the depths of evil in which mankind lives. It is a movement in which we feel the power of the Spirit calling us Christians together and thrusting us into the processes of human history as co-workers with God. This is the ecumenical movement of the twentieth century. The various organizations, stages of development, theologies, and personalities associated with the ecumenical movement as we know it should never be confused with the fundamental reality. At its deepest level the ecumenical movement is a spiritual reality in which we have a sense of living together in one Body, being obedient to one Lord, and serving one world.

Our task in Latin America is defined by the interplay of these three basic, given factors: the need for change in Latin America, the need for change in American attitudes and practices, and our common calling in Christ. Reflecting upon these matters, the Assembly of the National Council of Churches voted last December to concentrate the attention of its member churches upon four general subjects, of which world poverty, economic development, and justice was the first. As the Assembly did so, and with Latin America having been specifically called to mind, the Assembly commented:

Once-bold plans for true development seem to have shrunk into props for the status quo; in many nations the United States is viewed as the protector

of the status quo, and not the champion of freedom from the poverty we
ourselves abhor. Private investment too frequently does little to produce a
development that benefits the country concerned. Trade barriers remain.
Many countries are at the mercy of a price for their crops, raw materials, and
products over which they have little or no control. The basic point is that
vision, drive, and will seem to be lacking in our people, our church people,
and our government. National self-interest rides too high, and concern for
justice is low. One issue, of course, is the amount of money which is needed
for economic development, and the willingness of the U.S.A. to provide its
generous share. But the deeper issues concern the attitude of the American
people, the basic purpose of our nation in relation to this part of the world,
and the readiness of the United States to take any needed and sound action
for the correction of this injustice. The goal of justice requires us to transform mere self-interest by the dimension of sacrifice for the common good.
To that task, we propose that the churches put their hand with vigor, imagination, and competence.

And the Assembly added, "We shall need to join hands where
possible with brethren of the Roman Catholic Church."

I suggest that this means three things for our task in the United
States as it relates to Latin America. The first task concerns our
policy, the content of our Christian witness. The central issue is,
What should be our Christian response in the United States to
the need and fact of rapid social change in Latin America? Some
may ask, Why rapid change? Why, for instance, is not evangelism
our central witness? I would reply that evangelism, the proclamation of the Gospel, is our central witness, but that today the
decisive—not the only, but the decisive—proclamation of the Gospel must be in those terms which clearly affect men's lives. Those
terms are social. A Christian witness amid rapid social change, a
Christian witness in relation to rapid social change, and, where
there is gross injustice, a Christian witness that helps to produce
rapid social change is the decisive Christian witness. It is true that
we are by no means clearly and generally agreed on the content
of our Christian response to rapid social change in Latin America.
We must hammer that out. As we do, let us remember our common calling as God's Spirit moves afresh within the Christian
communities of our day. Let us strive to transcend a merely Protestant, or Eastern Orthodox, or Roman Catholic witness and
policy; let us transcend a policy merely of American Christians

or merely of Latin American Christians. Let us listen to one another, responsive to the Spirit who leads and gathers all the children of the Father. And let us do another thing as we formulate our witness. Let us not, citizens of a wealthy country and members of wealthy churches as we are, think merely of doing something for Latin America. Let us seek to respond to the social situation in Latin America freely, as God would have us do.

A second task concerns the education of our own church people. None of us needs to be told that our church people need education on matters of international affairs generally and Latin America in particular. Nor is it my purpose to exhort us all to do better along this line. A major aim of the International Affairs Program of the National Council of Churches is to improve and extend the educational efforts of the churches in international affairs. As we do so, I am confident that we shall have to come to grips with the major question of what our view of the world is to be.

I believe that educational work in our churches will amount to little unless ways are found to deal with this underlying question. What do our church members think the world is like? Do they think that the United States is the biggest and best nation in the world and that the sooner everyone is like us the better? Do they think that the world is divided between the good guys (us) and the bad guys (the Communists) and that everything should be done and judged accordingly? Do they think that the poor in the world are poor because they are lazy and will therefore probably always waste money and resources? Do they think that the Latin American world is a mixture of gauchos, juntas, revolutions, exotic women, and here and there a tourist spot? What kind of a picture of the world do people have within which to formulate their Christian obedience? I suggest that especially in the field of international affairs our thought and our educational work are dependent upon the picture we hold of the world in which we live.

A basic part of our educational task with church members surely lies here. For a Christian the ultimate understanding of the world is theological—the world created by God, fallen into sin, redeemed by Christ, and destined to a glorious consummation in the purpose of God. But this theological knowledge of the world must be carefully, relevantly, sensitively, connected to the world of today as it is. There is the crux of the matter. If Christians look at today's world, at today's Latin America, with prejudices or stereotypes, or half-truths, or mere tradition, they are wrong. The educational task is to help Christians see Latin America as it is and to respond to what they see in the light of the Gospel. That will rouse controversy; it will be costly; it may be painful to many. But it must be done.

Third, we must undertake action in the United States in relation to Latin America. What can we do? Vast economic and political powers are so entrenched as to make it seem all but hopeless for Christians to make any impact at all. To contemplate action seems little more than quixotic. Nevertheless, I think that there is action that can be effective. Action implies power. A Christian relies upon spiritual power and ultimately has no other. How may he use it? He may use it by passing resolutions in meetings; he may cry out from the housetop, street corner, or pulpit; he may organize ecclesiastical power. But there is another way in which Christians may behave so that the power of the Gospel is unleashed. Christians may create and engage in dialogue with the right people, on the right issue, and at the right time. Dialogue: a situation in which people struggle together to listen, to hear what God asks of them, and thus to try to discover the right thing to do. The right people for the dialogue: those who have power in the economic and political processes that affect Latin America. The right issue: rapid social change and the relation of the United States to it. The right time: now. There are hundreds, nay, thousands of laymen in our churches who have influence and power in relation to Latin America. Should we not create situations in which they confront the need for rapid social change in Latin America and in which they may listen afresh to the word of God in what they do? Those will be situations in which Latin Americans must be present to help us see Latin America as it is. And is it not likely that Europeans, especially those with experience in the Common Market, will be of great value in this coming dialogue?

What might be the subjects of this dialogue? Consider two illustrations. First, the total investment from the United States in

Latin America is at present about 13 billion dollars. What is the net impact of this investment? Does it work to produce the social change in Latin America in which human dignity grows, or does it tend to freeze a social situation in which human dignity is stifled? Sociological fact and economic figures may well show that in fact the aggregate United States investment in Latin America does not help to produce a healthy social change or does so to too small a degree. Christians thus have to ask themselves if it is right to acquiesce in that situation? Second, consider the issue of freedom. There are three alternatives, broadly speaking. First, it is possible to use our economic and political power in Latin America so as to increase our own freedom at home—that is exploitation, and we are doubtless not free of it. Second, we in the United States may view Latin America as a sphere in which to use our power to spread our distinctive American concept of freedom— that is the way of imperialism. Nor are we free of that. Or we may view Latin America (and other developing continents) as a place in which men secure the freedom to be free, to be themselves, to achieve their own particular form of dignity, and we may use our power to help them do so. The issue of freedom is fundamental in our relationships with Latin America. Should our dialogue not be about that?

With whom should this great dialogue be held, and in what context? A recent catalogue lists 2,500 American firms in commerce, industry, and finance doing business in Latin America. By 1975 it is estimated that one out of every one hundred Americans will spend part of his working life in Latin America. The same catalogue lists twenty-two UN agencies, twenty-seven Latin American development agencies, and forty-two agencies of the United States Government (of which one is the Alliance for Progress) operating in Latin America. Beyond these are thousands of intergovernmental, educational, agricultural, religious, labor, communications, philanthropic foundations, and professional organizations connected with Latin America. In all of these organizations there are thousands of Christians. Should dialogue about Christian response to Latin America not begin with them as they live, work, and plan in regard to Latin America? Here, I suggest, is a vast area of Christian witness, largely untapped. Surely it belongs to our joint responsibility to see to it that the Christians in these institutions become leaven and salt, in the name of Christ, in relationship to what they do in Latin America.

If we must work as American Christians in the United States we must also have a task in Latin America. For we are deeply involved, in our church life and through our missions, with the churches in Latin America. Therefore, we must speak strongly to ourselves, and act decisively among ourselves, in regard to the churches and rapid social change in Latin America. Where our piety has become a mere pietism, we must broaden it; where the paternalism of Christians increases dependence and hinders Christian freedom, we must reform; where (whatever specific confession or tradition) ecclesiastical alliances with power support the status quo, we must disengage.

The new, fresh winds of God's Spirit that we all feel in the Church call us to a re-examination of our mission in Latin America. I believe that will require us to see it as our mission to help create social change in Latin America, not to hide from it, nor to be on the side of the status quo. The conclusion seems to me inescapable: the churches and missionary agencies in Latin America must use every opportunity to help create those centers of power in Latin American social structures which will produce social change and contribute to the growth of responsible society.

We are in an historic moment of theological and spiritual openness. This is a treasured development, but ultimately it will be of little avail unless it leads to a common mission. That mission is to enter together into the purpose of God in human history to co-work with him in the affairs of men according to his ways that are not our ways. God is breaking us open to do that. I believe that in Latin America God is breaking open a society too long closed. Let us work together to break open every frozen situation of injustice in Latin America and in our own country's relations with Latin America for the purpose of securing that rapid social change which will enable men, with true dignity, to exercise their responsibility to one another, to the community, and to God.

PART FOUR

THE NATIONAL LEVEL

National Social-Economic Structures

ERNEST BARTELL, C.S.C.

When the subject of integration is applied to economic life, perhaps the most familiar area of concern that comes to mind is the subject of international economic integration. The goals, the effects, and the problems associated with the role of international trade in economic development, along with the problems associated with new structures such as common markets and free-trade areas, are perennial subjects of analysis by economists.

All of the attention directed toward institutional experiments to achieve international economic integration might easily overshadow the questions of domestic economic integration that remain nonetheless basic and essential to the achievement of goals of economic development. In this paper we shall attempt to outline some of the needs for and problems of domestic integration, particularly the problems of integrating the masses of people into the development process, that must be met if the developing economies of Latin America are to realize their growth potential under the economic and social constraints they now face. The economies of Latin America, of course, differ one from the other, so the problems raised here will not be equally applicable to every nation. Nevertheless as economic development increases the interdependence of nations, the domestic problems of one nation become the international problems of another, so that each does have a stake in the domestic development of the other.

In recent years stress has been placed on the importance for Latin America of involving the masses of people in the process of modernization and development. From political commentators like Victor Alba[1] to social movements like *Promoción Popular*[2] the recurrent theme is one of involvement of the people in the process of political and social change. What I would like to suggest here is that integration of the masses of people into the development process is not only defensible on moral, social, and political grounds but is also highly rational in terms of the conventional economic analysis of achieving goals of efficient maximization of output and income and optimal growth rates.

At one time domestic economic development may have been defined almost exclusively in terms of industrialization. Growth was synonymous with increases in the output of factories, mines, and steel mills. In a typical classical free-market model of development, industrialization depended upon the growth of an elite, an entrepreneurial middle class which would organize and promote this process of industrialization.[3] The engine of growth was, of course, the accumulation of capital by the entrepreneurial class out of the savings from profits earned in industry and commerce. High rates of capital accumulation depended upon the maintenance of high industrial and commercial profits, which in turn depended upon low costs of production.

The principal cost of production in this elementary model was the cost of wages, which could be pegged at subsistence levels as long as the supply of labor remained relatively unlimited, presumably through migration from the subsistence or traditional rural sector of the economy. The monetary value of wages at the subsistence level was seen to depend upon the cost of living in the modern sector, particularly upon the price of food. Hence, low food prices meant low wage rates, low costs of production, increased profit, saving, capital accumulation, and growth.[4]

Attention in rudimentary forms of this growth model was

directed to the traditional sector only insofar as that sector served as a more or less automatic supplier of unskilled labor and food to the developing modern sector. In the free enterprise version a rise in prices of food in the industrializing sector would presumably act as a signal to agricultural producers in the traditional sector to increase the production and supply of food products for the modern sector, and thereby lower prices and costs again. In the elementary version of centrally planned development the rural agricultural sector could be exploited as a source of forced savings to finance capital accumulation in the industrial sector through the use of such devices as the runover tax imposed upon centrally determined purchase prices of agricultural products from collective and state farms. The purchase price received in the rural sector was pegged at low levels, and in theory the turn-over tax was used to raise re-sale prices to levels high enough to perform a market-rationing function in the industrial sector.

That some growth is possible by concentrating resources in the industrial sector is indisputable. Nevertheless, failure to integrate growth of the rural sector into the overall scheme of domestic economic development can and has acted as a check on the growth of the industrial sector itself. First of all, in this type of analysis labor-to-land ratios are assumed to be high, and other conditions or agricultural production in the rural sector are assumed to be such that the marginal productivity of agricultural workers is too low to result in potential or actual decreases in agricultural output as the result of migration to urban industrial sectors. In many Latin American economies, however, these necessary assumptions are simply not verified.

Moreover, in the free enterprise model there is assumed a market mechanism to perform the integrating function of transmitting economic incentives from the industrial sector to the rural sector. Under conditions imposed by traditional patterns of land tenure in many Latin American countries such assumptions would simply be unwarranted. The absence of adequate market mechanisms, however, means that a rise in food prices and hence of wage costs in the industrializing sector accompanying the growth of the urban labor force will not induce offsetting increases in agricultural output. The rise in wage costs lowers profits and hence lowers the potential accumulation of capital out of profit-induced saving. Experience in centrally planned economies has shown that administered purchase prices of agricultural products pegged at low levels for purposes of maximizing public saving have resulted in an equally unresponsive agricultural sector.

In Latin America many economies have been especially subject to inflationary pressures from such sources as deficit financing of public expenditures and from the structural inflation resulting from bottlenecks that have accompanied domestic production policies of import substitution during the last two decades. Failure to integrate the industrial and agricultural sectors through development of efficient markets or other mechanisms simply adds one more serious structural bottleneck to accelerate the rate of inflation arising from other sources.

In most of the countries of Latin America the absence of a price mechanism sufficient for integration of the two sectors may be attributed at least in part to the traditional forms of land tenure that have acted as constraints to the domestic economic integration of agricultural production, and hence of the agricultural labor force as well. It is only necessary here to recall the foundation of the hacienda form of agricultural organization upon principles of economic self-sufficiency that are inherently resistant to domestic economic integration. An institutional form of land ownership that is at once both the basis of a self-contained economy and a model of social status rather than of economic efficiency cannot be the vehicle of domestic economic integration, since economic integration means specialization, trade, and economic interdependence.

The hacienda form of agricultural organization, on the other hand, sought to provide for as many of its own economic needs as possible. The agricultural labor force, in particular, was effectively insulated from the rest of the economy. The needs of the agricultural worker were provided for simply by the consumption at subsistence levels of the share of hacienda output that he could call his own. For the satisfaction of any needs beyond these he was dependent upon the institution and those who control it. In some cases money itself, the symbol of economic integration, was replaced by a nonconvertible scrip redeemable only at the *tiendas* of the hacienda itself.

Whatever trade existed between the hacienda and the rest of the economy depended upon the decision of a landowner whose goals, interests, and attitudes cannot typically be depicted as those of the classical entrepreneur through whose acquisitiveness markets were supposed to be developed and the sectors of the economy thereby integrated. The relevant model is rather that of the landed aristocracy marketing only enough output to maintain a traditional status-determined standard of living and to provide the export capital desired for the purchase of nonproductive imports and foreign securities. At the same time fertile lands not needed for these purposes lie idle, and the masses of agricultural workers cultivate marginal lands for their own subsistence. Under circumstances such as these the economic and social mobility of the population that is a prerequisite for domestic integration is necessarily absent.

The conservative subsistence farmer in this environment is sometimes caricatured as lacking the attitudes of thrift and profit-maximizing entrepreneurship necessary for effective behavior in a market economy. From an economic point of view, however, his conservative behavior under the constraints of inadequate facilities for marketing and credit, as well as the virtual absence of relevant information, may be viewed as economically rational risk minimization. The subsistence farmer who must pay exorbitant rates of interest for small amounts of capital, or who must pay as rent to his landlord a share of any increases in output resulting from innovation, while he bears the total of any losses due to failures of those innovations, may be quite rational in concluding that the personal value of any gains, properly discounted for personal risks, do not warrant the costs involved. The fact that at subsistence levels of income he has neither reserves nor market agencies upon which to depend in case of failure quite reasonably lessens the appeal of typical North American attitudes of pragmatic trial and error.

The commercial plantations identified with export crops in the tropical economies of the hemisphere, on the other hand, might appear to have been more fully integrated into the domestic economy of the country because of their more economically rational development and utilization of land for commercial purposes. Here again, however, the integration is often more apparent than real. Foreign ownership of these holdings has meant failure to reinvest agricultural earnings in domestic development and consequently failure to diversify the economic base of the development process.

For the domestic laborer the commercial plantation meant a dependence upon a paternalistic institution that is just as debilitating to social and economic mobility as the hacienda. Company-owned commissaries, hospitals, and even schools may have meant economic security, but not the economic independence necessary for an integrated process of development. Even when the foreign firm paid relatively high cash wages, and this was more true in the commercial exploitation of minerals than in agriculture, wage scales have not necessarily been conducive to the development of an efficient labor force.[5]

Foreign enterprises may tend to set wages at scales that are determined more by wage patterns in the economy of the parent firm than by labor supply conditions in the developing economy. This means, first of all, that labor is not likely to be used as intensively in all phases of production as local resource availability would permit. At higher wages the levels of employment by foreign firms, unlike employment on the haciendas, are likely to be set by conventional principles of profit maximization that weigh the value of the individual worker's contribution to the firm's output against his cost to the enterprise as a condition of his employment. The result may be open unemployment that is at least as inimical to economic integration as the disguised unemployment among *campesino* households dependent upon the hacienda.

In addition, higher wage scales set by foreign enterprise for more skilled technical and managerial labor may simply arouse expectations and create precedents that indigenous commercial agriculture and industry cannot afford to match. Such market imperfections hamper rather than help the orderly integration of the masses of people into the process of domestic development.

The dominance of the self-sufficient hacienda and of the foreign-owned, self-contained export agricultural and extractive industries provided little economic incentive for the expansion of efficient markets linking the modern to the subsistence sectors of the economy. Oligarchic domination of society by a landed aristocracy or by foreign enterprise determined conditions for the dominance of oligopolistic markets linking rural and industrial sectors. The absence of competition among buyers of agricultural products for distribution in urban industrial areas, for example, means that high prices for agricultural products due to increased demand in urban areas would not be self-liquidating as they would be if agricultural producers could respond to improved profit possibilities by increased production for urban consumption. Noncompetitive merchandising of agricultural output means instead that high prices for food products in urban areas will be reflected only in higher profits for the noncompetitive middleman, whose profit-maximizing interests under conditions of inelastic demand for food are best served by a nonresponsive agricultural sector.

The experience of the earlier land reforms in Latin America demonstrated that under such conditions the breakup of large landholdings and the redistribution of land, although a necessary prerequisite for economic and social mobility of the masses, were not sufficient to ensure an integrated economy conducive to growth. Hence, in recent years there has been greater concern for the development of new institutions to hasten the spread of markets to link major sectors of the economy in a balanced growth.

The cooperative movement, despite its relatively late arrival on a large scale in Latin America, presents from an economic point of view an alternative market mechanism which has the potential of more efficient integration of the subsistence farmer into the life of the economy that either existing free markets or collective alternatives under central planning. More recent land reform laws, such as those in Venezuela and Chile, incorporate provision for supplying to the new small landholder the economic and technical services necessary to ensure increased agricultural productivity. In addition, apart from the social and moral benefits of cooperative membership, the simple assurance of marketing and credit facilities helps serve the economic function of instilling in the new agricultural entrepreneur the willingness to bear risks, to save, and to invest, as well as the effective desire for economic achievement that are likely to make him a self-reliant member of a modern exchange economy. Perhaps the most distinguishing feature of the cooperative movement in Latin America has been the multipurpose agricultural cooperative that combines so many economic functions for these ends and purposes.

When properly administered, the cooperative form of business organization can operate efficiently to remove market imperfections that hamper balanced growth of industrial and agricultural sectors. By performing the function of middleman the marketing and consumer cooperatives provide a market mechanism for communicating economic incentives between consumer and producer in the two sectors, and thereby deter secular changes in the terms of trade between the two sectors that would tend to stifle the growth process. Moreover, by representing the interests of several small producers and consumer the cooperative can offer economies of large-scale operation that lower costs and increase the profitability of the small-scale agricultural enterprises which it serves.

At the same time there are reservations and qualifications that may be relevant to some of the more elaborate programs of cooperative organization that accompany Latin American schemes of land redistribution. Requirements that *campesinos* join cooperatives and participate in their educational, technical, and economic activities as a condition for receiving land or gaining title to lands received tend to violate one of the traditional principles of cooperativism, that is, the free and voluntary character of membership. It may thus be argued that mandatory membership in highly integrated systems of multipurpose agricultural cooperatives reduce the *campesino* economically to little more than the status of an agricultural worker on a centrally planned collective farm, especially where title to land is conditioned by cooperative membership.

Moreover, restrictions, like those in the Chilean law, that limit membership in cooperatives to *campesinos* tend only to perpetuate, rather than break down, traditional class barriers. Moreover, when transferred to urban cooperatives, such precedents may tend to create new class barriers where none had existed.

From one point of view such restrictions may appear egalitarian in interest by offering to the *campesino* an exclusive market weapon with which to redress traditional market grievances. However, such restrictions may simply offer economic reinforcement of social barriers already rooted in such sources as racial discrimination against the Indian component of the national population. The potential contribution to social and economic mobility rendered by de facto integration of members in the general assembly of an unrestrictive cooperative institution is too great to be overlooked in Latin American societies where alternative institutions for the same purpose have been traditionally lacking.

Moreover, restriction of membership limits the availability of qualified personnel upon which the management of the cooperative may draw and perhaps will leave an individual cooperative economically vulnerable to market competition which it may not be able to survive. This is particularly true where there is a possibility that local merchants who represent the most serious threat to the incipient cooperative might be induced to join the cooperative itself.

Schemes to provide an institutional framework for the integration of the subsistence sector into the economy require large amounts of capital, whether for education, land redistribution, agricultural extension, or the formation of cooperatives. Although some of the activities of some of these institutions, such as cooperatives, are self-financing, nevertheless public funds are usually required at some point in the initiation of all of them. The opportunity cost of such extensive projects often appears high in terms of immediate gains from alternatives that must be foregone in the industrializing sector. Hence, it is not unusual for operations to lag behind opportunities even where resistance is not met from affected vested interests. The cost of land redistribution in Panama, for one small example, was found so high that for a time even donated lands could not be accepted for redistribution.

Funds were simply not available to absorb costs of transferring ownership and titling as well as providing necessary auxiliary services. An economic appraisal of the efficiency of a land redistribution scheme may not, on grounds of costs, yield the same results as the appraisal of the moralist or the social philosopher.

Restrictions on the form of compensation for confiscated lands that are consistent with goals of domestic integration might include below-market nominal interest payments, nonredeemability and nonconvertibility features attached to the bonds used for compensation in order to minimize domestically destabilizing dangers of inflation and capital outflow. Where the bonds are marketable, the restrictions frequently drive prices far below par. Thus the costs, both public and private, of major policies of domestic economic integration run high.

The assumption is, of course, that eventually the public costs, and perhaps even the private costs, of initiating such reforms will be self-liquidating out of the increased productivity of the economy. Public costs can be recouped out of higher tax revenues from increased incomes. Private costs can be recouped by such devices as authorization to individuals to convert land-reform bonds into loans for productive private domestic investment.

Nevertheless, the role of public finance in the domestic integration of the economy can extend even further. The need for reform of tax administration in Latin American countries to ensure implementation of growth-oriented fiscal policies has been stressed often enough to warrant no further comment. With a workable tax administration, application of all the devices that have been used in more developed countries to stimulate productive investment—for example, investment tax credits and fast write-offs—can be considered for use in stimulating investment in the developing economy. Still, devices such as these are more applicable to the industrializing sector than to the traditional, rural sector, and hence they may be of only limited value in serving the purposes of domestic integration.

New measures of public finance must be devised that will assist in the integration of the emerging subsistence farmer. Thus, it is often insisted that savings for development will eventually have to reach the great masses of people. Credit unions, *bancos obreros, bancos populares,* and other similar savings institutions have served the function, among others, of introducing new classes of people to institutional saving, and thereby of mobilizing new sources of development financing. In their initial stages, of course, such institutions are not likely to mobilize large amounts of development capital. This is due partly to the relatively low income levels of the depositors and partly to the fact that credit union loans in the beginning must often be made for nonproductive consumer purposes as an incentive to induce new depositors to save institutionally.

In addition, at earlier stages of development the contributed services of numbers of people can be solicited in community development projects as a substitute for capital formation financed by voluntary savings. However the number of such projects that can effectively utilize disguised unemployment and contributed services without pressing upon constraints imposed by other and scarcer resources is probably limited. Experience has shown, moreover, that such community development projects must be geographically limited, since voluntary participation and the supply of contributed services are likely to be forthcoming only when the participants are assured of sharing *directly* in the benefits of the development projects.

Hence, new forms of mobilizing savings must be sought as integration of the traditional and modern sectors proceeds. Public saving in the form of income taxation may simply be too costly and inefficiently administered in early stages of development, while the regressivity of consumption taxes may be socially objectionable. However, as incomes begin to rise and tax machinery improves, the use of the income tax to mobilize public savings on a broad base becomes more feasible. Moreover, selective inducements favorable to growth and comparable to investment credits and tax write-offs in the industrial sector may be applied to the broad base of personal incomes. Thus, the burden of taxation on low incomes may be reduced by the issuance to the taxpayer of shares of ownership in new tax-financed business enterprises which may be operated by the government or in partnership with private enterprise. Taxation with compensation such as this becomes a form of quasi-private saving which can not only stimulate habits of saving but also ensure a broad base of income distribution for the future. This could be an important effect if it is true, as claimed, that incomes have become more, rather than less, concentrated in the hands of the few during the process of development of major Latin American economies.[6] At the same time a simple device such as this can perform an important educative role in the integration of the masses of people into a market economy. This type of tax and transfer mechanism has already been informally proposed by Richard Musgrave of Harvard in connection with a current study of the Chilean tax structure by the Harvard law and economics faculties.

As long as the agricultural and industrial sectors of the economy remain relatively separate social and economic entities, the need for comprehensive domestic planning may not be apparent, except perhaps as a political necessity in order to qualify for foreign aid. However, as the integration, and hence interdependence, of agricultural and industrial sectors of the economy proceeds, the necessity of comprehensive planning grows, both to test the consistency of individual projects and to compare the gains from alternative sets of development proposals. Political stability, however, remains a requisite for the implementation of any comprehensive development plan.

From an aggregate economic viewpoint, population pressure, as measured by labor to land ratios, in many countries of Latin America, especially in the larger countries of South America, is not as severe a problem as in the more crowded areas of Southeast Asia. Nevertheless, restructuring of land tenure and land utilization and the opening up of new lands through colonization, coupled with the rapid rates of population growth that characterize most Latin American countries today, imply considerable shifts in traditional patterns of population distribution. Already the lure of the capital city has meant that Latin American countries tend to be characterized by migration to urban centers in excess of what wage differentials for unskilled workers would tend to predict in a simple two-sector development model. It is estimated, for example, that in Latin American rural areas, where natural rates of population increase exceed 3 percent per year, the net increase in rural population, as a result of urban migration, does not exceed 1.5 percent.[7] The social cost of maintaining an unskilled labor force is likely to be greater in urban areas than in rural areas for several reasons. Provision for sewerage, public utilities, local transportation, police and fire protection, and other public services is likely to be more necessary and hence more costly in crowded urban slums than in rural areas. The social cost of provision for support of the unemployed is likely to be greater in the urban area than in the rural household, where unemployment compensation and old-age security means simply family redistribution of the agricultural output of the individual household.

There may be grounds to believe that greater integration of the rural sector into the process of development will result in a more orderly and economically rational rate of migration to urban centers. However, it is likely that present patterns of migration can be altered only by the extension of public services as well as economic opportunities into rural population centers. The magnitude of expenditures implied by such proposals along with the expenditures implicated in population movements associated with schemes of land redistribution and colonization strongly suggest the need for extensive regional planning.

Regional planning, however, implies much greater coordination between public authorities at local and national levels and between public and private economic institutions. Evidence in the more highly developed countries of Latin America like Mexico suggests that differences in levels of income among geographical regions of an individual country have not tended to diminish automatically even with growth in markets, infrastructure educational opportunities, and other indicators of overall development.[8] Hence, it may be the task of the regional planner to consider appropriate strategies of broadening the geographical base of domestic development. Possible policies that have been applied in various parts of Latin America include the domestic relocation of peoples living in areas of low development potential to unexploited areas with natural resource potential. A recent familiar example is the relocation of inhabitants of the arid north of Mexico down to jungle regions in the south after unsuccessful attempts to increase the productivity of the arid area.

An alternative geographical policy would relocate industry rather than people by means of selective tax exemptions and credits for industries that are willing to locate in outlying areas. This type of policy, used successfully in Puerto Rico, depends upon the efficiency of existing tax administration and upon the existence of an adequate infrastructure for profitable operations in outlying areas. A policy such as this can therefore be most effective only on the assumption of other policies upon which it depends, that is, in the context of a more comprehensive development plan. Moreover, there is likely to be a divergence between public and private costs, as well as between public and private benefits, accruing to policies of this kind. There is no assurance that the net private benefits, both economic and social, will be sufficient to induce the required participation in such projects without heavy government subsidy. A comprehensive regional development plan may be a necessary first step to determine whether the present value of the public benefits of such schemes over a period of time will warrant the necessary present expenditures and subsidies.

This same rationality must be brought to bear upon the geographical expansion of services that are considered basic to the integration of the masses of people into the process of development. No simple a priori answers can be given, for example, to a question of the allocation of funds for education despite broad consensus on the necessity of education in some form as an integrating force. Whether scarce resources, material and human, are to be invested in the characteristically mammoth Latin American urban universities, or in elementary and secondary schools at lower levels of urban and rural society, or in some combination of both on a regional basis, is a decision that cannot be made in isolation if it is to serve the purposes of domestic economic integration.[9] The same is true of decisions concerning the optimal mix of educational tracks ranging from universal primary education to selective adult vocational training. Costs and benefits of individual tracks may vary from region to region and can be properly evaluated only in the context of other domestic development policies.

The questions and examples that have been briefly raised here are intended simply to indicate that the integration of the masses of people in the Latin American countries into domestic economic development is a task that must be faced at every level of decision-making from the grass roots to national policy. Indeed, it is a task that may require reshaping not only of basic economic structures but also of political structures which have been beyond the scope of this presentation. Nevertheless, we have tried to point out that the importance of such domestic integration is so great to future economic growth that the vast scope of the effort required cannot be offered as an excuse for failure to meet the challenge.

NOTES

1. Victor Alba, *Alliance Without Allies* (New York: Praeger, 1965).

2. DESAL, *El Desarrollo Social de America Latina* (Santiago de Chile: Editorial Antartica, 1964), Vol. I.

3. See, for example, Joseph A. Schumpeter, *The Theory of Economic Development* (New York: Oxford University Press, Galaxy ed., 1961).

4. W. Arthur Lewis, "Economic Development with Unlimited Supplies of Labour," *The Manchester School* (May, 1954).

5. W. Arthur Lewis, *Unemployment in Developing Countries*, unpublished lecture to Mid-West Research Conference, October, 1964.

6. Ifigenia M. de Navarrete, *La Distribucion del Ingreso y El Desarrollo Economico de Mexico* (Mexico: Escuela Nacional de Economia, 1960).

7. Marshall Wolfe, "Rural Settlement Patterns and Social Change in Latin America," *Latin American Research Review*, Vol. 1, No. 2, p. 38.

8. Charles Nash Myers, *Education and National Development in Mexico* (Princeton: Industrial Relations Section, 1965).

9. Hector Correa, "Optimum Choice Between General and Vocational Education" *Kyklos*, 18 (1965), Fasc. 1; also A. J. Corazzini and E. Bartell, "Problems of Programming an Optimum Choice Between General and Vocational Education," *Kyklos*, 18 (1965), Fasc. 4.

The Movement Toward Integration

GUSTAVO LAGOS

This subject requires a presentation of the unfolding of the integration process, an attempt to evaluate its present status and to analyze future trends in the integration movement. The task calls for a great effort to synthesize, and it is highly probable that, in a subject as complex as this, I am bound to omit some of its aspects.

There is, I believe, a central unifying thought on which I shall base this effort to synthesize. The integration movement can be interpreted as the manifestation through the years of the various phases of an integrationist awareness and strategy taking shape as the process unfolds. It is true that these phases sometimes overlap. It is true that in some Latin American subregions, such as Central America or Greater Colombia, movements are under way within the confines of certain nations alone which seem to anticipate the general development of integrationist attitudes and strategies. I believe, however, that in Latin America as a whole it is possible to distinguish phases clearly characterized by the predominance, the emergence, or the absence of certain forms and trends of an awareness and strategy of integration.

In pursuing this central thought there are, in my opinion, five identifiable phases and trends. First, the age of the independence movements of the Latin American countries, when an integrationist attitude was evolved by the original generation of liberators, who lacked an adequate strategy for achieving Latin American unity. Second, the age of the emergence and growth of Latin American nationalism, which began with the passing of the liberator generation from the political scene and extended through the nineteenth century to World War I. This phase was characterized by the development of an integrationist trend at the highest level of Latin American thought but a perceptible weakening of integrationist awareness in governmental and economic circles. It was the age of integrationist awareness at the purely intellectual level, unsupported by political and economic groups that could provide practical meaning for a strategy and make it viable. In this phase of the process, toward the end of the nineteenth century, Brazil emerged from its monarchical era as a great Latin American republic that enforced the unity of its vast territory and developed an intelligent Latin American diplomacy designed to channel the country's foreign policy into continental enterprises and to win for it a prominent role in later phases and trends of the integration movement. Third, the age of development of an integrationist attitude on the political level, with a strategy of partisan involvement. This trend began in the 1920's with the creation of the *Alianza Popular Revolucionaria Americana* (APRA) in Peru and continues into the present day. It has been strengthened through the founding of Christian Democratic parties in several countries and the establishment of the Latin American Parliament in Lima in 1964. Fourth, the age in which the trend toward Latin American integration achieved expression in an economic awareness and strategy initially conceived on a limited scale, but later expanding to global proportions. This trend started in the 1930's, gained momentum with the establishment of ECLA, the Central American Common Market, and LAFTA, and was consolidated with the foundation of the Inter-American Development Bank.

Fifth, the present phase of integration, characterized by an overall consciousness and strategy of integration in the economic, political, and intellectual spheres, which could be considered a synthesis and ultimate expression of all earlier approaches. This phase began around the mid-sixties and is currently in full sway. In this lecture I shall endeavor first to explain the principal features of these five phases and trends, and then to define and diagnose the present state of the integrationist attitude and strategy, and close with the prospects for its future development.

Phases and Trends in the Development of an Integrationist Attitude and Strategy

(1)

The vision and awareness of Latin America as a whole, as a single geographic, historic, and cultural unit, the prevailing view of the liberators and of the forerunners and early advocates of integration, were derived from various sources: the political and economic unity existing in colonial times, the sense of belonging to a community of culture, religion, language, and customs, and the historical conviction, nurtured in ideology, philosophy, and the struggle for independence, of sharing in a single enterprise which with the passage of time would continue to rest on a common foundation and pursue common goals. In every document of the independence movement the word "America," referring to Spanish America, "the unity and fraternity of the Americans," takes precedence over the name of the individual country itself. "*La América toda existe en nación*," "America is all one single nation," said a verse from a Caracas song which later became the Venezuelan national anthem. San Martin's statement in 1819 that "all America is my country and I have the same interest in the United Provinces as in Chile" is no flight of lyricism, but a profound sentiment that arose from a conviction that he belonged to a great emerging nation. Miranda, Bolívar, Hidalgo and Morelos, Rocafuerte, Rivadavia, Monteagudo, San Martín, O'Higgins, José Antonio Miralla, and José Cecilio del Valle all thought of themselves as "Americans" because they spoke not only the same language of grammar but the same language of ideas to express a common aspiration and achieve a common goal.

There was a "common market" of freedom that covered all Spanish America in the struggle for and consolidation of independence, and armies, financial resources, and political and intellectual leaders circulated freely within it regardless of their place of origin. The sense of Spanish American solidarity was more real and more deep-seated than that of the nascent nationalisms.

The sense of awareness of unity was not, however, enough. Bridges had to be built with political and economic action in order to accomplish and preserve that unity. The great obstacle to the development of a realistic strategy of integration lay in the physical isolation imposed by vast distances, deserts, mountains, and jungles, the isolation of economies fragmented into simple consumer systems by the severance of their ties to the economy of the mother country, and the isolation of political systems, only recently emerged into independent existence and subject to the enormous tensions and problems of their own internal organization and their very survival.

It was inevitable that the Congress of Panama completely failed its task as conceived by Bolívar—to counteract the political divisiveness generated by isolation. Instead of demonstrating the cohesion of Spanish America it betrayed the degree to which disintegration had already advanced.

(2)

With the passing of the generation of liberators from the scene there was rapid disintegration of the unity forged in the struggle for independence. Latin America was split into more units than there had been administrative divisions under the viceroyalties and captain-generalcies in the colonial period. And so began the emergence of local nationalism. Rival groups consolidated their military, political, and economic power, and blocked every avenue for the development of an integrationist attitude. It was only when the threat of external aggression loomed that these narrow nationalisms were subordinated to a common show of unity in order to preserve independence. Such was the motivation for the treaty of confederation signed in 1848 by Peru, Bolivia, Chile, New Granada, and Ecuador. Like the earlier treaty signed in Panama, this pact aimed at guaranteeing the sovereignty and independence of its signatories. The Tripartite Treaty of 1856 signed by Chile, Peru, and Ecuador, although containing an integrationist language, was in reality simply another defensive alliance to ward off outside attackers.

But I wish to stress the point that underlying these documents was a "historic" feeling of identity, a sense of belonging to the same national group, with common roots and a common destiny. For example, the preamble of the treaty of 1848 states that the Spanish American republics "linked by the bonds of origin, language, religion, and customs, by their geographical location, by the common cause they have defended, by the similarity of their institutions, and, above all, by their common needs and mutual interests, cannot but consider themselves as parts of a single nation and should pool their forces and resources to overcome every obstacle to the destiny held forth to them by nature and civilization."

If the integrationist movement remained blocked by political nationalism, the idea certainly was not dead. It found expression in the intellectual sphere among writers and humanists, where it took refuge and grew. "There is a common cultural history in which the same idiom is spoken and the same problems are expressed throughout the continent. Great literary figures such as Bello, Sarmiento, Martí, Darío, cannot be walled off by narrow national boundaries, for their work encompasses and enriches all the countries. Almost all of them were the knights-errant of a 'Spanish Americanism' which lived on in the minds of men in spite of political turmoil. All Spanish America learned the legal and grammatical rules of Andrés Bello and delighted in the verses of Rubén Darío. Martí erected a kind of ideal pantheon for the entire continent in which Bolívar and Juárez, San Martín and Morazán, Heredia and Cecilio Acosta were venerated as the heroes and civilizers of a common fatherland."

This intellectual affinity for Latin American integration led to the foundation in 1862 of the Society for American Union, with branches in various Spanish American countries. Some of its more illustrious members were the Argentines Juan Gregorio de Las Heras and Juan Bautista Alberdi, and the Chileans José Victorino

Lastarria, Domingo Santa María, and Benjamín Vicuña Mac-
kenna. For the first time there appeared a strategic notion of
Latin American integration conceived as the gradual formation
of a single great nation. The relevant paragraphs of the Society's
charter read as follows:

What makes the formation of a great American nation seem impossible and
chimerical is that it is expected, it is required to spring into being all at
once, in a single instant, in all its titanic stature, girded by its vast waters,
crowned with its infinite skies and, armed with its omnipotent instruments
of labor, to sound the cry of peace and justice to a world amazed. But, while
this is a beautiful vision which will be realized by industry, commerce,
politics, art, and science in this exalted service of democracy, this is not what
can or should be undertaken at this time with our resources. . . .

Who has ever sought or could advocate that in order to establish our great
American nation, the laws governing the lives of individuals and people
be changed?

What we do seek, what we do hope for, what will be achieved, is the
gradual fashioning of that great nation that already has being in the emotions, the aspirations, and the ideas of almost every American individual and
people, and which is beginning to find concrete expression in opinions, plans,
projects, even in policies.

Along with the formation of Spanish American nationalisms,
in the late nineteenth century Brazil emerged from its monarchical phase and, having embraced the ideology and form of government of the other Latin American countries by becoming a
republic, made two contributions to the integration process. Unlike the former Spanish colonies, it managed to preserve its unity
under the aegis of the imperial Crown, which throughout the
nineteenth century provided a basis of legitimacy for its political
system and allowed it to nullify the separatist tendencies of districts and regions within its vast territory. And when Brazil
became a republic, it followed the policies of the Baron of Río
Branco and developed a highly intelligent and visionary diplomacy which gave the country a share in enterprises of continental
magnitude and enabled it to participate vigorously and with
signal success in the subsequent phases and trends of the integration movement.

(3)

The third historic phase is characterized by the development of an integrationist attitude in the political sphere with a strategy of penetration through parties, which began in the twenties and continues into the present day. It was the increasing contact with the United States which gradually led Latin America to think in terms of a community of interest of possible benefit to all the countries. Thus, for example, in the Pan American Conferences of 1923, 1928, and 1933, Latin America united to diminish the predominant influence of the United States within the Pan American Union and to condemn United States intervention in the Caribbean.

The anti-imperialistic ideology of Haya de la Torre, which emerged in Peru during the twenties, was partly an expression of this tendency to defend the common interests of Latin America vis-à-vis the United States. But there was a positive side to such pronunciamientos: *Alianza Popular Revolucionaria Americana* (APRA), a party founded by Haya de la Torre, represented a modern conception of Latin American integration as "the political and economic unification of the twenty republics into which the great Indo-American nation is divided."

This is not the place to examine the significance of APRA's activities, but it may be noted that this party, which is still active today in Peruvian political life, has influenced the entire southern continent. Its founder exercised, particularly during the early period, a leadership in intellectual and university circles transcending the boundaries of his country and charting courses of continental scope. In 1964, forty years after the drafting of the APRA platform, the party took the initiative in calling a meeting of Latin American parliamentarians to constitute the Latin American Parliament. The meeting was roundly successful. Delegations from fourteen national congresses agreed to establish a Latin American Parliament which would work for Latin American public opinion, economic integration of the region, and adoption of recommendations aimed at accelerating the integration process. Establishment of the Latin American Parliament received increasing political support from parties of the democratic left in Latin America, such as the Christian Democratic parties, which, like APRA, endorsed Latin American political and economic integration as it might be coordinated by regional organizations.

(4)

The fourth phase began as the 1920's drew to a close and developed during the following decades. It consisted of a tendency that ran parallel to the political trend of the third phase. Its characteristic feature was a change in the direction of the integrationist attitude from a political to an economic approach. Up to 1938 various plans were proposed to establish a Latin American customs union or partial unions, including notably the proposal of President Irigoyen of Argentina. Between 1939 and 1947 various lines of action were initiated but led to no practical result; these included a 1939 industrial and trade convention between Argentina and Brazil and a 1941 proposal for customs union of the River Plate countries. By the close of the forties a veritable network of bilateral agreements had sprung up among the southernmost countries of South America.

With the end of World War II the international situation underwent a radical change which was profoundly to affect the position of Latin America and the future development of integrationist thought and strategy. The United States and the Soviet Union emerged as the world centers of political, military, and economic power. "Today only these two nations have the economic stature needed to exercise the technological leadership which, applied to the military sphere, gives them undisputed predominance over the rest of the world and is leading to the widespread deterioration of the international status of the other nations." The technological revolution has divided the world into developed and underdeveloped areas, and Latin America has been relegated to the latter category. Although founded on the principle of universality, the United Nations did not escape the politics of the cold war, which tended to classify regions of the world into blocs. And Latin America, as it compared its characteristics with those of the rest of the world, began to define its own common features and interests. Just as there was an East-West bloc, for the first time in world power strategy there was talk of the "Latin American group," whose behavior received careful scrutiny under the bloc policy of the United Nations. It was in the negotiations leading to the establishment of the Economic Commission for Latin America that the Latin American group was to define itself by describing its common and peculiar economic, demographic, social, and political features. In his speech proposing the establishment of ECLA, the Ambassador of Chile now referred to the "Latin American community."

A powerful contributing factor to this awakening of the Latin American countries to their status as the constituents of a multinational group with its own well-defined characteristics was the way in which Latin America was received within the United Nations. There are countless indications that Latin America is viewed by the rest of the world as a group with its own peculiar characteristics. The salient features of the image of Latin America in the developed world appear to be its underdevelopment as a region, its political instability, its sharp contrasts between the rich and the poor, and its tendency to adopt, sometimes indiscriminately, ways of life and institutional models or patterns prevailing in more advanced regions.

ECLA was achieved only after it overcame a prolonged diplomatic struggle against opposition of the United States and other great powers. It represented the opening of a new era in which Latin America intensified its self-awareness through an analysis of its economic situation. The economic thought of ECLA attested to the capacity of a new intellectual elite to investigate the situation of Latin America with intellectual instruments of the Latin Americans' own making. Underlying all ECLA thinking was the basic premise that traditional economic theory could not be useful in analyzing and interpreting the Latin American situation. From this analytical attitude and from systematic research into the Latin American situation emerged the basic economic concepts of ECLA, independent of world ideologies and political rigidity. It was a continental strategy, and in the course of a decade it became an economic framework for examining and interpreting

Latin American development from regional rather than national considerations. In this sense the work of ECLA was the first important and significant expression of a Latin American group attitude, of the region's self-definition as a human group without regard for specific ideologies or political movements. Latin America now went beyond the approaches of the essayists and ideologists of the second phase to take up the analytical instruments of economic science.

Guided by the economic thought of ECLA, efforts were made to solve the common problems besetting the economies of the Latin American countries. There emerged at the close of the fifties the two basic arrangements for Latin American integration: the Latin American Free Trade Association (LAFTA), with Mexico and six South American countries (Argentina, Brazil, Chile, Uruguay, Paraguay, and Peru) as its initial members, since enlarged by the entry of Ecuador, Columbia, Venezuela, and Bolivia; and the Central American Common Market, which joins the five countries of Central America. For the time being, only Haiti, the Dominican Republic, Panama, and Cuba remain outside the general movement toward Latin American economic integration, but it is highly probable that Panama and the Dominican Republic will soon join one or another of the current systems, probably the Central American Common Market.

For the first time Latin American integrationist thought achieved concrete expression in an economic strategy limited, in its initial stages, to the problems of liberalizing trade among member countries of both associations. Moreover, while it is true that these two integration movements were established by international treaties signed by the governments and ratified by their parliaments, the economic integration movement remained almost exclusively at a technical level during its preliminary stages.

Like a chain reaction following the initial impetus given by ECLA, the establishment of LAFTA and the CACM led to the creation in turn of new teams and new centers of activity by which Latin Americans are awakening to their own identity as a cohesive part of the international community. Moreover, the fact that the concepts of ECLA evolved outside specific political ideologies has made them acceptable to vast sectors of the Latin American countries; indeed, ECLA's views have become representative of broad segments of intellectual and political groups within the new middle classes, which see in the studies and proposals of ECLA the most serious and fundamental approach to the problems of Latin American development.

The tensions generated between the United States and the Latin American countries as a result of the reaction of the latter to the postwar tendency of the United States to take Latin America for granted as a natural and unconditional ally provided a context of international conflict that helped the Latin Americans to become aware of the status their nations shared in the international system. The abuses inflicted on Vice President Nixon in several Latin American capitals were an irrational expression of this phenomenon, just as Operation Pan America, proposed by Brazil, represented a rational attempt by Latin America to achieve a redefinition of its relations with the United States.

These circumstances led to the creation of the Inter-American Development Bank, which furnished with its international secretariat a new context in which a staff of officials recruited from every country in the region were given the opportunity to influence one another and to experience in their living and working together a community that transcended their particular national interests. A framework of interaction was thus created within which the Latin Americans might progress and be consolidated by an institution of such rapidly rising importance that within five years after its establishment it was to become the principal international public source of long-term financing for economic and social investment projects in Latin America. In fact, the Inter-American Bank has become a bank for Latin American integration and has to date granted more than 100 million dollars in credit and technical assistance to finance integration projects. This implies the expansion of an economic strategy modest in the beginning, but now covering every economic aspect and spanning Latin America.

During the present decade the overall economic strategy of integration has already progressed far enough to find expression in new manifestations. The economic integration of Latin America has been recognized in the Charter of Punta del Este as a basic objective of the Alliance for Progress. The central banks of Latin America now work cooperatively; in Central America this has led to the establishment of a clearing house and a monetary union and, in the LAFTA countries, to the creation of a mechanism for the multilateral clearing of payments and the reciprocal extension of credit in convertible currencies under bilateral agreements between banking authorities. At the United Nations Conference on Trade and Development, Latin America, by acting in concert, bargained favorably among other developing areas to win more equitable conditions for its basic products and for its export of manufactured goods. In 1964 the Fourth Conference of the LAFTA member countries adopted a broad program of overall economic integration; they were behaving more and more like a common market or economic community. Agreement was reached on basic economic policy and on an action program in matters of foreign trade, zonal policy on industrial and agricultural development, financial and monetary affairs, and the coordination of development programs. The Central American Common Market achieved a complete liberalization of its intraregional trade, progressed toward a customs union, and coordinated more closely its development plans and policies. Studies were begun both in LAFTA and in the CACM for integration in the fields of basic industry and regional infrastructure. Border integration programs were initiated between the governments of Colombia and Venezuela, and Colombia and Ecuador, with the cooperation of the Inter-American Development Bank.

(5)

At the midpoint of the 1960's the various schools of thought of the integrationist groups began to converge noticeably and to influence one another, which led to the onset of the fifth phase in the evolution of integrationist thought and strategy, a phase which we might designate as one of overall awareness and strategy in the economic, political, and intellectual spheres, or a kind of synthesis and projection of all preceding phases. Speaking in Mexico in 1962, Raúl Prebisch, the director of ECLA, called for political decisions that would allow LAFTA to continue advancing. In that same year Felipe Herrera, the president of the Inter-American Development Bank, at the University of Bahia, Brazil, analyzed integration as an economic and political process. These two high-ranking international executives were urging that political decisions be taken so that the integration process might go forward. But when the Latin American Parliament or the President of Chile requested the economic advice of experts, it was now the politicians who were seeking the help of economists. Both experts and politicians invoked the past, the early stages in the development of the sense of oneness, for inspiration and justification. At the same time the international agencies which support integration, and the political parties represented in the Lima Parliament, were now joined by the trade unions, which through ORIT and CLASC convey the support of broad masses of Latin American workers for the goals of economic and political integration. Also, countless businessmen's organizations emerged from Mexico to Chile to promote the Latin American integration movement. The Latin American Episcopal Council (CELAM) recently added the voice of the Catholic Church to the great union groups that support the Latin American integration process.

Expressions of this new phase in integrationist thought and strategy are (1) the report submitted by the four economists, the leaders of the IDB, CIAP, ECLA, and ILPES, at the request of the President of Chile, making proposals for the formation of a Latin American Common Market. This report was sent to every Latin American president and helped the governments to become fully aware of the implications of the problem, and to move toward discussion of its economic, political, and institutional aspects; (2) the two meetings of LAFTA foreign ministers, where the new directions of economic integration were fully debated; (3) various meetings at the chief-of-state level held in 1965 and 1966 to discuss the problems of integration and to adopt multinationally concerted positions; (4) the Act of Rio de Janeiro, in which all the member countries of the inter-American system agreed to incorporate the goals of economic integration into the new OAS

Charter; and (5) the meeting of chiefs of state of the inter-
American system held in 1967.

Definition and Diagnosis of the Current Status of Integrationist Thought and Strategy

At this point it is possible to make a diagnosis of the state of
integrationist thought and strategy by pointing to a body of facts
which characterize and define them.

1. The two existing integration arrangements, LAFTA and the
Central American Common Market, have evolved far beyond
their earlier commercial objectives and now approximate a conception of an economic integration strategy on a continental scale.
In substance, both arrangements have accepted the establishment
of a Latin American economic community as an essential prerequisite to more rapid progress in the economic and social development of the Latin American countries.

2. An increasing number of national and international officials,
politicians, and business, trade union, university, and religious
leaders are coming to understand that the economic integration
of Latin America—through the formation of an economic community—is the only way for the region to assert its political position
and strengthen its economic relations in a world that is tending
to organize itself into blocs of continental size.

3. High-ranking and influential technical, political, and intellectual groups are convinced that the formation of the Latin
American economic community should be accomplished by the
Latin Americans themselves, within a long-range process chosen
and controlled by themselves, and aimed at bringing the common
man of Latin America into the enjoyment of material well-being
and into the full exercise of his human rights by effectively incorporating him into the political, economic, and social life of the
Latin American countries.

4. The process of regional integration is conceptually insepa-
rable from the national integration process as an essential instrument in the efforts of the Latin American countries to integrate
internally as national communities within a context of new eco-

nomic and social structures that will assure a maximum of prosperity and human dignity with equal opportunities for all.

5. The process of regional integration is also conceived as the essential means by which the Latin American countries may properly incorporate themselves into the world economy and into the broader political community of the nations of the world. The philosophy inspiring the process of Latin American integration is based, therefore, not on an autarchic, isolationist, or aggressive concept, but, to the contrary, on a universalist approach in which the integration of Latin America is viewed as part of a broader integration on a hemispheric, Western, and world scale.

6. There is an awareness that the integration of Latin America will be essential to the assertion and dynamic development of the cultural values and historical personality of the Latin American countries. On the intellectual level there is a conviction that an integrated Latin America, in offering a more commodious framework for the cultural development of its constituent countries, could contribute new dimensions to the way of life in all of Western civilization. And by reason of its experience in racial integration, its dual membership in the worlds of the white and colored races, Latin America could serve as a bridge between East and West, between the developing and developed parts of the world.

7. Only an integrated Latin America would possess the economic and financial base needed to give the Latin American countries full access to the knowledge and fruits of modern science and technology, and to allow them to benefit from scientific and technological progress.

8. Latin American economic integration has been recognized as one of the ultimate goals of the inter-American system in the Charter of Punta del Este and in the Act of Rio de Janeiro. The future OAS Charter, whose text is now under study and negotiation, will include economic integration among its basic provisions.

9. The United States, as a member of the inter-American system, now favors Latin American economic integration as a matter of policy. Its government has stated that the Latin American countries must themselves define and decide the direction and form

of the process. President Johnson has declared that "the effective unity of Latin America is vital to the needs of its growing population" and that the United States "is prepared to cooperate closely for the integration of Latin America."

10. In his message to the Latin American Episcopal Council at its 1966 meeting, Paul VI exhorted the Latin American Church to "spread the ideal of integration by awakening in Christians the conviction that individual national destinies will only be achieved in a framework of international solidarity, by forging a supranational consciousness and insisting, as the pontifical and Council authorities recently did, on the urgent need for world cooperation."

11. The integration movement is conceived as a voluntary and legal process unfolding by the mutual consent of the countries involved. As a voluntary process it must result from a spontaneous coordination of the interests and forces that move and guide it. As such, it is opposed to coercive integration, as represented in history by the multinational empire of Napoleon and by Hitler's expansionist concept of a New Europe. As a legal process, it must follow the rules of law governing the relations between the forces involved in the process. These rules, in order to be effective, must be based on a common outlook and on the recognition of mutual interest.

12. The international agencies operating in Latin America vigorously support the economic integration process. The Inter-American Development Bank, now the principal international public source of long-term financing for economic and social investment projects in Latin America, has strengthened its own internal structure by setting up two new instruments with which to satisfy more fully to meet the growing demands of the Latin American integration process: (a) the Preinvestment Fund for Latin American Integration, established to finance the study of multinational projects, and (b) the Institute for Latin American Integration, which will investigate formulas and means for accelerating development of Latin America by training technical personnel, advising public and private entities, and disseminating technical knowledge.

Prospects for the Development of Integrationist Thought and Strategy

The twelve foregoing points outline a diagnosis and define the present state of integrationist thought and strategy. In an attempt to identify future trends we shall pose the principal questions raised by the integration process at its present stage.

1. What are the present weaknesses or inadequacies of the integration movement?

2. Is there any general agreement on the means of remedying these shortcomings?

3. What possible alternatives are there if various strategies are proposed for the future of the integration movement?

4. What strategies could the Latin American groups in favor of integration develop to accelerate the process?

5. What strategies could the government and private groups in the United States develop to contribute to the success of the integration process?

(1)

When we diagnosed the present state of the integration process, we noted that increasingly numerous groups of officials, politicians, and section leaders are realizing that the economic integration of Latin America is the only way for the region to solve its problems. This fact, however, should not make us forget that while these groups are indeed growing and encompass all the leading sectors of Latin American society, economy, and politics, the broad masses and important segments in leading circles remain outside of, or indifferent to, the integration movement. The future history of the integration movement will be largely defined by the extent to which the feeling of unity expands and attracts larger segments of the Latin American population.

When he inaugurated the Institute for Latin American Integration, Felipe Herrera aptly summarized the obstacles to Latin American integration in the following principal points: (1) there are some today who think that action toward Latin American integration is confronted by insuperable difficulties, such as a resurgence of nationalistic orientations, the resumption of a trend toward narrow, bilateral relations, and a corresponding loss of faith in cooperation by Latin American countries as a means of realizing the economic and social justice sought by peoples of the continent; (2) the profound structural weaknesses of Latin American countries which have been repeatedly exposed and diagnosed over the last twenty years at international meetings have been seriously confronted only during the last five years; (3) the growth rate of the Latin American gross national product, although it has met the per capita goal of 2.5 percent per annum stated in the Charter of Punta del Este, remains very meager in comparison to that of other parts of the world; (4) foreign trade in Latin American raw materials continues uncertain, and international price fluctuations subject the Latin American economies to powerful tensions; (5) the foreign public debt of the Latin American countries has been rising at such a pace that its service amounts for some countries to between 20 and 30 percent of their foreign exchange earnings; (6) despite every effort in the international financial sphere, the flow of external capital into Latin America falls short of requirements; (7) within the countries, despite the many advances made to accelerate their development and modernize their economic systems, a tremendous population pressure continues to nullify such economic progress as has been made. In Latin America, two out of every three inhabitants is still in a permanent state of undernourishment, and per capita farm output is today lower than it was thirty years ago. At the present time in Latin America, two out of every five adults are illiterate.

Thus [Dr. Herrera declared] we should not wonder at the inflation, marginal social conditions, middle-class unrest, peasant agitation, and various types of tensions which seem to have grown worse and which have inevitably driven our governments to emergency action to overcome the difficulties and relieve the tensions of the present moment.

As the President of the Inter-American Bank pointed out in this lecture, this series of obstacles, rather than constituting a crisis in the integration process, justifies the need for it, since all the economic factors mentioned are symptoms of a Latin America in the throes of a political, economic, and social crisis stemming from the existence of weak and disjointed economies. Integration emerges as one of the remedies that would allow the national communities to overcome these problems. As Felipe Herrera said, "We do not know of a single case in which a rapid strengthening of the ties between our nations could not benefit in one way or another the several republics of the hemisphere." We will cite only one example.

We know that the basis of progress in the modern world is scientific and technological development. A Latin America divided into a congeries of national economies has been incapable of absorbing the technological and scientific progress generated in the industrialized world, much less of taking a hand in that progress. It is clear that the integration of human, financial, and material resources in this field would enable the region to modernize its educational systems more rapidly and to set up high-level centers of advanced education, technology, and scientific research.

Furthermore, while it is true that the obstacles we have noted affect the integration movement, they are not intrinsic to it, because even if the movement did not exist, those obstacles would still be present in the Latin American economies and societies.

The integration movement itself does, however, reveal weaknesses, obstacles, and inadequacies to which I would like to refer. Last year, when I explained to a United States audience at Georgetown University the importance of a new mentality, or consciousness, as an indispensable factor for integration, I said that a change would be required in the cultural systems of the Latin American countries to allow for the emergence of values, beliefs, and symbols that would legitimize the integration of the national economic systems and the creation of institutions needed to make the process possible. For, when regional economic integration movements seek the creation of larger economic spaces, they are laying the material foundations for new nations, for nations formed by nations, such as the United States or the Soviet Union today—or, possibly, the United States of Europe or the United States of Latin America tomorrow.

If the integration movement is to be successful, it is necessary to establish, along with the loyalty of the citizen to his own country, a new loyalty, an identification with a greater community formed by the integrating countries; hence, cultural change is essential, and the critical step in every integration process is taken when the political leaders embrace new values that permit the creation of the integrating institutions.

What is the current situation in Latin America with regard to a cultural and political change of this kind? On this point it may be said that, first, there is no institutional and juridical framework within which to relate the Central American Common Market, permanently and operationally, with the Latin American Free Trade Association, despite the fact that the Charter of Punta del Este has called for a closer link between the two. Second, the countries of the Central American Common Market are now actively engaged in an evaluation of the capacity of their institutional and juridical system to develop the commitments and policies derived from existing treaties and from advances made in the process of integration. Predictably, this evaluation will lead the governments to an institutional improvement enabling the Central American Common Market to continue at a satisfactory pace toward realization of an economic community. Third, the real problem of cultural and political change arises in connection with the LAFTA member countries, whose governments are cautious in their approach to any decision to set up institutions endowed with greater integration authority and, at the same time, seem to differ on the desirable pace of the process.

(2)

Analysis of this point leads us to answer our second question, namely, whether there is any general agreement on the means of removing the obstacles to integration.

As Director of the Institute for Latin American Integration, I have had the privilege of attending the two Conferences of Foreign Ministers of the LAFTA member countries, held in 1965 and 1966 at Montevideo, the headquarters of LAFTA. While it is difficult to gauge attitudes at a diplomatic conference, an interpretation of the declarations of the foreign ministers at those conferences leaves the general impression that while there is indeed general awareness of the economic, political, and social problems of integration and a conviction that a strategy needs to be developed to achieve the proposed goals, there is as yet no agreement on the means to be employed.

This lack of agreement is not surprising in view of the very recent initiation of the fifth stage in the evolution of integrationist thought and strategy, and of the fact that, consequently, the governments and political leaders in the Latin American countries have not yet had time enough for mature consideration of the form which national development could take to make its goals compatible with those of regional integration. The problem of harmonizing the strategy of national development with that of regional integration is posed on three levels: that of the large countries with the broadest markets in Latin America: Argentina, Brazil, and Mexico; that of the intermediate countries, such as Chile, Peru, Colombia, Uruguay, and Venezuela; and that of the relatively least developed countries, as for example, Ecuador, Paraguay, and Bolivia. It is essential that solutions be found to the problems on these three levels in order to facilitate cultural and political change, and to mobilize the support of the various sectors in the Latin American countries. It is almost self-evident that there will always be opposition to the integration process from sectors whose interests are tied to the structures of backwardness and underdevelopment in the Latin American countries. The important thing is to enlist the support of the forces favorable to change and to economic, social, and political growth. "Hence, integrating these objectives with the goals of development and the fulfillment of Latin America as a whole is indispensable to securing the support of these national forces for the regional integration process."

The search for formulas to harmonize the national development efforts of the several countries within the integration scheme is a task that properly devolves upon both the individual national governments and the integration institutions themselves. It is precisely here that discrepancies seem to arise. Some countries seem to be more able or more willing than others to encounter rapid means of harmonizing both types of development, while others seem to need more time to solve those problems either because they are at a different level of development or because domestic political trends or the socioeconomic pressure of urgent problems prevent or hinder long-range programming in a continental context. The countries which appear to favor more accelerated integration feel that this harmonization of national development with the economy of an integrated Latin America implies, in substance, the problem of harmonizing the common interest of the countries as represented by a developing and integrating regional economy and the national interest of each country.

The problem may be summarized in a question: Who is to define the common interest of the nations participating in this process? The advocates of a more rapid integration reply that only community institutions with political decision-making powers can do this. This stand is endorsed by the expert opinion of the four economists who head ECLA, the IDB, ILPES, and CIAP in their reply to the letter of the President of Chile mentioned earlier. Their document, now known in Latin America as the Report of the Four, proposed a set of community institutions similar to those of the European Economic Community. As the President of the IDB noted in a recent speech, these agencies could be the following: (1) a council of ministers with power to make political decisions in the name of the member countries and to supervise and guide the integration entities and agencies; (2) an exclusively technical executive committee of international officials which would operate independent of the member governments, submit proposals to the council of ministers concerning matters of common interest to the member countries, and exercise executive powers in certain fields; (3) a parliament to represent continental public opinion and provide high political forum for the introduction of recommendations regarding the advance of the process; (4) a court of justice to resolve conflicts arising in the enforcement or interpretation of community rules; and (5) an economic and social council and a cultural and technological council, both acting as consultative organs. The advocates of a slower pace reply that the need for community organs is beyond question, but they doubt that this is the politically appropriate moment for their establishment.

On another occasion I noted that the debate on integration in which Latin America is now engaged resembles to some extent the debate that took place in the United States with regard to approval of the new Constitution, or in Europe during the negotiation of the treaties of Paris and Rome to establish the Coal and Steel Community and the European Economic Community. In those cases, too, there was the problem, now besetting Latin America, of moving into a more advanced phase of integration by discarding weaker formulas for international cooperation which had proved inadequate to cope with common problems. The debate now taking place on the subject attests to the vitality of the process and to the fact that the integration movement is reaching a higher stage in its evolution. As an economic strategy takes shape, the governments and people for the first time begin to realize the need to re-examine an entire series of traditional concepts, since the very destiny of these countries is bound up in future stages of the integration movement.

The historical challenge to Latin America posed by the problems of integration is truly unique. For the first time since the division of the world into industrialized and underdeveloped regions, a group of underdeveloped countries occupying a vast geographic area is facing the problem of integration. The challenge and magnitude of the problems are gigantic in scope. The geographic area of Latin America is 20 million kilometers, more than twice as large as the United States sixteen times larger than the area of the European Common Market, and second in size only to the Soviet Union. In another thirty-three years Latin America will have a population of 625 million inhabitants, or two-thirds of the total population of the Western Hemisphere, which in the year 2000 will come to almost 1 billion persons. Consequently, Latin America will be the most heavily populated region in the West, exceeding the population of the United States and Canada combined, or all of the African nations, or the Soviet Union and Western Europe. When it is considered that this vast geographic area contains twenty national societies governed by political systems of different degrees of democratic maturity, and substandard postal, telecommunications, information and transport networks; that the socioeconomic systems are at different stages of internal development and integration; that the cultural systems exhibit certain subsystems that are highly Westernized and others that are extremely backward, then the integration process cannot always be expected to proceed smoothly.

We at the Institute for Latin American Integration believe that it is necessary to develop within the geographic area encompassed by the existing integration schemes centers that can foster an authentic sense of solidarity among different groups of individuals who are capable of projecting, inducing, and disseminating an attitude of solidarity highly integrationist in tone. In other words, we believe it is necessary to institute an integration strategy that will consist of setting up integration poles at strategic locations from which benefits will flow across the region. A multitude of examples could be cited of integration poles on the microeconomic and microsociological scale or on the macroeconomic or macrosociological scale. We would like to point out four classes of integration poles as examples: (1) subregional groups, (2) sectoral integration, (3) border integration, and (4) specific multinational projects or programs in the economic, educational, political, and social spheres.

In regard to subregional groups the strategy we are defining would lead to the identification of subregions whose sociological, political, and economic characteristics are conducive to establishing an integration pole. A typical example of this is the Central American Common Market, which might be followed in the future by other subregional groups now taking shape within Latin America, such as the intermediate-sized Pacific countries of LAFTA, the countries of the Southern Cone of South America, those of the River Plate Basin or of Greater Colombia. It may be noted that these subregional groups could provide a solution to the problems of the varying views held by the several countries as to the pace of the integration process. Subregional groups whose aims could be harmonized with the objectives of continental integration would allow countries desiring to advance more rapidly toward integration to do so without departing from the continental integration scheme.

In regard to sectoral integration the strategy of integration poles will consist of setting up sectoral integration schemes in the fields of the dynamic industries and of regional infrastructure to propagate the benefits of development and integration. By this means the relatively less developed or the intermediate-sized countries could enter into mutual agreements and proceed to establish broader markets for their industrial output by constituting larger units whose subsequent integration with those of the more developed countries could be accomplished under better conditions.

In regard to border integration the strategy of integration poles tends to identify border areas between two or more countries where there is an authentic feeling of solidarity. The border zone is viewed as a single unit where certain incentives are offered to the installation of production activities for a broader market beyond the boundaries. The Inter-American Development Bank has furnished technical and financial assistance for projects of this type between Colombia and Venezuela and between Colombia and Ecuador, and is currently considering similar assistance to the project for integration of the Gulf of Fonseca in Central America.

Last, with regard to the fourth type of integration poles, the strategy consists of preparing specific multinational programs in the economic, social, political, and educational fields. The Pre-investment Fund for Latin American Integration, recently established by the IDB, will provide valuable assistance in the identification of these projects in the economic and educational fields.

In our view, the strategy of integration poles affords opportunities for the individual Latin American countries to advance within the integration movement at the different levels of progress permitted by their political, economic, and social structures. This strategy may be divided into micro- and macrosociological and economic tactics to allow the participation of many persons and groups in the integration effort and so pave the way for mature evolution of the national cultural systems by generating within them a loyalty to the Latin American community in consonance with their ties of loyalty to the existing national community. At a later date this maturity will make it possible to take more decisive steps under the strategy of continental integration. The integration poles are the centers for the propagation of a sense of solidarity; they are milestones in the development strategy that should lead to the unification of Latin America into a great economic community, a great nation of nations.

Today, more than a century after the foundation of the Society for American Union, we can repeat with equal validity the assertion made in the constitution of this organization: "What we do seek, what we do hope for, what will be achieved, is the gradual fashioning of that great nation that already has being in the emotions, the aspirations and the ideas of almost every American individual and people, and which is beginning to find concrete expression in the opinions, the plans, the projects, even in the policies, of some."

The profound difference is that whereas a century ago these words were uttered by intellectual groups with no political or economic power, they now describe the very warp and woof of the present and future of Latin American society and involve every sector in the Latin American countries. They measure for us the extent to which we have advanced since the emergence of an overall integration attitude and strategy.

(4) and (5)

Finally, we need to answer the two questions we posed regarding the future development of the integrationist attitude and strategy: What strategy could the Latin American integrationist groups develop to accelerate the process? And what strategy could the Government and private groups of the United States develop to contribute to Latin American integration?

I would like to answer these two questions together, since this will allow me to clarify certain points relating to both. Some circles in the United States have conceived the idea of setting up action committees consisting of North and Latin Americans from the political, business, and labor sectors to promote the acceleration of Latin American integration. Although the intention behind this project is magnificent, we could not say as much for its political and psychological soundness. We already know enough about the operation of Latin American political systems to state with certainty that the cause of Latin American integration would be poorly served if the movement could be attributed to promotion and initiative from the United States. We know full well what the reaction would be in certain sectors of Latin American public opinion to such sponsorship. Just as Latin America has been slowly evolving its own integration strategy, so the more influential sectors and groups in the United States must also adopt a proper strategy for their cooperation in the cause of Latin American integration. This strategy has already been defined in broad outline by President Johnson, in his speech of August 17, 1966, at the headquarters of the Pan American Health Organization in Washington, when he said, "It is the Latin American countries themselves which must decide the type and form of the integration they want and the United States can only be called upon as a cooperating partner with Latin America in this great task."

To generate, publicize, and extend the movement of Latin American integration, it is the Latin Americans themselves who must mobilize action committees in business, political, labor, intellectual, and university circles, and every other basic sector of Latin American society, in the cause of integration, and establish integration poles—solidarities with which to bring about the steady evolution of a great Latin American nation.

In the development of integrationist attitude and strategy we might perhaps project a subsequent sixth stage in which the overall attitude and strategy now accepted among the political, technical, and intellectual elite of Latin America would spread throughout the vast geographic space of Latin America, into the many sectors and groups that comprise its societies, and so be transformed into a great popular continental movement.

This task cannot be undertaken by governments alone, though they do have a fundamental part to play, but must also be shared by every social sector. For today the task of reuniting "a great dismembered nation" requires the diffusion and propagation to every social stratum of a consensus existing among the leading elites. The voluntary and legal process that is Latin American integration can only be accomplished through voluntary and legal channels, that is, in essentially democratic ways.

In this great historical enterprise the United States, both at the government level and through private groups, can give invaluable aid through an external strategy in support of the internal strategy of the Latin American people and governments. At this historic juncture, only six years after the approval of the Charter of Punta del Este creating the Alliance for Progress, it seems clear that this Alliance, if it is to gain renewed momentum, must transform the spirit of the pact between the United States and Latin America by centering all its efforts on one of the goals stated at Punta del Este, and from an Alliance for Progress become an Alliance for Latin American Integration.

The basis for the new spirit of this hemispheric pact was superbly expressed by Vice President Humphrey when he said his country supports effective economic integration because it is essential to development under the Alliance for Progress, because the modern Latin America that can emerge from authentic integration would be a much more effective partner in all the great common world enterprises awaiting those of us who share the common values of Western civilization, because the mutually most advantageous and most fruitful commercial and financial relations of the United States are with industrialized and diversified regions, and, last, because economic integration is a fundamental part of the Alliance for Progress program, to which the United States committed itself in faith and loyalty at Punta del Este.

Inter-Americanism

JOSÉ IGNACIO RASCO

Introduction

How can Latin American integration be attained in a hemisphere where very opposite elements exist, where the great gulf between the Anglo-Saxon and the Luso-Hispanic worlds seemingly precludes the consolidation of the countries lying south of the Rio Grande? North of Mexico statistics show the highest progress in the world. But from Mexico down to the southern tip of the hemisphere there is a world of low production and underconsumption with tremendous contrasts of wealth and misery, culture and illiteracy.

In the United States the Revolutionary War started a process that culminated in the union of the Thirteen Colonies. In Latin America, on the other hand, the Wars of Independence started a process of disunion with the creation of a group of new republics. This is not the place to analyze this great historical phenomenon; I only point it out as a fact. But I think we should add that this fragmentation was politically inspired. The new frontiers did not erase the strong ties of common patrimony which had their origins in the colonial era.

In the 150 years since independence, however, many separatist interests have evolved. Common ties seem to have been cut by the political and economic rivalries of these "Disunited States of South America." And any attempt for the reintegration of Latin America will demand great energy to overcome such obstacles. The present call to unite is really a new war of independence against our atomized state. This explains the urgency and boldness of the talk on Latin American integration, on a common market, and on Latin American solidarity. Of what value can the United States be in this process? How can it aid the future destiny of Latin America? Such are the questions we propose to examine.

If the presence of the United States is felt in every corner of the world, one can well imagine how significant American technology, public and private investment, and economic and political pressures in general have been among its southern neighbors. It is not necessary to come up with an algebraic formula in order to gage the positive and negative aspects of this influence. Suffice it to say that it is too obvious and important a factor to be underestimated. This North American "invasion" is an element that elicits, perhaps as a self-defense mechanism, the response of integration. The example of the union of the Thirteen Colonies is also a case in point. As in many other historical instances, a foreign agent brings about the amalgamation of native elements.

It is no secret that such "stimuli" have produced a heavy artillery of anti-North American propaganda, which is to say that at first a feeling of opposition and hostility has accompanied this integrationist movement. I do not wish to burden these remarks with historical anecdotes that would elicit bad memories of the Big Stick, Manifest Destiny, or Dollar Diplomacy. But neither can we ignore history altogether. This anti-Yankeeism is a negative and circumstantial attitude, very much like the anti-Spanish feeling of the new Latin American nations during the wars of independence, or the aversion that the rebels of the Thirteen Colonies felt toward England.

Fortunately, Latin America has not stagnated in this negative feeling, just as the Thirteen Colonies moved away from a sterile hate against the mother country and the Ibero-Americans learned to appreciate Spain and Portugal. Reason has followed passion, and new perspectives have brought about a better understanding and the destruction of old prejudicies. A reaction favorable to the United States has emerged, an effort toward a positive meeting ground generated by the desire of the United States to rectify its Latin American policy. At this point we should also refresh our historical memory with such valuable examples as the Good Neighbor Policy, Point IV, and the Alliance for Progress. Above all we wish to avoid surrounding ourselves with a distorted exhibition of pictures that would only portray one aspect of reality.

From our own point of view, in the process of social-psychological "fixation," pro- and anti-North Americanism are concomitant factors in these relationships, and they frequently reappear in the American panorama. Both categories play a basic role in the conformation of the present and the future of all of the Americas. But both views—which can be useful in specific moments, as a soul-searching device when sizing up the unexpected—cannot be used as the guiding poles of any long-range strategy. They may be validly applied only as a "threat" or potential threat, as a self-defense measure that can serve as a stepping stone to negotiate from a more solid basis. Because of this, our view of the relations between North and South America cannot be summed up as either pro or anti. If we want to search for a prefix that affords greater realism, we should adopt "inter," which nowadays represents the hemispheric spirit much better than the deceptive pan-Americanism, a favorite until a few years ago.

Inter-Americanism is a more precise term and implies a two-way channel that best reflects the influences running in both directions through the Americas. Only in a condition of intercourse between equals can we find the solution to the riddle of Latin America's future. The integration of Latin America has to be based on inter-Americanism as a precondition for the suppression of protectionist tariffs and other barriers. These spring from ill-conceived national pride, which prefers to sacrifice man to the citizen, the essential to the accidental.

Inter-Americanism has to work first on a Latin American scale for the integration of the "United States of the South." At the same time it must be a necessary channel for a hemispheric integration with the United States of the north. The process will be an extremely complex one because the elements that are favorable or opposed to a Latin American integration are found both in the English and the Spanish and Portuguese sides of the Americas. Which is to say that there is a struggle of vested interests in both worlds. There are two North Americas and two South Americas.

The intricate pattern of interests moves today in a growing international scale, and social and economic factors escape more and more any local circumscription. This is why we have to talk nowadays of an international social justice. The internal struggle of every nation is no longer enough. Autarchy is a dream, particularly for those countries about to take their first steps in development. The integration of Latin America therefore presupposes a peremptory change in internal structures which in great measure are controlled by foreign hands.

Healthy voices throughout the hemisphere propose the formula of Latin American integration as reciprocally beneficial for the whole continent. In this respect Senator Jacob Javits has said:

Whether or not Latin America can produce the economic strength necessary to allow its people to attain their social and economic goals within a democratic framework depends on its willingness to make an early decision to work for meaningful economic integration for a truly effective Latin American common market.

Through the years, the United States has recognized this fact. Our commitment to Latin American integration has been affirmed by Presidents Eisenhower, Kennedy and Johnson, and even more recently by Secretary of State, Dean Rusk and Assistant Secretary of State, Lincoln Gordon. The formation of a Latin American Common Market is in the best political interest of the United States. It is a basic aim of the United States to create a world of free, strong and democratically organized nations and its post-war policies attest to this fact. The Marshall Plan, the World Bank, the United Nations and the European Economic Community have all found their justification, in our eyes, in the development of such a world.

Beyond economics and politics we must formulate the basic problem as one of international ethics. Only with a high sense of international idealism can we readjust the inter-American scene. We do not pretend to solve complicated problems with a utopian idealism, foreign to an all-too-material reality, nor do we seek to trample underfoot any legitimate interests. But we do think that only with a lofty concept of the moral responsibility that is latent in all human affairs can we harmonize the problems that both unite and separate the four Americas of which we are speaking. For the progress and integration of Latin America billions of dollars, plentiful technical assistance, and stable and reasonable prices are required; but the architectonic for the values guiding international politics must be the dignity of man.

This ethical rule should be applied not only in those cases demanding an investigation of a violent disregard of rights or of open aggression against local interests. It must also be applied to the more subtle ways by which external aid can bring about an archaic paternalism or exercise pressures flowing from the unequal power of nations. Needless to say, this ethical attitude must be adopted also by the nations receiving aid from the more developed ones. It is a well-known fact that smaller countries, armed with the strength of their own weakness, end up producing, by default and blackmail, an impasse.

The encyclical *Pacem in Terris* enunciates a moral principle that is all too often forgotten in international relations:

> The same moral law which governs relations between individual human beings serves also to regulate the relations of political communities with one another.

These words should be used as a cardinal principle in our day and age. One of the greatest privileges of a powerful nation is that of imposing the force of law over and above the right of strength. But in order to accomplish this, such a nation must avoid a messianic tone and preoccupation, to the detriment of genuine local solutions, with the imposition of a model, "The American Way of Life," as the only valid future.

Every juridical, and therefore moral, structure implies respect for the scale of values of a political community. In this respect John XXIII was unequivocal. In *Mater et Magistra* he declared that

> There is no doubt that when a nation makes progress in science, technology, economic life, and the prosperity of its citizens, a great contribution

is made to civilization. But all should realize that those things are not the highest goods, but only instruments for pursuing such goods.

Accordingly, we note with sorrow that in some nations economic life indeed progresses, but that not a few men are there to be found, who have no concern at all for the just ordering of goods. These men either completely ignore spiritual values, or put these out of their mind, or else deny they exist. While they pursue progress in science, technology, and economic life, they make so much of external benefits that for the most part they regard these as the highest goods of life. Accordingly, there are not lacking grave dangers in the help provided by more affluent nations for development of the poorer ones. For among the citizens of these latter nations, there is operative a general awareness of the higher values on which moral teaching rests— an awareness derived from ancient traditional custom which provides them with motivation.

Thus, those who seek to undermine in some measure the right instincts of these people, assuredly do something immoral. Rather, those attitudes, besides being held in honor, should be perfected and refined, since upon them true civilization depends.

From the foregoing, it will be seen that all international cooperation should be established on the basis of a dialogue and mutual exchange. The parties concerned must have not only a voice in but also the power to vote on the decisions that are being taken. A reciprocal interchange of opinion, as a rhetorical exercise, is not sufficient. Sometimes it is even preferable to omit consultations that will not have positive results. What we need is a dialogue in action, not an active dialogue.

Latin America proclaims the principle of multilateralism as a precondition for any dialogue of this kind. Bilateral agreements between the United States and individual Latin American countries—and both sides have been equally responsible in this respect —have resulted in the foreclosing of a long-term regional strategy. Bilateralism, because of its intrinsic disequilibrium, affords privileges and limited arrangements at the expense of the higher aim of integration. All bilateral treaties should be construed as a necessary corollary of the more inclusive multilateral agreements.

Ironically, this bilateralism is frequently justified in the name of a protectionist nationalism which thinks only of its own interests in this type of negotiation, even while it works against the equal rights of its neighbor countries. Such treaties are a flagrant sin against the principle of multilateral internationalism and are perpetrated with the complicity of the large and the small country in the mistaken belief that both gain by turning their backs to regional interests.

Frequently these bilateral sidetracks create a reaction and bring about the confusion of nationalism with nationalization, rioting mobs, anti-Yankee demonstrations, and the violent overthrow of the ruling accomplices of suicidal bilateralism. Under the common banner of an "independentism" that is really a tendentious "nationalism" there are often small oligarchic groups in infamous alliance with declared or undeclared elements in the Communist ranks who ignore the duties of an "interdependentism," so indispensable in our times.

Another obstacle that conspires against a mutual understanding between the English-speaking and Spanish- or Portuguese-speaking peoples is the reciprocal ignorance that exists between them. As Professors William Pierson and Federico Gil have indicated in their book *Governments of Latin America:*

> Lack of general knowledge about the social and political problems of Latin America, combined at times with irresponsible and oversimplified reporting on both sides, have often distorted actions and misinterpreted motives. Outside government circles, some business organizations, and academic institutions, the majority of the people have only superficial or inaccurate notions about their neighbors. These factors, often accentuated by language and cultural barriers, are at work on both sides against a sound foundation for policy.

This ignorance of each other's ways of being and of reacting is a constant factor in this permanent state of disequilibrium and maladjustment. We witness daily the unjust accusations and the use of platitudes and worn-out cliches about the idiosyncrasies of these cultures in the platforms of political parties and the declarations and speeches of well-known public personalities.

Sometimes, without falling into such extremes, it is merely a matter of misinformation. A recent case in point can be seen in the reciprocal misunderstanding that has arisen from the laudable effort of the Alliance for Progress. The shrewd observations of Senator Wayne Morse serve to illustrate this matter:

Our usual viewpoint, though partially valid, is defective on three counts: First, it attributes purely North American origins to the Alliance, when in fact its historic inspiration is the upsurge of reformist and revolutionary sentiment in Latin America. Secondly, and more important, it assigns an essentially passive role to the Latin American countries, when, in fact, the prospects of the Alliance depend overwhelmingly on the creative initiative of the peoples of Latin America and only to a very limited extent on assistance provided by the United States. Thirdly, the view of the Alliance as essentially a North American initiative perpetuates the myth that the interest of the United States in Latin America is something new, when in fact the United States has been profoundly involved in Latin America for over a century, and the Alliance, in historic terms, is not a radical departure but a continuation, by new and enlightened means, of traditional policies and involvements.

Such reciprocal lack of knowledge, which generates a whole range of theories based on prejudice and results in the cheapest kind of demagogy, is made ten times worse by the intervention of factors extraneous to the continent. With the bad faith that characterizes this intervention, a course of policy based on systematic struggle and hatred between classes is engendered.

Generally speaking, if the socioeconomic backwardness of Latin America is a grave problem, its psychological underdevelopment constitutes an even greater cause of concern. A strong dose of passion, of feelings of frustration, and past dependency compound this Latin American phenomenon. In the United States, too, there is a similar disproportion, a "cultural lag" between reality and opinion, since technology increases at a much greater speed than the awareness of many leaders of present-day problems. This tends to produce an attitude of contempt for the poorer relatives of the south.

Even though there have been many efforts in the past few decades to change these immature attitudes, certain stereotypes that reflect a great deal of mutual mistrust still persist. These preclude the rapid understanding of events with a concomitant delay in carrying out of programs.

The Latin American image of North America is evidently

deformed. Our literature attacks more often than praises. In the authors, and the actors as well, of the nineteenth century it is hard to avoid running across a systematic denunciation of United States diplomacy, often curiously combined with a great admiration for North American institutions, particularly the Constitution of the United States. Evidently there is a germ of truth in these analyses. The trouble is that nowadays many intellectuals persist in kicking a dead horse.

American writers have not depicted a very realistic Latin American picture either. An overemphasis on folkloric themes, ruins, and prehistoric relics ends up by portraying Latin America as a more or less colorful and photogenic site. Another factor, as José Figueres, the ex-president of Costa Rica, has pointed out, is that:

The United States is steadily moving further away from the underdeveloped world economically and, as a consequence of this, is moving further away psychologically. It is becoming more and more difficult for the United States as a nation to communicate with the rest of the world. When you have been rich for several generations, it is very difficult to gauge the emotions of people who have always been poor. There is bound to be a great deal of misunderstanding. The misunderstanding exists and it is growing worse. It makes me anxious about the future of inter-American relations.

Let us be realistic. A formula for the effective integration of Latin America cannot be achieved without the cooperation of the United States. Among other reasons Latin America does not have the technology and the capital resources necessary to modernize with the urgency required in order to attain a desirable level of development.

Felipe Herrera, president of the Inter-American Development Bank, has expressed this thought very clearly in the following terms:

An integrated Latin America could and should consolidate its association with the United States in a regional bond necessary to both. For despite the differences between them, they share common values and complement each other in ways that make this regional link natural and logical. There is no need for an economic inter-American issue to distort the true image of

Latin America. Inter-Americanism must not submerge or blur the identity of Latin America, but instead, should reflect the real image of the region.

Strong economic reasons recommend this relationship for the benefit of millions of people. We must not confuse this cooperation with a system whereby the rich give away "something for nothing" to the poor. As William Manger has so correctly pointed out, both Americas, the blond and the brunette, need one another:

Progress in one has its repercussions in the other; failure in one means failure in the other. If we wish to have strong political ties with Latin America, we must have, too, strong economic ties. If we expect our relations with Latin America to function effectively in the highly political field of peace and security—or in dealing with the threat of Communism—we must see that they also function effectively in the economic and the social field.

The principle of solidarity is a source of moral obligation. Aside from any material reasons that might make this thesis more attractive, the human basis, the right of a community to develop, demands a sense of international social justice among the nations that each day seem richer, and those that daily become poorer and poorer. This international solidarity and social justice implies a principle of self-help rather than an external transfusion as a lifesaving device.

Only with the thrust of a solid moral commitment can we break down the wall of interest, ignorance, prejudice, and irrationality, and ameliorate the resistance offered by the differences in culture, language, religion, customs, and history. In this connection it is indispensable to emphasize, as John XXIII has superbly done, a respect for indigenous traditions and a real altruism in all foreign aid:

It is indeed clear to all, that countries in process of development, often have their own individual characteristics, and that these arise from the nature of the locale, or from cultural tradition, or from some special trait of the citizens.

Now, when economically developed countries assist the poorer ones, they not only should have regard for these characteristics and respect them, but also should take special care lest, in aiding these nations, they seek to impose their own way of life upon them.

Moreover, economically developed countries should take particular care lest, in giving aid to poorer countries, they endeavor to turn the prevailing political situation to their own advantage, and seek to dominate them.

Should perchance such attempts be made, this clearly would be but another form of colonialism, which, although disguised in name, merely reflects their earlier but outdated dominion, now abandoned by many countries. When international relations are thus obstructed, the orderly progress of all peoples is endangered.

Genuine necessity, as well as justice, requires that whenever countries give attention to the fostering of skills or commerce, they should aid the less developed nations, without thought of domination, so that these latter eventually will be in a position to progress economically and socially on their own initiative.

These words should act as a constant guide for the platform of political parties, the preachings of churches, and the declarations of American leaders. Up to the present it can indeed be said that the idea of Latin American integration has been favored by many public personalities in the United States. President Lyndon Johnson, Vice President Hubert Humphrey, Secretary of State Dean Rusk, Senator Robert Kennedy, Senator Jacob Javits, and other high officials have shown great enthusiasm for such an idea.

The Catholic Church in Latin America has also in recent years been fighting very effectively in defense of social justice, against the exploitation of man by man. We are reminded here of the many sixteenth-century missionaries who proclaimed themselves defenders of the Indians against the abuses that were being perpetrated by the Spanish Conquerors.

Catholics today must feel, in all earnestness, the weight of this moral obligation. The force of public opinion generated by North American Catholicism, in alliance with the South American faithful, can favor a continental solidarity and nourish it with the loftiest ideals and with concrete and selfless efforts. This must be accomplished with the ecumenical sense of our times, without any arrogance, or false mysticism, or messianism, but with the genuine and real charity of which St. Paul so genially spoke.

PART FIVE

LATIN AMERICA
IN THE WORLD

International Trade

ANTONIO CASAS-GONZALEZ

Latin America, like other areas of the developing world, depends heavily on its export income to finance economic growth. A high degree of correlation therefore exists between growth of the gross domestic product, especially that of the industrial sector; growth of investment in infrastructure; and the capacity to import. For this reason an adequate rate of social and economic development in Latin America is not possible without a sustained expansion of exports. External financial aid plays a complementary role, and, although important, it will yield only short-run positive effects.

The dependence of the Latin American economies on the external sector, coupled with a high concentration of exports in a relatively small number of products (some fifteen basic products account for almost 75 percent of the total value of exports), has caused an excessive vulnerability on the part of the Latin American national economies to depressions occurring in international markets. The measures adopted by the Latin American countries in reaction to loss of export income have been remarkably similar, despite some marked structural differences between their economies. Indeed, the major differences among those measures have

283

been occasioned by the particular time and circumstances in which they were taken.

Knowledge of new techniques and the acquisition of new economic tools have influenced the kinds of policies being adopted. In recent years the application of corrective measures which take into account the need for integrated development have been gaining importance. In this paper I wish to discuss the role of foreign trade in the process of Latin American economic development and to point out its influence in the movements toward regional economic integration. It is useful to begin by briefly reviewing some phenomena which have not received sufficient attention in spite of their great importance and the fact that they have been recurring during the last thirty years. As a consequence of the world depression which began in the early thirties, and which brought about a violent contraction of world demand for traditional Latin American exports, almost all Latin American countries suffered grave balance of payments crises, which obliged their governments to adopt drastic measures to limit imports. These restrictive measures, aiming to reduce external purchasing to absolute necessities in order to avoid precipitating total economic paralysis, ranged from outright restraints on imports to the establishment of import quotas, prohibitively high duties, and complicated import license mechanisms.

Within this framework the more developed Latin American countries undertook their first sustained efforts at substituting for imports. It should be emphasized, however, that the resultant industrialization process was in no way a consequence of a deliberate developmental policy on the part of their governments, at least not as development is conceived of nowadays. It was instead the reaction of the private sector to restrictive measures on imports which resulted in a demand which could not be met. For that reason, industrialization was begun in the field of consumer goods, first in perishables and then in nonperishables.

The outbreak of World War II contributed, for different reasons, to the import-substituting trends and, in a large measure, consolidated the concept of "inward growth" which has characterized until recently the process of Latin American development.

When after the end of World War II the Latin American governments began to conceive of economic development and industrialization in more definite terms and took the first steps toward
setting up the institutional bases which would give impulse to the
process, the influence of unfortunate past experience in balance
of payments problems still persisted. The conceptual similarity
which is found in the legislations of that time in many Latin
American countries is notable, particularly in the high priority
which·foreign exchange savings receive with regard to the creation of new industry, in spite of the fact that there was no real
scarcity of foreign exchange at that time.

As one could expect, the industrialization process, which was
little concerned with establishing basic industries, in turn generated new and more urgent import necessities as a consequence
of the heavy demand for inputs which were not produced domestically. Thus, such a process demands a permanent increment of
foreign sector revenues. Unfortunately, the world market situation, except for very brief periods, does not facilitate the expansion of exports.

The fifties were characterized by almost constant declines in
prices of Latin American export products, with the exception of
two brief periods during the Korean and Suez crises. A look at
the indices of unit value for exports, calculated by the IMF on
the basis of 1958 prices equal 100, affords a clearer notion of this
problem. But the situation becomes even more critical during the
first years of the sixties. The index again declines, and only in
1964 does it show a slight upturn (101) compared to 1958. As
a result of the situation described, Latin American countries were
once again faced with serious disequilibria in their balance of
payments, which directly hindered their capacity to import and
resulted in additional difficulties in sustaining their developmental efforts.

The current outlook presents some disturbing factors which
further aggravate the situation. In addition to the traditional
needs for external financing are added these deriving from the
demands of existing industry and those arising from efforts to
accelerate development. The rising demand for new materials,

intermediate products, and services brought about by the industrialization process gives rise to greater rigidities in the import structure and thus decreases the possibilities of limiting imports in order to avoid balance of payments difficulties. Some highly complex and difficult to solve socioeconomic problems further aggravate the situation. For example, the sudden growth of an industrial proletariat, carrying greater weight in the political life of the countries than the old rural proletariat, makes it almost impossible to apply corrective measures, since these would result in a reduction of employment opportunities. Along these lines it should not be forgotten that an oversupply of labor, constantly aggravated by the accelerated population growth, is one of the most important determinants of political and social instability which characterize Latin America. Thus, despite some of the structural defects it manifests in its early stages the industrialization process is irreversible, since it constitutes the only means that governments have, at least in the short run, of assuring continuing sources of employment for the growing labor force.

In the early 1960's the majority of the Latin American nations created planning institutions and initiated programs fostering a rational policy for development. Nevertheless, those countries are finding great obstacles in overcoming some distortions deriving from the past. One of the most difficult to neutralize has been the lack of foreign income to satisfy development needs. This has become more acute as Latin America has entered a period of increasingly heavy external indebtedness, since the amortization of growing obligations further increases the need for export revenues.

To summarize, the following points should be underscored:

1. It was balance of payments crises which, generally speaking, initiated the process of industrialization in Latin America.

2. Therefore, industrialization, even that based on some type of development planning policies, recognizes, as its principal goal, the need for substitution of imports in order to save foreign exchange.

3. Industrialization, first and foremost, is oriented toward the production of perishable and nonperishable consumer goods and of some capital goods, with a certain measure of basic industries.

4. As a consequence, dependence on export earnings is increased by the expansion of demand originated by the process itself.

5. The export sector, lacking dynamism, is unable to assure financing of the development process already under way, which forces countries to look to foreign credit.

6. To the traditional financing needs are added increased demand for imports and servicing of the foreign debt.

7. Increasingly acute social problems prevent governments from adopting short-range reform measures which might cause cutbacks in employment opportunities.

8. And, finally, industry created in order to substitute imports encounters serious bottlenecks caused by the relative dimensions of the internal market.

Let us now consider the conditions Latin America faces in attempting to increase its exports.

Regional Economic Blocs

The emergence of regional economic blocs, as well as the protective policies adopted by certain industrialized nations since the postwar period, has created new obstacles to the expansion of Latin American exports. The members of the British Commonwealth have been enjoying access to the British market under favorable conditions. The same situation occurs within the COMECON countries. The European Economic Community through its policy of protecting agricultural production and granting preferential concessions to the associated overseas countries has made access to European markets extremely difficult for Latin American exports. To a lesser extent the liberalization of reciprocal trade between the member countries of the European Free Trade Association also limits the possibilities of expanding Latin American exports.

The policies of certain highly industrialized countries which are not members of regional blocs also contribute to limiting Latin American export trade. We may cite the agricultural subsidy program in the United States, which has contributed toward distorting world markets in agriculture, for example, in the case of cotton, which represents more than 5 percent of the total exports of Latin America.

Impact of Trade Policies Adopted by Industrialized Countries on Latin American Exports

A brief review of the current situation of the principal Latin American export products will give us a better understanding of the effects that the above-mentioned policies have had on Latin American foreign trade, and will provide us with a further justification for regional economic integration. Tropical agricultural products originating in Latin America enter into the European Common Market under disadvantageous competitive conditions compared with exports coming from the associated overseas countries. These benefit from preferential customs duties in addition to technical assistance and financial aid extended on very favorable terms. France, for example, has established restrictive quotas for imports coming from countries outside the franc area.

Sugar, which is an export product of sixteen of the twenty Latin American countries, is subject to quota limitations in almost all the developed countries to protect national production of associated territories. In the United States, legislation has tended systematically to diminish the reliance on imports in favor of local production. Agricultural products from Latin American temperate zones also encounter severe restrictions in the European Economic Community countries, and in the world market they must face the competition of subsidized products. This has meant that Latin American exports have been losing ground in world trade. Thus, for example, while in the first half of the 1950's the participation of Latin American exports varied around 10 percent of the world total, in recent years it has barely reached 6 percent, and there is evidence of a further deterioration of the relative position in the near future.

The rate of growth of the value of Latin American exports is insufficient to meet the development needs of the area. Between 1961 and 1965 the cumulative annual growth rate averaged

5.8 percent, with a minimum of 1.6 percent registered in 1961 and a maximum of 7.7 percent in 1964. In 1965 the growth was around 2.6 percent, and an even smaller rate is foreseen for 1966 and 1967. The outlook appears even more gloomy when one takes into account a new tendency for the decline of prices in the world market and a continuing deterioration of the terms of trade for the whole Latin American area.

In addition, there exists a structural factor which contributes to making the situation much more difficult: the great dependency of Latin America, for export finance, on food products with a low income elasticity of demand in the industrialized countries. We frequently hear mention of the world food crisis, but we must bear in mind that the areas with the greatest shortages do not have the means of paying for their imports. At present, and for many years to come, Latin America cannot consider those areas as true markets for its products.

Economic Integration of Latin America

Latin American economic integration is an old aspiration which culminated in 1960 with the signing of two treaties establishing the first zones of integration in the area. As a result of the initial groundwork laid over a period of several years, the treaty of Montevideo created the Latin American Free Trade Association (LAFTA). In December of the same year the General Treaty of Central American Integration was also signed.

Although both documents have the same goal, they present notable differences with regard to the means and the timing of their implementation. In addition, the geographic area which the respective treaties cover and the countries comprising them show significant differences. LAFTA, for example, is made up of ten, mostly large, countries: Argentina, Brazil, Chile, Colombia, Ecuador, Mexico, Paraguay, Peru, Uruguay, and, at the beginning of this year, Venezuela. In addition, Bolivia has expressed interest in joining the Association in the near future. The member countries of LAFTA comprise 89 percent of the population and 94 percent of the gross domestic product of Latin America.

The General Treaty of Central American Integration includes five small countries: Costa Rica, El Salvador, Guatemala, Honduras, and Nicaragua, which represent only about 5 percent of the population and 5 percent of the gross domestic product of Latin America. The objective of the treaty of Montevideo is the elimination of customs and other barriers limiting free trade between member countries. In order to avoid difficulties which might result from an immediate freeing of all trade, especially those caused by the varying degrees of development of the member countries, the treaty has established a graduated process of lowering duties and other barriers over a period of twelve years. To attain this objective, the treaty established annual negotiations as the mechanism by which reciprocal concessions at a minimum rate of 8 percent per year could be agreed upon. Although the treaty foresees the unconditional and unrestricted treatment of the most favored nation, it contains special clauses which assure an exclusive treatment in benefit of the relatively less economically developed countries, for example, Ecuador, Paraguay, and, when it joins, Bolivia. In accord with recently agreed upon conditions, it foresees also a special treatment for those countries with "insufficient markets" (Colombia, Chile, Peru, Uruguay, and Venezuela).

Products which have benefited with continuing lower duties in successive negotiations make up the so-called "National Lists." The lists became effective January 1, 1962, and once the sixth negotiation period of December, 1966, was finished, some 9,500 products had been incorporated. Furthermore, various agreements of industrial complementation have been subscribed, such as one for statistical equipment and electronic computers and another for electronic tubes, to permit the development of important industrial sectors.

The General Treaty of Central American Integration establishes free trade of all products originating in member countries with some exceptions. These refer mainly to some critical articles which are nevertheless subject to special preferential tariffs with respect to third countries, to certain quota limitations, or to specific trade agreements. However, the treaty calls for the removal of all trade barriers in a period of five years in order to build a true customs union. In the meantime the measures which have been adopted since the signing of the General Treaty consist of the elimination of certain quota controls, the amplifying of other quotas, and the concession of greater duty preferences among the member nations. These have diminished greatly the significance of a good part of the existing exceptions to the treaty. In addition, the General Treaty establishes the adoption, in a period also of five years, of the common external tariffs which would apply to imports coming from countries outside the trade zone.

In Central America the impact of CACOM is very widespread and very direct. Advertising signs speak no longer of "the best soft drink of Honduras," but of "the best soft drink of Central America." Workers in El Salvador know that the canned goods they produce may be sold in Nicaragua or Costa Rica. Five years ago capitalists would never have invested their funds in a neighboring republic. There was a legacy of suspicion, prejudice, distrust. My own father-in-law, from El Salvador, used to speak of integration as "a crazy idea," and assured me he would never put a cent in Honduras or in any other Central American country. But only last year he joined with some other Salvadoreans in making investments in Honduras in one of the industries being set up there under CACOM. His attitude has completely changed, and he is one of the great defenders of integration.

There exist marked differences between both integration movements, especially in the institutional, financial, and regional development planning aspects. In very broad terms we can say that the General Treaty of Central American Integration goes much further than the treaty of Montevideo, which is practically limited to establishing a zone of free trade.

The Development of Export Trade and Latin American Regional Economic Integration

The traditional structure of Latin American foreign commerce, comprised primarily of raw materials, fuels, and foodstuffs, has caused the trade patterns of these countries to be oriented toward the developed countries. Before the integration treaties became effective, commerce within LAFTA countries, and within the Central American nations, varied between 6 and 11 percent of their total foreign trade. The major trade patterns were those between the countries of the temperate southern zone and their neighboring countries to the north, since trade among tropical countries was relatively small. On the other hand, countries which were producers of mineral raw materials were limited in their possibility of exporting to other Latin American nations because of the relatively low degree of industrial development in the region. This, in part, explains why Latin America only now has begun to establish an infrastructure adequate to satisfy the needs of intraregional trade.

Our own attitude in the Inter-American Development Bank toward road building has changed a great deal. I remember that when I went with a delegation to see President Belaunde of Peru three years ago, we were not very impressed with his plans for a Marginal Road of the Andes. I thought he was imagining things and that he needed to come down to earth. But he kept on insisting so hard that the Bank agreed to finance some studies, if only to avoid political problems. And now we are financing 450 kilometers of that road system. In less than three years this dream, about which I was so skeptical, is going to become a reality. We have also financed a road from Valparaiso in Chile to Mendoza in Argentina, and are studying a road to link Buenos Aires with Yacuiba in Bolivia. The Bank, which in its three years of operations had not financed a single road, is now financing more than $25 to $30 million in roads, and by the end of 1967 that figure will be about $100 million. And along with this increase in financing goes greater skill and sophistication in the planning of these projects.

A clearer idea of the relative isolation in which the Latin American countries developed may be obtained by bearing in mind that until a short time ago, banking operations accompanying commercial trade between Buenos Aires and Lima, for example, had to go through New York; the same situation prevails today for telegraphic and telephone communications. Added to these obstacles are others of an economic, financial, and even political nature, the solution of which is not simple.

Among those of an economic nature perhaps one of the most serious is that brought about by the varying degrees of development among the Latin American countries. Their differential characteristics are such that the elimination of trade barriers is not sufficient to assure a balanced development of the region. Significant advances have been made, but the majority of the problems remain to be resolved. The recognition of special conditions within the framework of LAFTA for the relatively less-developed countries and those with insufficient markets, although a positive step, has not yet produced the expected results.

The chronic monetary instability which troubles many Latin American countries constitutes another barrier against financial integration. Although a mechanism has already been established among the Central American countries, much remains to be done within LAFTA. The only tangible gains of LAFTA have been the establishment of credit mechanisms and bilateral payment agreements.

Political instability, also a characteristic of many Latin American countries, has prevented the adoption of the necessary high-level governmental decisions. The traditional concept of national sovereignty, deeply rooted in Latin America, delays the adoption of some urgently needed steps which would afford greater dynamism to the process of regional integration.

Despite these obstacles, the integration movement, already under way, constitutes an irreversible process. Let us remember what was said at the beginning about the continuous damage to Latin America's participation in world trade as a consequence of the protective policies and subsidies of the intraregional economic blocs and certain industrialized countries. Latin America has been challenging these and has participated in the United Nations Conference on Trade and Development (UNCTAD) and in other international organizations. Short-run results, however, cannot be expected from the deliberations of the Conference. If indeed the industrial countries are now more favorably disposed than in the first meeting of the UNCTAD in 1964, an enumeration of specific measures to be adopted for the benefit of the developing countries is still forthcoming. The negotiations of GATT, and especially those carried out in the Kennedy Round, have so far failed to produce results which can bring solutions to the problems of Latin America. Meanwhile the attitude and policies of the economic blocs outside of the Latin American region, especially the European Economic Community, offer little cause for optimism. New measures tending to protect domestic meat production can be cited as proof of this. If, therefore, Latin America cannot find a favorable short-run answer to its problems of trade and development in the international sphere, it has no other alternative but to intensify its efforts to expand its trade within its own region.

The problems of Latin American industrial development have also been increasing with some degree of urgency. It has been shown how the process of industrialization was initiated in large measure with the goal of substituting imports. That process, which at the outset grew rapidly, has recently been losing its dynamism. Despite the fact that there still exist possibilities for expansion, this is becoming more and more difficult. The necessity of providing a more rational dimension to existing and future industry in order to improve its competitive capacity is now evident. This can only be attained through expansion of markets by freeing intraregional commerce and by complementing and integrating the economies of the region. This process is presently being carried out rather rapidly in Central America and a bit more slowly in the LAFTA countries. Some idea of the possibilities of expansion which integration of Latin American markets offers can be given by the fact that in the field of foodstuffs alone, Latin America imports more than 700 million dollars annually from outside the region.

The advances which have been made in expanding intraregional trade since 1960 are significant, despite the fact that the value of this trade is still rather small. This situation points to the future possibilities for growth, which should be considerably enhanced with the perfection of existing mechanisms.

It would be useful to examine some of the facts related to the development of trade within the integration treaties. For convenience it is preferable to examine separately those corresponding to LAFTA—with the exception of Venezuela, which just recently became a member—and those of the Central American countries.

Trade between member countries of LAFTA has traditionally been, for reasons already discussed, of rather small significance. Before the signing of the treaty of Montevideo many of the Latin American countries channeled their commerce through bilateral trade and payments agreements. During the period 1953–1955, in which the former treaties were still in effect, trade among these countries constituted barely 10 percent of their exports, with a great concentration in the reciprocal trade between Argentina, Brazil, and Chile. After 1955, when these treaties were abrogated, the proportion of intraregional commerce fell significantly, to reach a low of 6 percent in 1961.

Beginning in January, 1962, when the first National List of LAFTA went into effect, regional trade began an accelerated rate of expansion, evidenced by an accumulative annual growth rate of 12 percent in 1962, 23 percent in 1963, 27 percent in 1964, and around 20 percent, according to provisional data, in 1965. In addition, the participation of intraregional trade as a percentage of all commerce also improved and in 1965 represented more than 10 percent of the total.

Another fact which should be emphasized is the establishment, since the signing of the treaty, of regular and growing trade patterns between Colombia, Ecuador, and Mexico and between countries of the South Atlantic coast. As a consequence of the treaty a gradual change has also been effected in the structure of intraregional trade. In 1962, 84 percent of transactions corresponded to foodstuff and raw materials, while in 1964 this proportion was reduced to 77 percent, with a corresponding increase in manufactured products.

In summary, the following benefits may be attributed to the treaty: an increase in trade within the Latin American zone, the beginning of a process of diversification of exports, and the establishment of trade patterns among countries of the area which in the past maintained very irregular and insignificant commercial traffic. Finally, it should be emphasized that more than half of the increase of total commerce noted in the last five years can be attributed to the expansion of the intrazonal trade.

The General Treaty of Central American Integration has been a dynamic factor of great importance in the expansion of trade of its member countries. According to estimates of the Secretariat of the treaty (SIECA) such trade was responsible in 1964 for 16.5 percent of the gross industrial product of the region, while in 1962 the relation was only 10.7 percent. The freeing of trade likewise contributed to a notable diversification of exports, as we may see from the fact that in 1963, 70 percent of intraregional trade was comprised of manufactured products.

Since the program of freeing trade was put into effect, intra-regional commerce has been growing rapidly: in 1961 by 13 percent, in 1962 by 37 percent, in 1963 by 31 percent, in 1964 by 59 percent, and in 1965 by 25 percent. This trade has also increased its participation in the general trade totals, from 7 percent before the treaty went into effect to more than 15 percent last year. The outlook for the next few years is for an acceleration in the rhythm of growth of intra-Central American trade as a result of the development of industrial activity favored by the widening of markets. The expansion of intra-Central American trade in the last five years provided almost a third of the growth of the total foreign trade of the area.

Much has been said about the possibility of joining the two separate efforts for Latin American economic integration. Nonetheless, the economic and political implications which are present in the short run will probably delay the adherance of Central America to the treaty of Montevideo. In the meantime, the secretariats of each treaty have been exchanging information and seeking ways of cooperating to solve problems of common interest.

The present decade will be remembered by Latin Americans as the period when the foundations of the system by which future generations will enjoy a better life were laid. All of us who consider integration as the best solution to the economic problems of Latin America are sure of this.

International Communications Media

JOSEPH MICHENFELDER, M.M.

Social communications can be described as the art of communicating simultaneously with large numbers of men through media which are not dependent upon interpersonal contact. The term encompasses the four major mass media—press, radio, television, and films—along with their many elaborations and refinements such as computers, satellites, cable services, radio schools, closed-circuit television, publications, records, and filmstrips.

It is hardly necessary to justify the involvement of Christians in social communications. But it might be pointed out that the Christian views social communications not as a weapon of conquest but as an instrument of service. The Christian objective in utilizing instruments of social communications is not mass control, image-making, commercialism, manipulation, or an apostolic *quid pro quo*—which translates into media jargon as "the Gospel hook." Rather, the Christian objective is the presenting of truth (with a small "t") to as many persons as possible—truth which forms and informs, elevates and inspires, instructs and entertains. Just as the Christian loves his fellow man because he *is* man, and feeds a hungry man because he *is* hungry, so he engages in social communications because man *needs* to communicate. Such total commitment to the real world of real men responds to the total visions of the Second Vatican Council. Christians now realize that prior to the Council it was quite difficult for the Church to fulfill her mission within the modern world because she did not seem to be a part of it. She regarded herself, rather, and was often regarded by others, as a maverick, a foreign element. Conciliar Christians must consequently keep themselves open for any historical change because history is the way of the spirit. As soon as Christians cut themselves off from historical developments, such as the communications revolution, they stiffen into antiques, quaint museum pieces. And the Church, instead of living and working as the soul of human society, evolves into a kind of establishment whose members become fixated upon themselves and speak clearly, perhaps, to one another, but in indecipherable code to the rest of humanity.

I should like now to discuss some pivotal factors vis-à-vis international communications and a continent such as Latin America. The twenty republics involved must be described as "in integral development" socially, politically, economically, spiritually, and, to an extent which most North Americans and Europeans fail to realize, ideologically. In my analysis I shall depend heavily upon the research and writings of Dr. Wilbur Schramm, director of the Institute for Communications Research at Stanford University. His volume *Mass Media and National Development* bears every mark of the classic study, or, if not that, at least a significant prototype.[1]

In treating the world flow of information, Schramm discovers what he calls "repetitive patterns as regular as trade winds." He then concludes that these patterns are not at all favorable to new and developing countries in urgent need of information, which is one of the essential factors in genuine integration. The broad picture is this:

1. The great avenues of information exchange are owned by a few countries. The five major world news agencies, that is, are owned, publicly or privately, in four nations. The Associated Press and United Press International are United States agencies; Agence France Presse is French; Tass is Soviet; Reuters is British.

2. Ownership of long-distance telecommunication facilities,

though not quite so restricted as that of the world news agencies, is still in relatively few hands.

3. Less than one-third of the countries of the world are the major producers and custodians of the technology on which modern society depends.

4. The concentration of wealth in certain countries makes it possible for their people to support the industries and enterprises of communications media, and to produce the equipment and the personnel which an efficient flow of information requires.

This formidable matrix produces the patterns, and indeed, like the trade winds, they *are* predictable. Schramm's worldwide analysis of newspapers over a designated period of time reveals that the overwhelming percentage of news flows from Europe and North America to the other continents. He also demonstrates that the United States, France, the Soviet Union, and England, the four countries that are homes of the five world news agencies, dominate this immense flow of information.

It would be a simplistic error, of course, to read into such an analysis some kind of conspiratorial meaning. It so happens that the sheer potency of these four countries, by reason of the dynamics of their diplomatic relations, economic strength, trade, science, technology, and art, ensures that almost anything of significance that occurs within their borders is likely to be of interest to smaller, less potent countries throughout the world. In one sense it is not unlike the comparative imbalance of true power between the Security Council and the General Assembly of the United Nations.

I think we should not be nearly so disturbed about the heaviness of news flow from a few countries as about the thinness of the flow from many others. For instance, Mr. Hal Hendrix, Latin American editor of *The Miami News,* made an analysis of the news flow of one United States wire service from Latin America during the month of February, 1962. Hendrix concluded that if the February wire file were "the only source of enlightenment for the rest of the world, then Latin America would be considered to consist mainly of Cuba." During that month of February most other countries of Latin America were represented newswise by a few so-called "events" such as the arrival of Prince Philip in Bolivia, the arrival of Billy Graham in Chile, a bus accident, a plane crash, and a flood in Peru. From several countries there was no news whatsoever.[2]

A further observation should be made here in reference to the nature of news dissemination within a developing country. While news and information are readily available in the capitals and urban centers of Latin America, the flow of supply to the rural areas drops off enormously. No matter where one travels in the provinces one has the feeling of being isolated from the major movements and ideas that encompass what we call modernity. And then when one remembers that it is there, in the rural provinces where the masses live, that these people sustain the spiraling birth rate, subhuman living standards, and illiteracy, human *dis*integration in the most oppressing sense of the word, one tends to view the educational potential of social communications and media instruments with new respect and expectations. As Pin and Houtart point out in their book, *The Church and the Latin American Revolution,* it appears to be the radio, more than the printed word, which shatters the news-information-awareness barriers which condemn rural Latin Americans to a seventeenth century civilization. I quote:

The power of radio in recent years simply cannot be overemphasized. And now, with the advent of transistors, the boom in radio broadcasting is bound to become even more pronounced. The radio has not merely enabled the marginal populations to shed their ideological limitations in national affairs, it has put them in contact with life around the world. The immediate effects of this can be exaggerated, but the long-range influences are extremely important. . . . The consciousness of living in abnormal conditions is day by day seeping into the mentality of these people. Already their minds have begun a process of transformation.[3]

However, Daniel Lerner, who commands a reputation similar to that of Schramm, cautions media technicians with the following insight based on his studies of a village in Egypt. When the Nasser Government directed Radio Cairo to the community, Lerner claims that nothing *really* changed except the people's expectations. He comments:

This is the typical situation that over the last decade has been producing the revolution of rising frustrations. The mass media have been used to stim-

ulate people in some sense . . . by raising their levels of aspiration—the good
things of the world, for a better life. No adequate provision is made, however, for raising the levels of achievement. Thus people are encouraged to
want more than they can possibly get, aspirations rapidly outrun achievements, and frustrations spread.[4]

As a corollary to this, Gino Germani points out in one of his
sociological studies that a society which is isolated and quite out
of communication is not underdeveloped from the subjective point
of view of its own members. They do, however, consider themselves underdeveloped when they are given the means—in Latin
America, mainly transistor radios—to compare their condition with
that of a more developed society. This sudden awareness, which
Houtart and Pin say is at the base of the present transformations
in Latin America, this awareness by the continent's *dis*integrated
and disfranchised population is what creates the explosive ideological situation. Even if to the casual observer, journalist, or
tourist their traditional "pattern of life" does not appear to change
with the advent of the transistor radio, it is still *not the same* as
it was before the awareness of underdevelopment. We have,
then, the perennially valid distinction between an objective need
and the felt need. In terms of ideological forces in Latin America
the Marxists have exploited this simple sociological dynamic with
far more effort, tenacity, creativity, and success than the West.
The illiterate Peruvian or Colombian or Brazilian peasant clutch-
ing his transistor radio listens not only to his national programs
but also to those of Radio Moscow, Radio Peking, and Radio
Havana. And not infrequently the programming from Marxist
countries is of much higher interest-and-attention caliber because
it is almost totally directed toward the creating and accelerating of
the felt need. The keynote is revolution now! The formula for
change is spelled out. Thus for the peasant the Marxist mystique
is charged with real meaning, however simplistic and naive it
may appear to urban sophisticates or to USIS monitors. The West,
more specifically the United States, has forged really one instrument of rebuttal, the Voice of America. And it is curious to discover how many rural inhabitants of Latin America never listen
to its programs, mainly, I suspect, because the Voice of America

communicates neither the deeper ideological currents of the United States nor the authentic revolutionary aspirations of Latin Americans. (As a footnote, it may be added that the Vatican Radio, which also beams to Latin America, is utterly ineffectual in terms of program content and cannot be considered as one of the forces for change.)

Houtart and Pin conclude their investigation of the phenomenon of the radio with the prophecy that the rapidity of the revolutionary movement of the masses toward a fair share of the twentieth century's wealth and well-being will perhaps depend upon "the degree of awareness of their relatively low condition (and) consequently, upon the development of the means of communication."[5] Many in the field of communications have done studies and amassed experiences when, indeed, just a few short years ago the radio could be described as the single most important media instrument in creating awareness and forging the new patterns which would assist mightily in the integration of Latin American society. I thought so myself a few years ago. I no longer do. I would like, therefore, to devote the remainder of this paper to a brief, cursory examination of the reasons for this uncertainty as it now prevails among increasing numbers of Americans to the north and the south.

Radio (along with the printed word) will undoubtedly continue to play a major role as a media instrument in Latin America. But in terms of the overwhelming impact which communications is expected to have upon developing countries of Latin America— widening of horizons, focusing of ideological attention, creating of a climate for development, changing strongly held values and attitudes, enforcing social norms and educating vast numbers of illiterates—radio will most certainly assume a quite secondary importance and yield to television as the prime integrator of the masses of men toward and into the twenty-first century.

There is ample evidence by way of recognized prophets. Herman Kahn—who specializes in crystal gazing on a highly scientific level by projecting from the known to the feasible and therefore to the probable—claims that by the year 2000 there will be "ten likely and important technological innovations." Four of them are in the field of communications—from inexpensive high-capacity communication and data-processing hardware, such as satellites and lasers, to pervasive techniques for monitoring citizens . . . right out of Orwell's nightmare.[6] (But that is another problem!) Even more visionary than Kahn is E. B. White, who writes:

> I believe television is going to be the test of the modern world, and that in this new opportunity to see beyond the range of our vision we shall discover either a new and unbearable disturbance of the general peace or a saving radiance in the sky. We shall stand or fall by television—of that I am quite sure.

I say "more visionary" because White wrote that statement in 1938. Finally there is the recent, rather fatalistic, statement of England's W. F. Deedes, who, referring to television, said: "It has within its power to decide what kind of people we become. Nothing less."[7]

Let me say, in passing, that I would indeed like to cite here some pertinent passage—scientific, prophetic, or even theological —from the Second Vatican Council's Decree on the Instruments of Social Communication, some passage which reveals on the part of the institutional Church an awareness of the electronic revolution which the conciliar generation has witnessed and must help nurture and guide to maturity. I read the document in vain. Of course, we know that very shortly the Pontifical Commission for Social Communications will issue a pastoral instruction that will hopefully amend the conciliar decree. Which recalls the words of Francis Bacon: "Hope is a good breakfast but a lean supper."

It comes down to this: in the contemporary world the name of the game is modernity. And because this is the name of the game, if the Church is truly going to collaborate with the world of communications, first she must know that world. If not, the Church runs the risk of speaking to the world in terms quite reminiscent of Marconi and Edison.

There are, thankfully, in Latin America some centers and institutes under Church auspices which recognize the dimensions of the electronic revolution. ICODES in Bogotá, under the direction of Father Gustavo Perez, comes to mind, as does the *Instituto*

Bellarmino in Santiago. Both centers, well grounded in theory and in personnel, are moving steadily into the mainstream of audio-visual production. The writings and activities of a North American Jesuit, Father Neil Hurley of the *Instituto Bellarmino* of Santiago, place him among the more visionary of Catholic communications specialists on the Latin American scene. Much of what follows is based on Hurley's research in the field of satellite telecommunications. Hurley's preoccupation must, I think, become the preoccupation of all of us involved in communications, as well as all of us who believe in accelerating integration in Latin America in order to strengthen what Bishop Manuel Larrain often and lovingly referred to as "our hemispheric solidarity, the fraternal covenant among nations."

Hurley's position, simply stated, is this: although the system of satellite communications is still in its infancy, it is growing at at an incredible pace. Now is the time, perhaps the only time, for determining *how* satellite communications should be employed. The strands of what he calls "an electric cocoon" are now being woven around our planet, and these strands

once woven, intertwined and knotted, will not be readily unraveled. Whether we are aware of it or not, the present generation will have to determine the nature of communications for the entire planet. Future generations will be held in the vise-like grip of whatever system of satellite communications we mold now.[8]

David Sarnoff of the Radio Corporation of America has blueprinted the phase development of global satellite communications in this manner:

Phase One: By 1970 the world will possess a system of low-power, synchronous satellites, making it possible to realize direct telephone dialing as well as transmission of telegraphic and data-processing messages, and closed-circuit television.

Phase Two: By 1980 orbiting satellites powered by nuclear energy will accommodate some 10,000 voice or six television channels, and satellite communications will be within the economic reach of small nations and private users.

Phase Three: Beyond 1980, but not too many years beyond, man will have overcome most time-space barriers on the planet. A system of five to ten manned satellites, atomically powered, each possessing 500,000 voice and 500 TV channels, will enable any person, wherever he finds himself, to see or be seen, speak to or be spoken to, by any other person in the world similarly equipped.

Consequently, it is inevitable that "the moving image as projected by the communications satellite will emerge as the constitutive, representative and decisive experience of the human race on earth."[9]

Can any of us who have experienced the birth and rapid adolescence of United States television, for example, seriously doubt that the picture, the kinetic image, more and more fills the waking hours of North Americans? Commercial television broadcasting began in 1946, with six stations serving eight thousand families. As of January 1, 1966, the Television Information Office of the National Association of Broadcasters offered these dimensions of the medium: Some 54 million homes, or 94 percent of all family units, are equipped to receive television. There are 700 stations on the air, with 124 others under construction and 179 applications on file. The year-round per family average of daily television viewing is now estimated at five and a half hours. Viewers have a total investment of 27 billion, 500 million dollars in their receiving sets, and the networks and stations have invested 800 million dollars in transmitting equipment. In 1965 the gross income for TV broadcasters, all from advertising, was just under 2 billion, 500 million dollars, with a 3-billion-dollar projection for 1970.[10]

By the same year, the average eighteen-year-old American will have seen the equivalent of two solid years of televiewing (about eighteen thousand hours in all). Add this to other visual experiences, mainly movies, and it is evident that the image will occupy a large part of the waking day of space-age man.[11] It will be, in fact, man's most important activity after sleeping and working. Thus, for reasons too numerable to treat here, the moving image is now becoming the global teacher, the unspoken but universal language, passing across national boundaries with the surety and ease of sunrays, converting the globe into what Hurley calls a "world village." Above and beyond educational and entertainment programming via satellite, the electronic flow of information will so increase throughout the planet as to cause the disappearance of insular institutions and closed societies. And Hurley is quick to point out that "the hunger for information, catharsis and direct experience is especially acute among those who, for one reason or other, could be called underprivileged—the illiterate, the unskilled, the young and the poor."[12] What these people see in movies and on television shapes their view of both their immediate and their remote environment. Once formed, this new environment begins to reshape their characters, their thought patterns, and their institutions. Hurley, rather grimly to my mind, says that "with the creation of a global system of satellite communications, man and the machine will be definitively integrated—a wedding with no possibility of separation except through a world catastrophe."[13]

It is useful at this point to refresh memories of recent communications history. Five years ago, after it had been proven technically feasible to orbit satellites as relay stations, the United States Congress passed the Communications Satellite Act of 1962. This created COMSAT, the Communications and Satellite Corporation, a broad-based enterprise of private and public investors with capital of 200 million dollars from stock issued in June, 1964.

COMSAT'S commitment is threefold:

1. To develop a global communications satellite system and sell communications services at a profit.

2. To represent the United States in INTELSAT, the International Telecommunications Satellite Consortium, of which more than fifty nations (including Vatican City State) are now partners.

3. To act as manager of INTELSAT on behalf of all of the participating entities designated by the representative countries.

(COMSAT, then, is not a United States Government agency. It is a private corporation responsible to its shareholders, just like the older United States communications companies.)

To operate the global satellite system, COMSAT maintains extensive and growing facilities. Among them is Early Bird, the 240-channel synchronous satellite presently stationed in equatorial orbit over the east coast of Brazil, and joining North America and Europe. Launchings are programmed through 1970 according to blueprints which closely resemble the Phase I development predicted by Mr. Sarnoff. It is important to note that the global system managed by INTELSAT will be available to any country, regardless of whether or not it is signatory to the agreements, simply by paying a fee. Important also is the fact that there is a guarantee that each recipient nation will have the option to decide how and by whom its television facilities are to be owned and operated.

The critical element in establishing a viable inter-American television system is the construction of the ground stations necessary to receive signals transmitted by satellites. During 1967 and 1968 Brazil, Argentina, Colombia, Chile, and Venezuela plan to build such ground stations at a cost of between 4.5 and 6 million dollars. No one seems to doubt that rapid and secure financing of ground stations will be easily obtained. The Inter-American Development Bank (BID) is on the verge of completing a broad survey which will establish criteria for loans to Latin American countries desiring to commit themselves to INTELSAT.

It is obvious that our major concern here is not the technical and financial aspects of INTELSAT, but rather the fact that the creative genius of man has made available technical components that can blanket the world with ideas. By 1980 man will be able to communicate instantaneously, in sound and light, with anyone, anywhere. People in Buenos Aires, Lima, London, Tokyo, Quebec, and Berlin will be able to ask for and receive, almost at once through computer exchange, copies of documents, contracts, blueprints, and photos from anywhere on this planet. Students in any part of the world will be able to hear and see classes at the University of Santiago, the University of Mexico, Oxford, Harvard and Moscow universities by closed-circuit television. Renowned scientists, without leaving their laboratories, will be in sight-sound contact with their colleagues. The same applies to delegates to the United Nations. The same will be true for the international leadership of the Church.

What is the significance of such a communications system as it relates to the integration of Latin America? As an educational instrument for the disseminating of knowledge regarding literacy, hygiene, nutrition, vocational skills, and universal primary education, there is no more revolutionary means than satellite telecommunications. And the most immediate and most practical application of educational telecommunications would seem to be in Latin America, a region that enjoys a homogeneity of culture, tradition, faith, and purpose, and a rather impressive technical structure of radio, television, telephone, and telex.

The heart of the matter is this: How do we want the pan-American telecommunications system to perform? The question must be faced by the business and university communities, by the Church and even by the military. Is there not the likelihood that the system will be dominated by the United States in the same way that the wire services, moving-picture distribution, and exported television programs are now dominated? Is there not the danger that propaganda of all kinds, subtle and crude, hard and soft, may be presented in an almost irresistible way to untrained minds? Yes, there are many risks, many dangers. The great potential for mutual understanding and the sharing of knowledge could rather easily boomerang into deepened hatreds and hysterical tensions—unless the Church makes its presence felt as nations come to grips with the problems of international regulations, unless the Church's need to participate in a satellite communications system is evaluated in terms of the highest possible good for man's spiritual enlightenment, unless, as Hurley suggests, the Church initiates a massive program of collaboration and integration on the programming level.

I, personally, have no idea where or how to begin. Hurley offers a possible beginning, the establishing of

a joint venture among nongovernmental institutions to gather the capital, conduct research and development on high-priority information needs, supervise television programming, maintain an international "sight-sound-data" bank for use by member institutions, and negotiate international agreements. In other words, we need a cooperative in communications, a confederation of cultural agencies to overcome the political obstacles and to command, through adequate payment, that portion of the available band-space which is needed for the spiritual, educational and cultural priorities of international society.[14]

Such imagination and enterprising initiative must be inspired and guided by the guardians of man's mind, heart, and soul. The Church is among those guardians.

I shall close what I hope has not been too haphazard an approach to a vital subject with the separate, but not unrelated, statements of two gentlemen, both of whom surely qualify as guardians of man's mind, heart, and soul. I am speaking of the vice-president of the Columbia Broadcasting System, Mr. John A. Schneider, and the Father General of the Society of Jesus, Father Pedro Arrupe, S.J. Mr. Schneider asserts that:

In ten years we will have an instant communications capability, world-wide. But as to what we are going to say to the world when we have their attention, I'm not certain yet. That's the thing that worries me.

Father Arrupe, for his part, warns that

I am afraid that we (Jesuits) may repeat yesterday's answer to tomorrow's problems, talk in a way men no longer understand, speak a language that does not speak to the heart of living man. If we do this, we shall more and more be talking to ourselves; no one will listen, because no one understands what we are trying to say.

(In response to questions, Father Michenfelder made the following comments.)

Some of the prophecies I have quoted may sound utopian, impossible. But there are only extrapolations of existing trends, a projection of what is already happening. Until the advent of the transistor radio, for example, that medium was considered an interesting instrument, but one of no use in rural areas. Nobody considered it an educational tool until Monsignor Salcedo came along in Bogotá. He found that he could buy Japanese transistors for $16.70; that forced American companies to cut prices, and now we can buy a fairly good American transistor radio, assembled in Arequipa, for $18.50. The same thing is going to occur in transistor television. And the possibilities for educational use, for commercial use, are going to be enormous. When you remember that there will be 600 million Latin Americans by the end of this century, and recall that 94 percent of North Americans now have access to a television set, you can see the tremendous potential there. And as a Roman Catholic, I want to look to the presence of the institutional Church. I want the vision, the authority, the prophetic pastoral mission of my bishops present in this new medium.

But so far I feel that nearly everything that the Church has issued as official documentation on the subject of media is highly unrealistic. Communications specialists exist now in Latin America, laymen and laywomen who will gladly embrace the Church's programs. But the Church must pay them a just wage, a professional wage. The Church in Latin America, the Church in the United States, makes the mistake of planning a very advanced program requiring great technical skill and then asks for volunteers to carry it out. These projects demand well-paid, highly trained specialists. I feel that if we cannot pay the same salaries as COMSAT and RCA, if we cannot think in those terms, we are not going to be in the ball game. Communications is expensive, and yet the Church has often treated it as a kind of minor issue, something to be handled by volunteers in their spare time.

We might begin by bringing together five or six qualified people from Latin America for a year and giving them a variety of experience in genuine communications work. And if they show talent and inspiration, a really Christian dedication, after they return and go to work, than we might consider higher education to make them really qualified beyond the technical level. But our desperate need right now is for qualified people who can do technician's work and who should be paid for it. And beyond that we need people who can produce programs to which people will want to listen. Otherwise, although we may get space on the radio band, we will not be on people's sets.

NOTES

1. Wilbur Schramm, *Mass Media and National Development* (Stanford: Stanford University Press, 1964).

2. *Ibid.*, p. 63.

3. François Houtart and Emile Pin, *The Church and the Latin American Revolution* (New York: Sheed & Ward, 1965) pp. 62–63.

4. Lerner, in Pye, *Communications and Political Development,* pp. 344–345.

5. Houtart and Pin, *op. cit.,* p. 64.

6. Herman Kahn, *Some Comments on Development and Violence* (New York: Hudson Institute, Inc.).

7. William Ferry and Harry S. Ashmore, *Mass Communications* (Santa Barbara: Center for the Study of Democratic Institutions, 1966).

8. Neil P. Hurley, S.J., "Satellite Communications," *America,* August 27, 1966.

9. Neil P. Hurley, S.J., "Picture of the Future," *America,* February 13, 1965.

10. Ferry and Ashmore, *op. cit.*

11. Neil P. Hurley, S.J., "Communications Revolution: Its Impact on Our Ministries," *Woodstock Letters,* Vol. 95, No. 4 (fall, 1966), 458.

12. Neil P. Hurley, S.J., "Picture of the Future."

13. *Ibid.*

14. Neil P. Hurley, S.J., "Communications Revolution," 460.

International Military Relations

MICHAEL FRANCIS

Militarism in Latin America is a controversial and complex subject, and the international influences on the military establishments of Latin America constitute but one aspect of this subject. No claim is made that these are the most important influences on the behavior of the military. However, these influences should not be ignored, and have significant effects on the integration process of man and society in Latin America.

To begin this discussion, the nature of the defense commitments of the Latin American states should be outlined. The Charter of the United Nations and the Inter-American Treaty of Reciprocal Assistance are the two major agreements which commit the states of Latin America to use their collective military force under certain circumstances. Latin American representatives played an active role in writing the United Nations Charter at San Francisco in 1945. They were particularly concerned with strengthening the role of regional organizations. They hoped also to weaken the Security Council in order to make the United Nations somewhat less blatantly a club run by Russia, England, France, China, and the United States. As a result of the veto power in the Security Council and the development of the East-West deadlock, the commitment to assist the United Nations militarily has not proved demanding. A few Latin American countries participated with small forces in the Korean War, although not nearly as much as the United States would have liked. During this conflict only Colombia, then under the heel of Dictator Laureano Gómez, sent military aid. At the time several Latin American states claimed that their constitutions would not allow them to send troops outside their borders. A more important factor was a lack of interest in becoming involved in such a remote area of the world. The states of Latin America felt then and feel now that their own problems are too important and too far from solution to allow them to become entangled in extrahemispheric problems.

Under the Rio treaty of 1947 the American states are bound to cooperate in sanctions if a two-thirds majority so decides. The lone legal exception is in cases of sanctions involving the use of military force. In these circumstances a nation is only committed to participate if it voted with the majority favoring the military sanctions. Thus far the Rio treaty's provisions for the use of military sanctions have not been utilized. The principle of nonintervention runs deep in Latin American international law, particularly when the United States is a possible threat to the hemisphere. Also, no clear-cut case has arisen within the inter-American system demanding the use of military sanctions, although in several instances a small peace-keeping force might have been very helpful.

The concept of a possible peace-keeping force is one that has caused considerable controversy. One of the first groups to advocate this idea was the United States Senate Foreign Relations Committee headed by William Fulbright. In 1959 the committee recommended that 31.5 million dollars be set aside for the development of such a group. It described the concept as follows:

> The force ideally should be an international force in fact—that is, one which is actually composed of units from various countries—rather than an international force—that is, one which simply has units from various countries committed to it, or earmarked for it, under various contingencies. The

important thing, however, is to make a beginning with whatever kind of arrangement is initially possible.

It need not be a large force, but it should be adequate to provide for international security within the Western Hemisphere and to make a contribution to the defense of the hemisphere from outside attack. If the first mission were actually carried out, the cost of the force would be more than offset by the reductions which would become possible in the domestic military budgets of the Latin American countries.

The committee recognizes, of course, that such an international force cannot be created overnight. If it is possible at all, it will take time to work out the necessary agreements within the OAS.[1]

However, the recommendation was not well received by certain isolationist elements in the Congress and was opposed by the Department of State and various military officials who saw no particular advantage to the plan.[2]

The idea received new impetus in 1965 as a result of the United States intervention in the Dominican Republic. The convenience of such a force (assuming the OAS would have agreed to its use in the Dominican Republic) began to appeal to the Johnson administration as it tried to free itself from its Dominican embroilment. The United States planned to discuss the formation of such a force at the foreign ministers meeting in Rio de Janeiro in November, 1965, and had the support of Brazil. Mexico and Chile, however, spoke out strongly against the plan on the grounds that it presents a threat to the sovereignty of the Latin American states, and the United States decided not to press the idea. In March, 1966, at a meeting of commanders of Latin American armies in Buenos Aires, Brazil quietly abandoned the plan in the face of Argentine opposition. Military men apparently opposed the concept because of their traditional distrust of the United States and because they did not feel the OAS was sufficiently anti-Communist.

The interrelationship between the military men of Latin America is an interesting question. Undoubtedly there are some linkages. Recent events in Brazil and Argentina are too similar to be purely coincidental. Military leaders in the two countries obviously admire and emulate each other. In addition to formal areas of consultation, such as the Inter-American Defense Board, there are informal personal contacts between the officers of the Latin

American countries. Military take-overs obviously have repercussions across state borders. One of the reasons for the hesitation
of the United States to recognize the military coup in Peru in
1962, for example, was a fear that quick recognition would
encourage a military coup in Venezuela.

The strongest international influence on the Latin American
military leaders is undoubtedly the United States. It is important
to understand the form this influence takes and the problems it
presents. The United States program of military aid to Latin
America and the reasons behind it are important to this understanding. For many years the justification given in the United
States for giving military aid to the Latin American countries
was that they were participating in a joint hemispheric defense
plan. The failure to develop an effective program of cooperative
defense led to increasing resistance by Congress toward the
expenditures. Therefore, the justification was changed. The new
explanation for the program is that it (1) helps to "profession-
alize" the Latin American militaries, (2) encourages participation
by military forces in economic development projects, or "civic
action" programs, and (3) provides the "internal security" necessary for economic growth.

The professionalization justification hinges on the idea that the
Latin American soldiers should be trained in United States-
operated schools or exposed to advice from United States soldiers
in order to gain a respect for civilian authority. United States
Secretary of Defense Robert McNamara has said that "the expo-
sure of the military officers to our schools acquaints them with
democratic philosophies and democratic ways of thinking which
they, in turn, take back to their countries."[3] McNamara has also
declared that

In all probability the greatest return on any portion of our military assistance
investment—dollar for dollar—comes from the training of selected officers in
U.S. schools and installation. . . . They are the coming leaders of their
nations. It is beyond price to the United States to make friends of such men.[4]

The Secretary does not comment on whether or not these men
should be the "coming leaders of their nations."

The approach may be commendable in theory, but there are

a number of practical difficulties connected with it. The strict separation between military and civilian authorities which supposedly exists in the United States would be a good model for Latin America. The problem is that even in the United States the military frequently become involved in political and diplomatic policy making. The United States military establishment exerts enormous behind-the-scenes pressure and sometimes comes into the open to disagree with some aspects of civilian control. The dispute between President Harry Truman and General Douglas MacArthur during the Korean War is a valid example. Today in Viet Nam many military officers are vocal in their desire to be "turned loose" to win the war without having to worry about diplomatic considerations. Much of the controversy which has surrounded McNamara grows from his attempts to be the first Secretary of Defense to actually control the military.

Although it is difficult to document, the military advisory groups the United States sends to assist Latin Americans are often suspect. There are frequent rumors of their helping or encouraging the overthrow of elected governments.[5] While many of these rumors may simply be anti-American propaganda, it is not illogical to assume that in certain cases some United States officers assigned to Latin America might well encourage the overthrow of an elected government. A United States officer may be shocked at the graft and rumors of graft which permeate Latin capitals. He may be repelled by demagogic politicians in Latin America and fail to recognize that in many instances these men have their parallels among politicians at home. He may also come face-to-face with "real Communists," in or out of the government. It is relatively easy to function in the United States without ever coming into contact with an individual who claims to be a Communist. But in Latin America such persons are more numerous, and do not have quite the same stigma as in the United States. The United States officer may be critical of a government which allows such an individual to function in society, and this may lead him to "look the other way" when a coup is hatched.

The testimony of a United States general before the House Foreign Affairs Committee in 1966 substantiates the idea that

Latin American officers may be influencing United States Officers and advisors as much as they are being influenced by the others.[6] The general stated that on the basis of the twelve thousand miles he had traveled throughout Latin America he was convinced that the military did not want to be dictators and were "trying to get constitutional government established." He then went on to say, "Castello Branco does not have a military government. He resigned from the military services." The United States general was pleased to report that many of the Latin American military officers would like to be in Vietnam. He praised the high degree of professionalism of the Brazilian army and said, "I hold the Brazilian forces in high regard." He maintained that the sale of jet airplanes to Argentina would help "improve the professionalism in these forces. They have old beat-up-type aircraft and they are going to need new ones." He was pleased with the sophistication of the Latin American officers. He said, "in some cases they are more sophisticated than the American officer, particularly when you are dealing with political problems or political economic problems." This last statement runs completely counter to the idea of civilian-military separation. The key to the United States system has been that the military men are supposed to stick to their guns and leave "political-economic problems" to the politicians. The general also seemed to accept the idea that some type of veto should be retained by the United States over candidates for high public office in Latin America. He stated that "a most difficult decision that faces our policy makers during the next ten years" is trying to identify "the motives of people that are being brought to power."

The second category of United States military aid to Latin America is civic action programs which channel the time and energy of the military into economically useful activities such as road building. This idea grew from a dilemma faced by the United States Government after the formation of the Alliance for Progress. The United States felt that the Latin American military establishments needed assistance in order to provide the stability necessary for social and economic development under the Alliance. However, strengthening the security forces in Latin America meant support for the groups which often strongly supported dictatorships. Therefore the military needed to become part of the process of economic development so that it would not wish to overthrow the government. This program was to have the secondary advantage of improving the national image of the armed forces and thereby strengthening the popularity of the central government.

There are several problems basic to this program. In the first place there is a feeling that civic action programs are included in foreign aid bills because the United States Congress will vote for military aid to Latin America under this guise. In the last hearings before the Congress an administration spokesman claimed that "The greater emphasis on civic action will require a continuing allocation of funds to insure an adequate capability for this important program."[7] However, the figures given later in the hearings show a steady decrease in civic action expenditures in Latin America since 1963, which would indicate that the Pentagon is not so interested in the program. In 1963 about 14 million dollars went for civic action, while only 8 million dollars was requested for the fiscal year 1966.

It should be pointed out that if the military image is sufficiently refurbished, it may make military intervention in politics more acceptable. The image of the Brazilian military, for example, has always been comparatively good, but this has only served to make intervention easier. Finally, there is no strong evidence that is less expensive to use the military for projects of economic development. A recent comprehensive book on the subject of these civic action programs is generally pessimistic and concludes that "there is no undisputed proof of the success of civic action."[8] The entire program bears disturbing similarities to these programs which accompanied the Caribbean interventions by the United States Marines prior to the coming of the Good Neighbor Policy.

Essentially the civic action and professionalization justifications are subsidiary to the third goal of the military aid program: to provide for internal security. There is a prominent group of scholars who believe that the development process is very destructive to the fabric of society, and more of a threat to social stability than poverty itself. During this period of anomie the threat of Communism is particularly great.[9] However, the "keeping of order" has been used as an excuse for too many military coups and dictatorships in Latin America to be well received. Many doubts exist as to the army's ability to distinguish between democratic reformers and Communists. A study of seven military coups between 1962 and 1964 found that in all interventions "the armed forces sought to justify their actions . . . as a necessary mission to save their respective nations from the menace of Communism and from ineffective civilian government."[10]

The entire question of internal security is more complex than either the opponents or proponents of the program suggest. Some order may well be necessary for progress in Latin America. It is true that weapons not purchased in the United States usually will be obtained elsewhere if the United States refuses to sell them. The fact that the United States furnishes military aid is not the reason for the large Latin American military establishments. The United States obviously sees the entire military aid program as a method of putting pressure on Latin America's militarists. McNamara has stated that

> We think we stand a much better chance of achieving that objective [of preventing Latin America from wasting too much money on military expenditures] by maintaining this very, very modest military assistance program which gives us considerable leverage over their military planning.[11]

The former commander in chief of the Southern Command, General Andrew P. O'Meara, has testified that the "amenability" of the Latin American officer "to suggestions from American forces can be very important in the future."[12] The United States Government has argued that the dependence of both India and Pakistan on the United States for replacement parts cut short that recent conflict—a rather dubious example. The fact remains that over 50 percent of the military assistance which the United States gives to Latin America goes for "internal security" and that the phrase has an ominous ring to it. This figure compares to approximately 16 percent for civic action programs and another 16 percent for maritime defense.[13]

There has been some discussion of a possible multilateral agreement among the Latin American states to reduce armaments. Former Costa Rican Ambassador to the United States Gonzalo Facio and former Chilean President Jorge Alessandri were two of several Latin spokesmen to endorse such a move during the late 1950's. Most elements of the U. S. Government were favorably disposed toward the idea. At the 1957 Economic Conference of the OAS in Buenos Aires the head of the United States delegation said that his country favored arms reduction in order to speed economic growth.[14] This remained the stated objective of United States policy, although doubt can be cast regarding how vigorously the idea was pushed. During Eisenhower's 1960 trip to Latin America he declared in Santiago, "I assure you that my Government is prepared to cooperate in any practical steps that may be initiated by the Government of Chile or any of her neighbors to reduce [arms] expenditures."[15] Both the 1959 Santiago meeting of foreign ministers and the 1960 meeting in San José passed United States-supported resolutions favoring some type of reduction in military forces. There was, however, some opposition from military elements in Latin American governments. The Council of the OAS put the question on the agenda of the oft-cancelled Eleventh Inter-American Conference.

Christian Democratic President Eduardo Frei of Chile has been very vocal in calling for arms reductions. However Chile purchased twenty-one British Hawker Hunter jet fighters in 1966, and Peru reacted by planning to buy supersonic British Lightnings. This caused the United States Department of State to begin pressing for further discussions of arms reductions out of fear of an armaments race in Latin America. The United States would like to see some tapering off of arms expenditures of some types, but it also hopes to keep up internal security forces in Latin America. In practice these two goals conflict. Another basic problem is that most of the arms proposals call for a reduction in the number of armaments *above* the level needed for the maintenance of internal order and the preservation of territorial borders. The question inevitably arises as to who can decide what is "above" the necessary level. From Peru's point of view Chile's purchase of twenty-one jets was unnecessary, but it obviously was not unnecessary from the point of view of certain important elements in Chile. One thing is clear: this type of aircraft is *not* designed to combat insurgency.

It should be pointed out, however, that there are very few cases of military coups where the military acted without the backing or encouragement of important civilian interests. The 1963 over-throw of Juan Bosch as the president of the Dominican Republic is a typical example. Important elements of Dominican society never accepted the election results and kept urging the military to overthrow Bosch until the army staged its coup. Rafael Caldera, Venezuelan Christian Democratic leader, defined the problem by saying that

Venezuelans are so accustomed to see the army as a factor in their daily lives, so accustomed to make the army the arbiter of their political contests, that at each moment the most varied groups for the most dissimilar ends attempt to involve the army in new adventures to change our political reality.[16]

One method of increasing Latin American governmental stability would be to convince groups which have failed to win elections not to try to change the situation by pressing for military inter-vention. In the long run, interventions will cease when most of the principal groups in the political arena are willing to accept defeat rather than destroy the system.

The idea that overthrowing an elected government is not con-ducive to the development of political freedom is a simple one, but it is not always easy to accept in practice. An example will make the point clearer. In the 1958 presidential election in Chile Salvador Allende, candidate of the Communist-Socialist coalition (FRAP), polled 356,000 votes. He lost to Jorge Alessandri by only a little more than 33,000 votes. In 1964 Allende polled 976,000, almost three times as many. However, he lost again, this time to Eduardo Frei, who received 1,400,000 votes. Suppose the Frei vote had been split into four or five different parties and it appeared the Chilean Congress was about to name the FRAP candidate as president. Difficult cases such as this separate those willing to accept a democratic system, and thereby accept the Communist-Socialist candidate, and those who favor democracy only so long as it favors them.

Military overthrows of elected governments must be assumed to be against the best interests of the country unless proven otherwise. Regardless of how benevolent it may appear at the outset, a government that attempts to rule without popular support will not represent the people. Several of today's outspoken critics of the government of General Juan Ongania in Argentina did not lift their voices in protest when he overthrew President Arturo Illia. The coming to power of Gustavo Rojas Pinilla was well received in Colombia in 1953. Later this government proved to be one of the most inept in modern South American history.

A recently published article by a prominent United States political scientist helps to lift the curtain of confusion and altruistic statements surrounding military coups. He suggests that the pressure for military takeovers greatly increases during a declining economic situation. Another point of danger is election time.

As elections have become representative of the sentiments of a wider range of the population, coups d'etat have tended increasingly to occur in the period immediately prior to a presidential election and the subsequent inauguration, to be conservative in policy orientation, to be directed against constitutional governments. . . .[17]

This type of intervention usually centers around the prevention of the election or inauguration of an individual the military finds unacceptable. Often this is because the individual constitutes a threat to the military's institutional standing. According to military folklore, civilians are supposed to leave the military alone. Part of the Latin American military's violent anti-Castroism stems less from Communism as a doctrine than from the fact that Fidel Castro exiled, jailed, or executed many Cuban professional military men. A major reason for the Peruvian military's unwillingness to tolerate the Aprista party dates back to an assault by *apristas* on an army garrison in Trujillo after a rigged election in 1931. Fear of the return of Juan Peron by high-ranking Argentine military officials who toppled him in 1955 helps account for the ouster of Arturo Frondizi in 1962 after the President allowed participation by *Peronista* parties in the elections.

The tacit assumption of this paper is that the present political structure in Latin America can be modified to promote integration and does not need to undergo a violent revolution.

Its conclusion must therefore be an attempt to answer the question, "What changes can be made in international military relations to help prevent military interventions against elected governments and thereby better the chances of democratic representation for the average Latin American?"

On the part of Latin American countries proof must be offered that a country which greatly reduces its military budget will not suddenly find itself the loser of a border dispute. Other countries should shun governments established by a military takeover of an elected administration. Other pressures can also be applied, but it is difficult to apply pressures against a military coup in another country if your own government is threatened by the same fate.

The United States can also do a number of things. If it feels it must continue military aid, more care should be taken in its administration. Requests for arms purchases must be closely examined, and military advisors in Latin America must adhere to the policy of the Department of State. The United States, through public and private statements, should actively attempt to dissuade military coups and punish governments which are militarily dominated unless they make sincere efforts to restore free elections. The continual talk about the Communist threat in Latin America does not help the situation. A number of governments receiving military aid for "internal security" are not threatened at all by Communist takeovers. Economic assistance to prevent interventions triggered by domestic economic difficulties will also help.

Possible military intervention is not the only, or even the principal, roadblock to the integration of man and society in Latin America. Militarism is more a symptom of the basic disorders than the disease itself. The problem of military coups can best be solved, as it has been in Mexico, through good leadership and a government which convinces the people—as Mexico was certainly convinced during the presidential term of Lazaro Cardenas—that it has their interests at heart.

NOTES

1. Senate Committee on Foreign Relations, *The Mutual Security Act of 1959*, Rept. No. 412, 86th Cong., 1st Sess., 1959 [Majority Report], p. 11.

2. For a fuller discussion of the question see Michael J. Francis, "Prospects of Military Aid to Latin America," *Southwestern Social Science Quarterly* (March, 1966), 448–450.

3. Senate Committee on Foreign Relations, *Hearings, Foreign Assistance Act of 1962*, 87th Cong., 2d Sess., 1962, p. 76.

4. House Committee on Foreign Affairs, *Hearings, Foreign Assistance Act of 1965*, 89th Cong., 1st Sess., 1965, p. 782.

5. For example, see "Soldiers All," *Newsweek* (November 14, 1966), p. 56, and Edwin Lieuwen, *General vs. Presidents: Neomilitarism in Latin America* (New York: Frederick A. Praeger, 1964), pp. 118–119.

6. House Committee on Foreign Affairs, *Hearings, Foreign Assistance Act of 1966*, 89th Cong., 2d Sess., 1966, pp. 423–454.

7. House Committee on Foreign Affairs, *Hearings, Foreign Assistance Act of 1966*, p. 426.

8. Williard F. Barber and C. Neale Ronning, *Internal Security and Military Power: Counterinsurgency and Civic Action in Latin America* (Columbus, Ohio: Ohio State University Press, 1966), p. 244.

9. Adam B. Ulam, *The Unfinished Revolution* (New York: Vintage, 1964); Lucien W. Pye, "The Roots of Insurgency and Commencement of Rebellions" in *Internal War,* ed. Harry Echstein (New York: Free Press, 1964), pp. 157–180: and Eric Hoffer, *The Ordeal of Change* (New York: Harper & Row, 1963), pp. 96–100. Some non-Communist groups even argue that the old social structure will probably have to be demonished before true social change will take place.

10. Lieuwen, *op. cit.,* p. 105.

11. Senate Committee on Appropriations, *Hearings, Foreign Assistance Appropriations, 1965*, 89th Cong., 1st Sess., 1965, p. 232.

12. House Committee on Foreign Affairs, *Hearings, Foreign Assistance Act of 1965*, p. 351.

13. Senate Committee on Appropriations, *Hearings, Foreign Assistance Appropriations, 1966*, 89th Cong., 2d Sess., 1966, p. 146.

14. Department of State Bulletin, XXXVII (September 16, 1957)

465. For a critical outline of the United States position as stated before the OAS see Victor Alba, *El militarismo* (Mexico City: 1959), pp. 234–238.

15. Dwight D. Eisenhower, "Texts of Eisenhower's Speeches in Santiago and His Letters to Chilean Students," *New York Times*, March 2, 1960.

16. Quoted in John J. Johnson, *The Military and Society in Latin America* (Stanford: Stanford University Press, 1964), p. 120.

17. Martin Needler, "Political Development and Military Intervention in Latin America," *The American Political Science Review* (September, 1966), 624.

International Food Problems

EDWARD O'BRIEN

World Food Problems

Prior to World War II the less-developed countries of the world were net exporters of 11 million tons of grain. This past year of 1966 they imported approximately 25 million tons of grain. The less-developed countries are clearly losing the capacity to feed themselves. Will there be sufficient food in the future to feed the rapidly expanding population?

Since new lands are no longer available for solving mankind's food problems, the real problem facing the world today is the gap separating the existing body of known technology from its application. In essence it is a productivity problem. The fact that such productivity has materialized as yet in only a small part of the world does not indicate that it cannot take place in other parts of the world. Nor should it require the same period of time. This is our reason for optimism.

Our world food problem is closely associated with the recent acceleration in the population growth rate. Throughout history a high birth rate was necessary to offset the high death rate and insure the continuation of the human race. But with the reduction in death rates resulting from the widespread application of medical technology, population is now growing rapidly. From the time of Jesus Christ until the end of the sixteenth century world population grew an average of 2 percent to 5 percent a *century*. Since 1960 the world population has been growing almost 2 percent per year. And population growth is concentrated in the less-developed regions—regions less able to afford these population increases. An estimated 2 billion people will be added to the present population of the less-developed countries between now and the year 2000.

The impact of population on food supplies in developing countries is aggravated by the concentration of people in cities. The extremely rapid growth of urban population compounds the problem because it imposes the difficult task of improving the distribution system so food can be moved from producing areas to urban areas. To accomplish this task, incentives must be used to bring farmers into the commercial economy. Not only must there be an increase in food production, but marketing facilities must be built to transport, process, store, and distribute the farm products. If this task is not accomplished, urban centers will have to rely on imports for much of their food supplies.

Over the past thirty years food production has increased in the less-developed countries at a rate of a little more than 2 percent per year, about the same rate of increase as in the developed countries. But most of this increase in the less-developed countries has been offset by expansion in population. Two-thirds of the world's people now live in countries with inadequate average diets. The diet-deficit areas include all of Asia except Japan and Israel, all but the southern tip of Africa, part of South America, and almost all of Central America and the Caribbean.

Grain is a good indicator of food output and consumption. In the diet-deficit regions, if recent trends continue, grain production can be expected to increase almost 3 percent annually, just slightly better than population growth. Yet consumption has been increasing at a faster rate than production, and this growing gap has been made up by increased imports. A continuation of these trends of production and consumption for another two decades is clearly unacceptable, both to the diet-deficit countries and to the conscience of most of the diet-adequate countries. Food consumption would continue to be below nutritional standards, and there would be increasing dependency upon the United States for food. The cost of American aid to these countries would spiral without a development of their ability eventually to take care of themselves, and the capability of the United States to aid these countries would reach an end.

It is clear, then, that the most reasonable course of action to improve food consumption in the diet-deficit countries is to encourage programs to increase food production in these countries themselves. Food aid should be used to encourage such development. To achieve the target of adequate nutritional standards within the next decade, and at the same time to begin to cut down the rate of increase in imports, grain production in food-deficit countries must be accelerated from a 3 percent annual increase to an increase of 4 percent per year by 1980. That this goal is not unreasonable is shown by a recent study of twenty-six of these less-developed countries, twelve of which have achieved an annual increase in agricultural production of more than 4 percent. As Secretary of Agriculture Orville Freeman puts it:

> There is no inherent reason why most of the newly developing countries cannot within the next decade or two increase their food and fiber production so as to meet the increased demand of their citizens and to have enough food or food-producing resources to spare to contribute substantially—through trade and non-farm employment—to general economic development.

Over much of the world's history the amount of land under cultivation has increased with population. But in most of the diet-deficit countries of Latin America new lands are no longer available at reasonable cost. Agricultural development therefore requires improvement in yields per acre. This is difficult to accomplish with a largely illiterate labor force, high interest rates, and a lack of technicians.

There do exist, nevertheless, many opportunities for application of technology that can benefit the countries in the diet-deficit class. In the developed regions there is a vast reservoir of knowledge and an abundance of improved technology which, if properly

adapted to the specific conditions of the deficit countries, could increase the production of food. However, the problem of introducing it into the producing sector of another country is complicated.

Fertilizer probably provides the best potential for rapidly increasing crop production in the less-developed countries. In the
United States crop output per acre has increased 50 percent since
1940, and almost one-half of this increase is the result of increased
use of fertilizers.

In some countries the most significant aspect of the problem
may be the inability to process, store, and transport food products
from producer to consumer rather than an inability to produce
adequate amounts and varieties of food. The marketing problem
in some countries is made more difficult by the fact that the major
areas of production and consumption are far removed from each
other. The so-called breadbasket of Brazil in the southern state
of Rio Grande Do Sul, for example, is two thousand miles from
the drought-ridden state of Para in the northeast. Developments
now only in the beginning stages, such as preservation of food by
radiation and dehydration, could have a major impact in such
areas in the long run.

Food Assistance

Even before the peace treaties of World War I were signed, a
relief mission, triggered by the United States and headed by President Herbert Hoover, was set up to attend to the urgent assistance and reconstruction needs of the devastated and starving
nations. Immediately after World War II the Marshall Plan was
an example of new international cooperation. During the 1950's
and 1960's our Presidents and Congress continued to approve
foreign aid programs. The United States is, by a considerable
margin, the largest contributor to the World Food Program and
the Food and Agriculture Organization of the United Nations.
The most significant legislation in the area of food is Public Law
480, in effect since July, 1954. It authorizes the transfer of American farm abundance to friendly nations through sale, barter, and
donation. This program has filled the food void and warded off

starvation in many needy countries of the world. During the first decade, within the donation sector alone, where the people-to-people impact is greatest, P.L. 480 has made available to governments and to registered American voluntary agencies a total of 23.8 billion pounds of foodstuffs valued at 2.7 billion dollars. These foods were distributed to approximately 62.7 million needy individuals in 131 different countries all over the world. Latin America shared in this program to the extent of 4.1 billion pounds of food valued at 468 million dollars.

It is my privilege to serve these needy millions in my role as a member of the staff of Catholic Relief Services, the official overseas aid agency of the American bishops and American Catholics. In conjunction with other voluntary agencies, religious and secular, and in cooperation with the Agency for International Development and the United States Department of Agriculture, our agency combines the generosity of American Catholics and the United States Government into a powerful instrument of direct assistance to the poor and hungry.

In recent years voluntary agencies devoted to giving food to the hungry of the world have been putting increasing stress on technical assistance programs that will lead to social change in the underdeveloped countries. Recognizing that meaningful accomplishments in these nations must have the participation of the people, the agencies attempt to insure that the poor themselves are active in these projects. Priority is given to programs of community development, cooperatives, and leadership training; and every available technique to promote active participation by the people in programs where they will be helping themselves is utilized. Emphasis is currently placed on experimental farms, resettlement programs, rural cooperatives, and the introduction of new seeds, fertilizers, tools, and farm techniques. These agencies are steadily augmenting their staffs overseas with technical specialists, many of them volunteers. Their function is to assist local organizations in working out social development projects, to use food and other supplies in more effective ways for the improvement of their community, and to help establish associations and organizations which can give continuity to this work.

In return for their labor in special projects, participants receive a ration of food in proportion to the number of hours they work. The project could be one of road construction in Bolivia, wells and irrigation canals in India, hog production in Korea, land resettlement in Paraguay, leadership training in Venezuela, school construction in Panama, slum clearance in Peru, and reforestation in Chile.

Latin America

If Mexico, Uruguay, and Argentina are excluded, Latin America cannot feed itself. Why is this so?

One reason is that too many Latin American countries have one-crop or one-product economies. Brazil, Colombia, Costa Rica, El Salvador, Guatemala, and Haiti, for example, are dependent on coffee exports to earn the foreign capital required to purchase the foods necessary to help feed their own growing population. Bolivia depends on its exports of tin, Chile on copper, Uruguay on wool, and Venezuela on oil. In short, Latin America's main exports are either agriculture or extracted products (minerals), the so-called primary commodities purchased and utilized by the more developed industrialized countries. These primary export products are the very lifeblood of most Latin American economies. It is not too difficult to visualize what happens to the economy of Colombia when the world price of coffee fails, or to Bolivia when the world price of tin is depressed, or to Chile when copper is not in world demand. Foreign exchange, vital for the purchase of food and manufactured consumer goods from the industrialized and more efficient producing countries of the world, is drastically reduced, and in the face of a steadily increasing number of mouths to feed the results can only be disastrous.

Latin America is, however, in the throes of its own industrial revolution. Traditionally it has been an agricultural and mining area, with much of the land cultivated by antiquated methods and under ancient social relationships. The industrial countries' search for raw materials and food, however, has resulted in the development of a modern agricultural sector and of an up-to-date mining industry. Through these developments the countries have become somewhat more closely tied to the world economy. Economic life in Latin America is now rapidly broadening with the growth of service industries, banking, and all the other phases of a modern economy. Moreover, the peoples' aspirations for better living standards are rising even more rapidly than the economy. The widespread popular demand for rapid economic change outruns the change itself.

The demographic explosion, which gives Latin America the most rapidly increasing population of any comparable area of the globe, intensifies the urgency of the situation. This sudden increase in numbers has led to two complications. First, the low income countries need large amounts of capital for new investment. Their imports of capital goods, already heavy, must increase over the near future as they attempt to increase their productive capacity before the next generation catches up with them. Second, many of them are now, and will be for some time to come, weathering a period during which they are dependent on imports of food. Newly implanted industry can take advantage of modern technology, but traditional agriculture is extremely resistant to it. Food production is likely to lag, which means that Latin American nations will have to concentrate on the export of goods to earn the foreign exchange with which to buy imported food. They will be compelled, in other words, to emulate the British pattern of growth in the nineteenth century rather than that of the United States.

Exports trades have often served as a powerful stimulus to economic progress. An export industry imposes standards of quality and general efficiency on a commercial community which are not usually found in traditional society. The nucleus of exporters, if they are successful and influential people, may then become pacesetters for the rest of the economy, as was the case in Japan during the 1920's and 1930's. On the other hand, Latin America is full of instances where the beneficient example of the exporters has failed to spread to the rest of the economy. And even if it could be proved that being forced to export was necessarily good for a country in this early stage of development, the question remains as to how rapid an increase in exports is feasible over a short period of time. Export markets for the traditional primary products of the underdeveloped countries have been growing much more slowly than the rest of the world export trade. This is largely the result of the new technology, which helps the industrial countries to get along with less raw material for any given volume of output. Synthetic fibers and plastics replace traditional materials, and a given amount of material is made to go a longer way. This is one reason why the gap in living standards between the developed and underdeveloped countries continues to widen.

Markets for automobiles, computers, and airplanes are much more buoyant than those for coffee, copper, and tin. We have also been outstandingly successful in applying technology to the production of food. Sheltered behind tariff walls, American farmers have increased their efficiency tremendously, and are now producing substantially more food with far fewer people than before World War II. The result is that the volume of food and materials which the underdeveloped countries can sell is reduced.

Then, too, the Latin American states are by nature and tradition among the most parochial. To persuade them to think of sacrificing some small segment of the national commercial interest for the sake of the greater good is a difficult matter. The Economic Commission for Latin America (ECLA) has made strenuous efforts to persuade Latin Americans that something radical must be done to stop the waste of the continent's resources caused by the barriers to trade within the area. There is a growing acceptance of the idea that they must trade more with one another and cease to regard their short-term national interests in commerce as absolutely paramount.

Hitherto, the trade channels of the Latin American countries have seemed to be almost deliberately designed to bypass one another. The value of the goods which they buy and sell among themselves represents about 10 percent of the total trade of Latin America, and there are historical reasons why goods flow outward to Europe and North America rather than inland. The export trade was originally developed by foreigners, Europeans and North Americans, with their own markets in mind. The specialized production of crops like cocoa and coffee, or minerals like copper and tin, was in any case unsuitable for any large-scale development of trade on a regional basis. The markets were in the rich countries outside. Because the trading relationships with the developed countries were well-established and worked smoothly—sea transport being easier and cheaper than opening new roads into the hinterland—imports into the neighboring undeveloped countries, even of goods which they could have supplied to one another, tended to move along the same old trade routes.

Latin American countries must commit themselves to act together to increase their trade by granting mutual commercial favors. They can help to relieve the pressures on their balance of payments by trading more among themselves. It is not simply a matter of taking in each other's washing. Surplus production of a commodity runs to waste in one country, while in another country people go short of it because the mechanism of exchange fails to function efficiently.

Even if the underdeveloped countries make a successful effort to stimulate trade among themselves, they are still going to need foreign capital. The shortage of available capital resources in the private sectors of the Latin American economies is a major reason for the fact that the governments of the area have participated so extensively in the process of industrialization and general economic development. They have done so out of necessity. There are few private enterprises in Latin American countries capable of raising sufficient funds to build utilities, steel plants, and railroad systems. Rather than leave these projects to foreign investors, the governments and people prefer to negotiate loans from international lending institutions which provide the foreign exchange necessary to buy capital equipment.

It should be recognized that the diversity of the underdeveloped areas in Latin America makes it difficult to apply a single formula for speeding development. The resources, stage of development, culture, and organization must be considered in preparing plans and programs for economic progress. Nevertheless, there appear to be several important requirements that any country must meet if rapid economic progress is to be made.

Perhaps the most crucial among these requirements is a reasonably stable and reliable government. While a stable government does not insure economic progress, the forward-looking decisions necessary for progress cannot be made rationally without reasonable stability. Leaders in less-developed nations all too frequently emphasize industrialization rather than agriculture, and usually out of all proportion to their needs and capabilities. And the crops they do concentrate on too often are those which bring hard currency from overseas: coffee, sugar, bananas, cotton, and so on. Those in a position to make important decisions affecting programs of development must try to see the development process as a whole and resist the temptation to adopt simple formulas, such as a concentration on heavy industry, to the neglect of less glamorous but often more important measures.

Democratic governments should exhibit a genuine concern for social justice, to maintain stability, and to gain the enthusiastic support of their people for development programs. A wide distribution of benefits is important because the development of a modern industrial society requires mass markets to stimulate efficient production.

It is not sufficient simply to bring additional acreage of arable land under the plow in these nations. There is a very real limit to expansion in that direction. The real need is for changes in age-old agricultural practices, for the training of illiterate farmers, for better irrigation, for increased fertilizer production and use, for better seed strains, for insecticides and pest control, for expansion of transportation and storage facilities, for risk capital and credit extension, for better distribution and marketing facilities.

Another essential factor is the development of research aimed at the special needs of the underdeveloped countries. Science and technology must be adapted to the physical, economic, and cultural characteristics of each area. Most of the underutilized agricultural land is in the tropical and subtropical zones of Latin America, where United States agricultural experience is of secondary value. Some research has been done on tropical agriculture, but little success has been achieved in increasing the productivity of these soils. A Bolivian-grown potato, for example, is about the size of an egg.

In most cases industrial development must accompany agricultural development. Without industry a country cannot produce the fertilizers, pesticides, and machinery that make high agricultural yields possible. Then, too, industrial development is necessary to absorb the labor which will leave agriculture as it grows more efficient. We must remember, also, that economic change is costly to certain vested interests. A UN report by a panel of economists some time ago stated that

> there is a sense in which rapid economic progress is impossible without painful readjustments. Ancient philosophies have to be scrapped, old cultural institutions have to disintegrate, bonds of caste, creed, and race to be burst, and large numbers of persons who cannot keep up with progress have to have their expectations of a comfortable life frustrated. Very few communities are willing to pay the full price of rapid economic progress.

It is clear, now, that Latin America's role in world affairs is going to be much more important in the years to come than it has been in the past. Its fast-growing population will make up a larger proportion of mankind. It is further advanced on the road to economic development than Asia and Africa, and has taken great forward strides since World War II. Its rising economic weight will be felt much more in the future than heretofore. At the same time it will be an important part of that two-thirds of the world that is seeking help to raise its production levels, its standards of living, and its strength. Previously an isolated area more or less off the stage whereon the future of the world was being determined, Latin America is now moving out of the wings and onstage. Let us applaud our progressive neighbors of the Alliance for Progress.

Latin America and the Universal Church

LEON JOSEF CARDINAL SUENENS

When I received the invitation to contribute to this discussion, I felt within myself a certain hesitation. How could I treat this subject of the challenge of Latin America among a group such as this? But then I realized that the entire logic of the Second Vatican Council means for all of us involvement with the whole Church of God. We stand before the world as coresponsible with Christ and with one another, with the Vicar of Christ and with every Christian. We are not meant to be alone, enclosed in our own problems and successes, be they personal or national. We share a life, the life of Christ, and together we are Christ for the world. My family is humanity, my spiritual family is the Church, and half of that family, in thirty years or so, will be Latin America. Lacordaire once said, "A Christian is a man to whom Jesus Christ has confided responsibility for other men"; or as a monk of Mount Athos once put it, "My brother is my life."

We cannot, therefore, remain indifferent to the joys and hopes, the griefs and anxieties, of half our family. We, the Church, are faced in Latin America with a reality, with a problem equally immense and profound. I would like to discuss these problems of

337

Latin America with you, so that we may more profoundly understand and more actively contribute to the alleviation of the sufferings of Christ in Latin America.

It is true that Latin America must be saved, but we are not
discussing this problem as though we were ourselves "already
saved." It may be that the salvation of North America and all the
world depends upon the response we give to Christ in Latin
America. Christ will say to us one day, "What you did to these
my brothers you did to me." In some ways we are the poor ones,
and this chance given us by Christ to serve is meant to be the
source of our wealth.

The Church and the Social Problem in Latin America

We find in Latin America a poignant concretization of the number one social problem of our time: the gap between the rich and
the poor. There is a tiny minority of rich within each country in
control of a vast proportion of its nation's wealth. And there is
a tiny minority of wealthy nations enriching themselves still further at the expense of the rest of the world to such a degree that
at this moment two-thirds of the human family, our family, live
in conditions which are subhuman. This gigantic disparity, this
"insult," in the Pope's words, "flung in the face of humanity" is
the most urgent problem facing the world today.

It is not only that this disparity exists in proportions hitherto
unheard of, but that now "les miserables" of the human family
see and experience daily the difference between their lot and
ours. As Nehru once said, "It is not hunger and misery which
are new. What is new in India is that men are aware of their
hunger and misery." And we Christians, for our part, continue
to live in what can be called a comfortable global ghetto, while
the great majority of the world, which is non-Christian, awaits
some sign from us, some gesture, which indicates that we have
taken a stand, a Christ-stand, in regard to their misery. Yes, we
must help by all the means at our disposal to alleviate the suffering of our brother. But deeper than all this, the poor nations of the
world want to know what stand we take. They are right in using

this criterion to judge the authenticity of our Christian preaching. At the Council nearly one hundred of the Council Fathers, in their interventions, stressed this scandal and appealed to our consciences to remove the social, collective mortal sin of the modern world in which we Christians share.

This is the social problem which exists so acutely in Latin America; the *estancias* and the *favellas,* the rich industrialized nations getting richer and the poor South American nations getting poorer. And all of this transpiring within a situation where the population continues to mount at the rate of a 90 percent increase every twenty-five years.

As you and I face this problem and allow its realities to penetrate our understanding, we are forced to recognize that we have a duty, a responsibility before Christ and before our fellow men, a duty imposed upon us by the very fact of the privilege of our vocation as Christians. We can describe this duty under three different aspects.

There is first the duty of denouncing social injustice.

There is second our duty to aid every effort which attempts to insure social, economic, and human equality and also to see to it that the young are educated and formed in a social conscience.

And third, we must promote and aid research into these problems so that adequate solutions will be found which go to the very root-cause of the disease.

1. The Denouncing of Social Injustice.

On the day of his consecration every bishop is addressed by his consecrator in words heavy with the meaning and experience of centuries. These call him to a love of the truth, "never betraying it, no matter what the pressure of praise or fear. That he never make of darkness, light; or of light, darkness. That he never call evil, good; nor good, evil." These words equally express the vocation of all Christians.

There is a negative aspect of this duty: not to be content with silence. We do not have the right to be silent; we cannot indulge in the luxury of passively accepting the status quo, passively accepting the established disorder, passively accepting inertia. There is no such thing as a right to exercise nonintervention. The priest and the Levite had no right to pass by the wounded man as they made their way to Jericho. When Christ asked who the wounded man's neighbor was, he placed upon every human being the choice, not of determining his neighbor, but of accepting or rejecting the fact that he himself is the neighbor of every man. We speak of sin as though it were the infraction of some rule, the transgression of some abstract law. But in our heart, we know that it is the refusal to love. The gravest sins that men commit are the sins of omission. We cannot simply accept the status quo in Latin America and consider it impossible to change.

The Church must baptize the world, not stand silent before its evil. The time is short. There is already a gap between events and our modes of thinking and of acting. We carry the torch of the Gospel, yet sometimes others see better by its light. I am thinking about what happened in the nineteenth century. The misery of the poor was there. The *Communist Manifesto* of Karl Marx was written and published in 1848. The encyclical *Rerum Novarum* came to save the honor of Christianity but came fifty years later. We must never forget that. We must enter deeply into the spirit of the Council and wash ourselves clean of the dust we have accumulated through twenty centuries of pilgrimage. It is something wonderful, really, to contemplate a Church enduring for two thousand years, but there is a price to pay. From time to time you have to clean off the dust.

There is a positive aspect of our duty: the obligation to speak.

The Church has spoken. John XXIII in his encyclical *Mater et Magistra* has set the markers along the road we must follow. But in Latin America the very core of this insight is yet to be fully realized. But can we not look forward to another pontifical document, or better and more solemn yet, a document coming from the synod of bishops along with the Pope which would awaken the conscience of men in regard to these problems and provide, as it were, a *Rerum Novarum* for the Third World, that two-thirds of humanity that is forced to live in conditions which belie their human dignity.

The Church has spoken. The Council has taken to its heart the suffering of Christ in the poor of this world: "The joys and the hopes, the griefs and the anxieties of the men of this age, especially those who are poor or in any way afflicted, these are the joys and hopes, the griefs and anxieties of the followers of Christ."

The reality of world poverty was present in the minds and souls of the bishops at the Second Vatican Council when they called for the establishment of an organization "to stimulate the Catholic community to foster progress in needy regions, and social justice on the international scene." (*Gaudium er Spes,* Section 90)

The principal goal envisaged by the Fathers of the Council for this organization is that of awakening the conscience of Christians to Christ's suffering in their fellow men, so that they work together to build a world which is truly human. It would be the means through which the Church could commit itself to the overcoming of the enmities and the injustices of the modern world. It would be the organ through which the Church could exercise its service by aiding men of this age in their efforts to establish a true family of mankind in love and in peace, in mutual trust and concern, so that men may rejoice in their recognition of one another as brothers. The Holy Father has set up a secretariate as the Council wished it, and has thus declared to the world the Church's intention to enter side by side with all men of good will in the struggle against poverty and its causes and thus erase the scandal of our affluent age.

But the Church is not only the hierarchy. Each member of the Church is obliged to speak and to make his personal witness and irrevocable stand as a Christian. I am thinking here especially of all those whose activities contribute to the forming of public opinion:

Journalists in their interviews and reporting so that they do not write only what people want to read, and so create by the tone of their writing an impression which dulls the impact of the truth.

The radio, television, and film industries in whose power it lies so to present the truth that people are led to a deeper understanding of the real issues confronting us.

The universities and centers of higher learning which wield such a large influence over future leaders and can by their attitudes and publications create an atmosphere of pseudosophistication and irresponsibility.

2. Working for the Social Renewal of Today and Tomorrow.

For Today. There are beginnings in evidence everywhere, and we greet them with joy. We see, for instance, the work begun by our late, beloved Bishop Manuel Larrain, to whom we all owe so much, and all the pioneers in the work for social justice in South America. Their struggle was long and painful; they were denounced and labelled "communist." But now we see that they were and are the men of the future. Their ideals for justice, human dignity, and equality are those which are now championed by the Church. They deserve our praise, admiration, and allegiance.

For Tomorrow. But if we wish these beginnings to arrive at a full fruition, and social reform to become ever more and more a reality, then the youth of today, both religious and lay, must become sensititve to the demands imposed upon them by Christ and the modern world. They must be formed through instruction, through a gradual indoctrination, and by real contact with their brothers who are suffering. We must eliminate the scandal of rich young men and women graduating year after year from our Catholic schools utterly oblivious of the true meaning of their own existence and the responsibility this entails of serving and caring for their brothers. They must stop thinking in terms of "aid to foreign countries" and "assistance to the underprivileged" and realize that their salvation depends upon their capacity to answer the call of Christ and ennoble themselves through service. As Louis Lavelle once said, "The greatest gift we can make to others is not to communicate to them our riches but to reveal to them their own." But for such an attitude really to become part of our youth, they must learn that paternalism is the very negation of authentic life, and realize that true growth whether in the realm of social justice or economic development, comes from within. Perhaps we should institute real examinations and grant academic degrees in "Social-Religious Apostolate."

3. Providing for Research into the Evils, Their Causes and Remedies.

Research today is a matter not of individual genius working

independently, but of teamwork, the combined efforts and intelligence of many laboring toward the same goal. The insight needed today in order to understand and resolve the vast and complex problems of science requires multiple contributions which can only be achieved by the combination of many aspects of the problem. This intelligence is the possession and fruit of many working together: witness the space program, cancer research, and nearly every other area of scientific endeavor. Our efforts in Latin America are no exception to this. Their dimensions are worldwide; their complexity touches upon many personal lives. We ourselves must learn first how to work together and then foster and sustain research teams dedicated to the people of Latin America.

We need research on the socioeconomic plane. In Latin America, as in nearly all parts of the world today, the key problem is that of international commerce, the relationship between the wealthy nations and the emerging nations, especially in regard to the flow of basic goods. The regulating of this question spells life or death for Latin America. We need only read Gilbert Blardone on the Prebisch Report to see the true dimensions of what can justly be called the scandal of our relationship to Latin America. In the period from 1950 to 1961 approximately 13.9 billion dollars left Latin America for the rich nations of the world. This was caused by the disparity between foreign capital investment and foreign capital gain and the simultaneous rise in the price of finished products and the fall in the price of raw materials. For example, as Doctor Carlos Saenz de Santamaria has pointed out, the price of a jeep in Colombia, which was the equivalent of 14 bags of coffee in 1962, now costs the equivalent of well over 40 bags of coffee. And as you are well aware, such figures can be cited for nearly every commodity. If this continues, the rich nations, blinded by the illusion of rapid wealth, will not only ruin the economic stability of millions but ultimately contribute to their own impoverishment.

Laws are needed, but more fundamental than this, a whole new outlook is required, based not upon immediate self-interest but on the long-range realization that no man and indeed no nation can deprive others without ultimately depriving himself:

"my brother is my life." The wealthy must cease maintaining the poor by paternalistic aid while preserving them in a state which robs them of their human dignity. Cooperation, not aid, is the way that men must relate to one another, with each according the other the dignity and freedom given to him by God. There must be a true "Alliance for Progress" and not a subservience for wealth.

The true wealth of a man or of a nation lies not so much in material things as in an awareness of dignity and a capacity for self-determination. The contribution of a nation cannot be extorted; it must be given freely and received by equals. If men are to live as brothers, they must know that their contribution is needed. If a poor nation is forced to provide for the needs of another nation simply in order to exist, both nations are impoverished, but the wealthy nation more deeply than the poor.

The principles are clear, but their day-to-day application must be made concrete and equitable. There must be research into the very roots of these problems, and solutions proposed which safeguard the rights and dignity of those on both sides of the hunger curtain. If a nation needs bread, it should be given, but only so that this nation may be strong enough to learn to grow its own bread and meet in the family of nations as an equal with something to give and something to receive.

We also require research in the sphere of demography. The problem of economic disparity is rendered more poignant with every hour that passes by the simple fact that the population among the world's poor is increasing at a rate three-and-one-third faster than that of the rich. As Monsignor Gremillion has pointed out in his volume *The Other Dialogue,* "There are about 31 million more additional persons in the poor nations each year than there are in the rich nations." In a world whose population required 500,000 years to reach the level of one and one-half billion, we saw in the last sixty years the doubling of that figure, which could be quadrupled by the year 2000. These are not facts to be taken lightly.

The Second Vatican Council has made a solemn appeal to research centers, and in particular to Catholic universities throughout the world, to combine their efforts at research in this vital field of birth regulation. It is easier to indicate ways that are blocked, to point out what roads must not be followed, than it is to show the way which leads to the goal.

The University of Louvain heard this appeal of the Council, and for its part created an International Center for the Study and Research of Human Fertility. As chancellor of that University, I appealed to the Ford Foundation in the United States, which responded with a generosity that I am glad to acknowledge here publicly. Thanks to its aid, five scholars, under the direction of Professor Ferrin, have dedicated themselves to a five-year study to establish beforehand the exact date of ovulation and to devise a simple means available to all for determining it. This is but one effort which needs to be integrated in an overall program.

At this high level of scientific research, Catholic Americans, with their tradition of technology and scientific competence, have an important role to play and a leadership to assume. We greet the achievements already realized here in the United States: the studies which have been published, the centers which have been established, and, in particular, the initiatives undertaken by the Archbishop of Boston, Cardinal Cushing.

There is no question here of trying to alter the law of God because of pragmatic problems. It is rather a question of hearing the voice of God in history, allowing the vision of overpopulated poverty really to enter our souls, and, with the energy given us by faith, coming to a deeper understanding of the mystery of human personality and bodily existence in the light and the freedom of God's self-revelation.

The Church and the Religious Problem in Latin America

We all know the religious situation in Latin America, the long traditions now imperfectly understood, the customary Catholicism, the flashes of true heroism and generosity, the patience and simplicity of the poor, the fiestas—little more than an emotional release—the fervent practice and the social inertia, the cultured piety and the superstition, and, permeating it all, the mysterious presence of Christ who somehow, through all these centuries and all their vagaries, has never left his people.

All of this forces us to rethink the nature of the Church's eternal mission in the light of the Church's modern needs. And this not only in Latin America but throughout the whole Church, for which Latin America is, as it were, the model and the workshop, the theater of so many daring initiatives fired by the audacity of faith and the drama of so much left to do. The pastoral mission of the Church must be rethought in the light of the true missionary needs of South America, the needs of its people with their real problems and aspirations. It is a question, not of promoting our understanding of Christianity, but of making Christ present to all men of good will. Christianity is not an idea; it is an event. The Church's missionary activity is not propaganda; it is the sacrament of service through which the power of Christ's Resurrection becomes present and available to all men in the uniqueness of their freedom.

But we must bear in mind that we are speaking of the missionary activity of the Church, that charge given to the whole people of God and not only to the clergy, who will in a few years be but one of every seven thousand Christians in Latin America. We have discussed the humanizing effect of the good news, yet men must see the depth from which this human compassion and concern really flow. The Church must be committed as a whole to the love of man, but in a way which reflects Christ's love for man. If the Church loves man as God loves man, we will all be willing to die for man. This means that the sacred principle in the Church, the hierarchy, must assume its responsibility for the animation and enlightenment of the whole People of God of which they are a part. It is a matter, not of allowing the laity to supply for the lack of clergy, but of conferring upon them that share in the total mission of the Church which is rightfully theirs by Baptism and a commission of Christ.

The Church's pastoral mission must be rethought in terms of the historical reality within which God in his providence has placed the Church. The Church's juridical structure must be the expression of its inner life in relation to the life situation amid which it exists. Law, like language, is meant to be an expression that facilitates and sustains an inner life. But law, like language, can be an obstacle to communication unless it learns to bend and adapt itself to the demands of true intuition. If Church law, as it exists in Latin America, does not facilitate the expression of the Church's true life, which is of the Holy Spirit, then our obligation is twofold: to enter more profoundly into that life, live it more completely, and from this experience derive that inner sense of how this life must achieve its juridical expression.

The Church's reality in South America confers upon it a unique pastoral role. It is as though Latin America were a magnifying glass concentrating the light of the Gospel and enkindling new flames of response. We experience the light and heat which has been already generated. It is with emotions of admiration and gratitude that we greet:

A Church which in northeast Brazil has established several parishes where teams of religious lead the community in accomplishing all the tasks of evangelization, the nonsacramental acts of cult, and the spiritual and corporal acts of mercy. It is a seed whose growth indicates the direction along which renewal of the religious life must go.

A Church in Chile where the postconciliar period has given rise to various manifestations of the true Church: a laity served by its shepherds, and diocesan councils with laity participating in the preparation and making of decisions.

A Church which ten years before most other Christian countries organized their episcopal colleges had organized CELAM, an episcopal college on a continental level comprised of more than six hundred bishops who had already begun to work together to accomplish the great tasks facing them in Latin America.

A Church in Brazil where a group of bishops and faithful proposed to their government that in the northeast, one of the poorest regions of the Latin continent, a colossal development plan, which would aid 30 million people, be undertaken and brought to a successful conclusion.

A Church which in Riobamba, anticipating the formation of deacons, has in its villages and mountains established communities of faith, prayer, and apostolic action that are led by lay people with priests to serve them and to maintain their communion with the local Church by means of the Eucharistic celebration.

A Church in Colombia and Brazil where Christians, by the tens of millions, dispersed and lacking adequate means of communication and transportation, are able, thanks to the radio, to hear the Word of God and the prayers of the liturgy from the lips of their bishops.

A Church in which the pastoral consequences of the Council are already becoming a reality because of traveling pastoral teams which go from region to region to stimulate the thought and the activity of the People of God.

Latin America, by the very fact that it is poor, has its own mission to exercise in regard to the rest of the Church. The poor are the chosen vessels of Christ and bear in a mysterious way the sweet fragrance of his presence and witness to a world, anxious to insulate itself from insecurity, that salvation was accomplished by Christ "Who was rich, yet for our sake became poor, so that through his poverty we might become rich." (2 Cor. 8:9)

Christ, who lives in his Church, lives in each local church some aspect of his life with a particular intensity. Christ in the Church of Latin America is the poor Christ who lacks human means of accomplishing his redemptive work. He is the Christ who has nowhere to lay his head, the Christ born in a stable and dying on a cross. He is the Christ, the little man, whom circumstances force to be patient, meek, dependent, and, at times, in danger from civil authority; the Christ whose soul is tempered by the daily experience of man's true state before God, the real Christ preaching the Gospel with his life. It matters little somehow that so many thousands of these Christians do not "practice" their faith. It is true that though they do not practice, their very lives preach; and they are baptized and sealed with the image of Christ.

The Church in Latin America, just because it is poor, has a prophetic role to play within the People of God. The Church is not just a people of prophets; it is a prophetic people. Not only do prophets arise in her from time to time, but the very community itself is prophetic. History abounds in examples of nations, cities, newly founded orders, and movements which have borne the burden of the Word of God, "facing jeers and flogging, even fetters and prison bars; they were stoned to death, they were cut in two, they were put to the sword, they went about dressed in skins of sheep or goats, in poverty, distress, and misery. They were too good for this world." (Heb. 11:36–37) Often these groups made their witness, unaware that through them the Word of God was set loose in history to heal and sustain the people of God.

It is in this light that the Church in Latin America must rethink the poverty within itself so that it becomes aware of its true mission and, amid the acquisition of the goods of this earth to which it has a right, never loses the sense of its vocation to bear in its body the dying of Jesus so that the life of Jesus may shine forth. We already experience some of the effects of this charism which Latin America possesses. How many of the PAVLA workers have come, very conscious that they received much more than they gave? One can read in nearly every report emanating from the Peace Corps not only the great contribution that contact with the people of Latin America has made to the Peace Corps Workers themselves but also a gradual shift in orientation within the Peace Corps. It is a question no longer of merely doing for others in South America, but one of establishing a relation of friendship out of which there grows cooperation toward achieving the goals desired by the people themselves.

For it is the prophetic role of the whole Church of God to rely ultimately, not on human means, but on the power of the Spirit of Christ. We know that only God can satisfy the longing of every human heart and of the whole human family. The true meaning of human existence lies in neither despising nor clinging to the goods of this earth but in seeing this cosmos as ultimately destined to be radiant with the glory of the risen Christ shining through those who are bound to him in love. A Church truly poor brings to the world that witness which calms the anxiety of men who can see visibly before their eyes that God's power is brought to its perfection in weakness.

Conclusion

Latin America presents to the Church, in a concentrated form, the double challenge confronting the Church throughout the world. This challenge forces the Church to look more deeply into herself and seek to discover that unique source which can respond to this twofold problem, this problem with two faces, the social and the religious. The source of life within the Church is the Spirit of Christ, who died not to save souls but to save men, whose power brings men to "share his sufferings being conformed to his death" in order to know the "power of his Resurrection" by which he "transfigures our lowly body, conforming it to his glorious body." Thus, the Church has a twofold role springing from this single source, that of evangelizing the world and of humanizing it.

Evangelization means more than setting forth a doctrine; it is the setting loose of life, and this life is a seed whose full flowering is the perfect humanization of man. For so long a time we Christians have held an anxious grasp on the status quo and kept ourselves aloof from movements which we now see are noble and in conformity with the deep aspirations of man. Now our task is to be so committed to these ideals that men are forced to look deeply to find the source which drives us. There they must find the spirit of Christ, the glory of God shining on the face of Christ Jesus, and this must be their introduction to the Father.

This means that by the very force of our faith and the audacity and optimism that it confers, we the Church must not merely join such movements and attempt to deflect them into channels more familiar to us. We must rather respect the intrinsic nobility of these human ideals and enshrine them in the light of Christ. What is needed is not conformity but revolution. The need in Latin America is too great, and the pace of the change is too fast, for us to content ourselves with arriving late on the scene with "corrective measures." There must be a revolution, but a revolution of peace. If the power and compassion of Christ do not permeate these social changes, there may be revolution, but it will be a revolution of blood.

The World of God is being addressed anew to God's people.

We are free to accept or reject this Word, but our existence can never be the same again. A man who rejects responsibility is no longer neutral. We are called upon to permeate and sustain this peaceful revolution whose ultimate goal is a world befitting the dignity of man. Every step in the progress of technology, literacy, and medicine which alleviates human suffering is an extension of the Redemption. The living source of the power needed to effect this extension is found in the Gospel and reflected in the documents of the Second Vatican Council such as the Constitution on Church in the Modern World. But ideas are not enough; they must live in the souls of dedicated Church leaders whose deep poverty and freedom from human structures, no matter how venerable, will allow them to follow the delicate yet dynamic movement of the Spirit. Change in itself is neutral. Mutation is not life, yet there is no life which does not involve transformation. The role of the Church's leaders is not only "to tear down and to uproot" but also "to build and to plant." (Jer. 1:10)

The Church has the mission of Christ, upon whom the Spirit rested to "announce the good news to the poor." The fire of Christ transforms the world, but it is not merely the sum of human energies and striving. It is a force from without whose transcendent source is the very life of God. Christianity is not a social messianism, but the continuation of that mission of the Messiah who has made available to men a power and a goal which transcends them, and yet whose existence within them makes them more human.

Christ's kingdom is not of this world, that is, it does not arise from forces intrinsic to man or the cosmos. He died, not to make a paradise on earth, but to make of life's experience a sacrament conferring upon the whole human family a joy which surpasses all understanding. Christianity is not a form of social work or a temporal messianism but a call to a higher life, to free men to be truly human, compassionate toward one another, and to aid one another in their journey to the Father.

I tried elsewhere to make it clear how much in error those thinkers are who believe that the preaching of the full Gospel of Jesus Christ to the poor should be postponed until their lot has been improved by social action and they have thus been rendered receptive to the Gospel message. One has only to recall the words we have already cited: "the *poor* will have the Gospel preached to them." To feed a man is an act of Christ; to imagine that he must be well fed before he can receive the life of Christ is a denial of Christ.

The Christ who once refused to turn stones into bread and declared that it is not in bread alone that man lives but in the Word, the Life of God, is also the Christ who fed the multitudes in the desert. We are faced with this twofold mission in Latin America. We have to give men bread *and* the sacred host. We have to teach them the alphabet *and* the doctrine of Christ. We have to offer them social security *and* the providence of God. We have to save men, not only souls. We need social pioneers who are saints.

The Crusades of the past had for their goal the liberation of the tomb of Christ, and this goal was noble and sacred. Today the crusade for the Third World wishes not only to liberate the tomb of Christ but also Christ himself whom Christians must discover suffering in hunger, sickness, and misery, in the rejected two-thirds of humanity.

We do not have the right to pass Christ by and not recognize him: not extend our hand to him, not cover him, not feed him in the person of the poor. He is our Brother—our life.

This is the challenge of our time, the challenge of Latin America to the Universal Church.

Index